Complete Works vol.3 (2011-2018)
KAZUYO SEJIMA RYUE NISHIZAWA SANAA

Monograph featuring Louvre-Lens and after (2011–2018)
including many projects first appered.
Permanent book collection for your archive

276 pages
307×300mm

永久保存版
¥5,900+tax

妹島和世，西沢立衛，SANAAの完全作品集第3弾
ルーヴル・ランス以降，現在までの約70のプロジェクトを収録

未発表
プロジェクト
多数収録

Republishing after 40 years.

These 10 volumes of *Villages and Towns* series are the result of 10 years of preparation by *Yukio Futagawa*. White washed houses and streets of villages on Aegean Islands; baroque decorations on walls of farm houses amongst the Alps; Italian towns with beautiful squares; cave-dwellings of Andalusian villages; Adriatic towns with their main orientation to the Sea. Many of villages and towns introduced in this series have been forgotten for centuries, being kept undisturbed by modern progress. They are rare and precious architectural specimens. Spaces and forms which make up these villages and towns are the result of ages of constant improvements by experience, and they have many ideas to offer and warnings to give to today's architecture although some of them have disappeared in these 40 years.

40年の時を経て, 復刻。

《世界の村と街》シリーズ全10巻は、ヨーロッパ地域を中心として二川幸夫が10年の歳月をかけ企画・編集・撮影したものです。エーゲ海に浮ぶ白い集落、アルプス山中のバロック風の壁絵のある村、イタリア半島に点在する美しい広場を持つ街、自然と家並が一体となったアンダルシアの村、海を玄関として構成されたアドリア海の街など、ここに登場してくる村と街は現代文明に置き忘れられたためにかろうじて人間の生活の匂いを残している、個性あふれた貴重な集合住宅群です。今日、姿を消してしまったものもありますが、だからこそ、これらの村や街は、繁栄だけのなかから生れたわれわれの住空間に幾多の警告やヒントを与えてくれるでしょう。何故なら、そこにある住空間には人間の生活のための長い経験や知恵の中から生れた確かな造形があるからです。40年を経てもなお。

Villages and Towns
世界の村と街

Editing & Photographs:
Yukio Futagawa
編集・写真：二川幸夫

Recommendation by Jasper Morrison
For anyone who has correctly dreamed of the Mediterranean Sea and its relatives as a paradise on earth, these are the instruction manuals for appreciating the towns and villages which surround them. I can think of no other documentation which so perfectly describes the structure of a way of life we would all do well to learn from.
Jasper Morrison (Furniture/Product Designer)

ジャスパー・モリソンさんに推薦いただきました。
本書は、地中海とその周りに広がる村と街を、まさに「地上の楽園」として夢見てきたすべての人々に向けた鑑賞マニュアルです。我々一人ひとりが学ぶべきことの多い地中海での生き方のしくみを、これほど完璧に描写した記録を他に知りません。
ジャスパー・モリソン（家具／プロダクト デザイナー）

NEW

#5 *Italy*
イタリア半島の村と街 II

Location: Alberobello, Cisternino and Ostuni
Introduction & Essays: Makoto Suzuki
掲載地：アルベロベッロ、チステルニーノ、オストゥーニ　序文・解説：鈴木恂
136 pages

For worldwide readers, English translation texts are newly-added
多くの方にご覧いただけるよう、新たに英語訳を加えました

with Original Case, English and Japanese texts, 300×228mm
¥3,800+tax

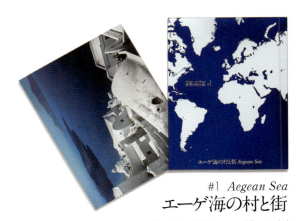

#1 *Aegean Sea*
エーゲ海の村と街
Location: Mykonos and Santorini
Introduction: Arata Isozaki   Essays: Makoto Suzuki
144 pages

#2 *Adriatic Sea*
アドリア海の村と街
Location: Dubrovnik and Venice
Introduction & Essays: Tadashi Yokoyama
144 pages

#3 *Mediterranean Sea*
地中海の村と街
Location: Procida, Bonifacio, Medenine and Takurouna
Introduction & Essays: Makoto Suzuki
136 pages

#4 *Italy*
イタリア半島の村と街 I
Location: Siena, San Gimignano and Assisi
Introduction & Essays: Tadashi Yokoyama
144 pages

GA JAPAN

Global Architecture

日本の新しい優れた現代建築のエッセンスを発信する隔月刊の建築専門誌。
建築思想,理論,哲学,技術思想を多面的に照射しつつ,建築の本質に迫る本格的建築総合誌です。

Japanese Text Only / Size: 300×228mm

¥2,333+税

151 GA JAPAN MAR-APR/2018
100 details

150 GA JAPAN JAN-FEB/2018
特集 総括と展望 建築二〇一七/二〇一八 流行る建築展

149 GA JAPAN NOV-DEC/2017
PLOT 設計のプロセス

特集:100 details——百の納まり
最近5年間に紹介した建築を中心に,気になる建築や「○と×」座談会で取り上げた力作まで,100件の建築をディテールから振り返る
伊東豊雄,長田直之,米田明,SANAA,平田晃久,新素材研究所,小川晋一,アルファヴィル,藤野高志,D・チッパーフィールド,島田陽,北川原温,三家大地,中山英之,日建設計,CAt,佐藤総合計画+安田アトリエ,有馬裕之,中川エリカ,福山博之,山下貴成,SALHAUS,百枝優,城戸崎博孝,隈研吾,o+h,三分一博志,松島潤平,堀部安嗣,H&dM,竹中工務店,萬代基介,山本理顕,原広司,窪田勝文,他
インタヴュー:西沢立衛,吉村靖孝,佐藤淳,遠藤政樹
コラム:山梨知彦,鈴木了二
連載:地球の景色20/藤本壮介,ロボットはコンピュータの夢をかたちにするか? 22/アンズスタジオ

240 pages

特集:[総括と展望]建築2017/2018
座談会:西沢立衛×平田晃久×藤本壮介×二川由夫
特集:流行る建築展
——12人の識者による建築を巡る展覧会のはなし
安藤忠雄,隈研吾,藤本壮介,長谷川祐子,原研哉,三宅理一,長谷川逸子,日埜直彦,田根剛,藤森照信,寺田真理子,藤本貴子
作品:SANAA+新穂設計+石川設計 荘銀タクト鶴岡(鶴岡市文化会館),北川原温/ナカニシ新本社R&DセンターRD1,有馬裕之/きふね
PLOT:大学の多目的広場 石上純也,明治神宮ミュージアム 隈研吾
連載:地球の景色19/藤本壮介,ロボットはコンピュータの夢をかたちにするか? 21/アンズスタジオ
GA広場:torre 01/長田直之,新潟の集合住宅/細海拓也,(仮称)弘前市芸術文化施設 田根剛

184 pages

特集:PLOT 設計のプロセス
——17組の建築家たちから発せられた,ナマな言葉で紡ぐ設計のプロセス
中川エリカ,妹島和世+西沢立衛,隈研吾,平田晃久,藤本壮介,赤松佳珠子,大西麻貴+百田有希,安藤忠雄,三澤遼,北川原温,周防貴之,杉本博司+榊田倫之,乾久美子,日建設計,有馬裕之,大江匡,藤原徹平+針谷將史
作品:小嶋一浩+赤松佳珠子/京都外国語大学新4号館,佐藤総合計画+安田アトリエ/京都女子大学図書館,日建設計/国際藝術リソースセンター,藤森照信/低過庵
連載:地球の景色18/藤本壮介,ロボットはコンピュータの夢をかたちにするか? 20/アンズスタジオ
GA広場:ジャンクスペースを越える革新はあるか 編集部

188 pages

Our subscription is available worldwide.
年間購読のご案内 どこよりも早く確実にお手元にお届けいたします

Please visit our website: http://www.ga-ada.co.jp
Contact us: sales@ga-tbc.co.jp (Overseas) / order@ga-tbc.co.jp (日本国内)
詳細はウェブサイトをご覧下さい。

GA HOUSES
Key to Abbreviations

ALC	alcove
ARCD	arcade/covered passageway
ART	art room
ATL	atelier
ATR	atrium
ATT	attic
AV	audio-visual room
BAL	balcony
BAR	bar
BK	breakfast room
BR	bedroom
BRG	bridge/catwalk
BTH	bathroom
BVD	belvedere/lookout
CAR	carport/car shelter
CH	children's room
CEL	cellar
CL	closet/walk-in closet
CLK	cloak
CT	court
D	dining room
DEN	den
DK	deck
DN	stairs-down
DRK	darkroom
DRS	dressing room/wardrobe
DRW	drawing room
E	entry
ECT	entrance court
EH	entrance hall
EV	elevator
EXC	exercise room
F	family room
FPL	fireplace
FYR	foyer
GAL	gallery
GDN	garden
GRG	garage
GRN	greenhouse
GST	guest room/guest bedroom
GZBO	gazebo
H	hall
HK	house keeper
ING	inglenook
K	kitchen
L	living room
LBR	library
LBY	lobby
LDRY	laundry
LFT	loft
LGA	loggia
LGE	lounge
LWL	light well
MBR	master bedroom
MBTH	master bathroom
MECH	mechanical
MLTP	multipurpose room
MSIC	music room
MUD	mud room
OF	office
P	porch/portico
PAN	pantry/larder
PLY	playroom
POOL	swimming pool/pool/pond
PT	patio
RE	rear entry
RT	roof terrace
SHW	shower
SIT	sitting room
SHOP	shop
SKY	skylight
SL	slope/ramp
SLP	sleeping loft
SNA	sauna
STD	studio
STDY	study
ST	staircase/stair hall
STR	storage/storeroom
SUN	sunroom/sun parlor/solarium
SVE	service entry
SVYD	service yard
TAT	tatami room/tea ceremony room
TER	terrace
UP	stairs-up
UTL	utility room
VD	void/open
VRA	veranda
VSTB	vestibule
WC	water closet
WRK	workshop/work room

PROJECT 2018

157

Global Architecture
GA HOUSES

A.D.A. EDITA Tokyo

16 **Aires Mateus:** House in Monsaraz
アイレス・マテウス：モンサラズの住宅

111 **Kentaro Takeguchi + Asako Yamamoto/Alphaville:**
Nishi-Oji Town House
竹口健太郎＋山本麻子／アルファヴィル：西大路タウンハウス

158 **Hiroyuki Arima:** In Park Slope
有馬裕之：In Park Slope

120 **Bercy Chen:** Arrowhead House
ベイシー／チェン：アローヘッド・ハウス

148 **BGP Arquitectura:** Jojutla House
BGPアルキテクトゥーラ：ホフトラ・ハウス

32 **Tatiana Bilbao:** Ways of Life
タチアナ・ビルバオ：生活の方法

72 **Will Bruder:** Palms Treehouse
ウィル・ブルダー：ヤシの木ハウス

92 **Chenchow Little:** Unfolding House
チェンチョウ／リトル：展開する家

133 **Steven Ehrlich + Takashi Yanai:** Baxter Street Residence
スティーヴン・アーリック＋柳井隆：バクスター通りの住宅

60 **Ensamble Studio:** Ca'n Terra
アンサンブル・スタジオ：カン・テラ

116 **Sou Fujimoto:** Tree House Tokyo
藤本壮介：ツリーハウス東京

28 **Takashi Fujino:** Scaffold
藤野高志：櫓

154 **Shigeru Fuse:** House in Hitachinaka
布施茂：ひたちなかの住宅

114 **Sean Godsell:** Drone House
ショーン・ゴッドセル：ドローン・ハウス

50 **Grupo Aranea:** Casa Muchavista
グルッポ・アラネア：カーサ・ムチャヴィスタ

25 **Grupo SP:** Cidade Jardim House
グルッポSP：シダーデ・ジャルジン・ハウス

54 **Tomohiro Hata:** House in Goshikiyama
畑友洋：五色山の家

126 **Irisarri + Piñera:** Surf and Yoga Monitor
イリサーリ＋ピネェラ：サーフ＆ヨガ・モニター

98 **Alberto Kalach:** Casa en Monterrey
アルベルト・カラチ：モンテレイの家

103 **Alberto Kalach:** Casa Brisas
アルベルト・カラチ：カーサ・ブリサス

96 **Hirotaka Kidosaki:** Villa in Nanjo
城戸崎博孝：沖縄　大西邸

57 **Mathias Klotz:** Hites House
マティアス・クロッツ：ハイツ・ハウス

130 **Katsufumi Kubota:** K-Villa
窪田勝文：K-Villa

106 **Kengo Kuma:** Suspended Forest
隈研吾：Suspended Forest

178 **Keisuke Maeda:** House in Onnason
前田圭介：恩納村の住宅

69 **Shingo Masuda + Katsuhisa Otsubo:** Mark the Land
増田信吾＋大坪克亘：Mark the Land

81 **Gurjit Singh Matharoo:** Sound Architecture
グルジット・シン・マタロー：サウンド・アーキテクチャー

162 **Andra Matin:** Pererenan House
アンドラ・マティン：ペレレナン・ハウス

166 **Andra Matin:** Omah Jati
アンドラ・マティン：オマー・ジャティ

123 **Satoshi Matsuoka + Yuki Tamura:** EBISU project
松岡聡＋田村裕希：EBISUプロジェクト

74 **Erika Nakagawa:** Tower and Onomatopoeia
中川エリカ：塔とオノマトペ

13 **Ryue Nishizawa:** I House
西沢立衛：I邸

GA HOUSES 157

152 Nitsche Arquitetos: Ilhabela House
ニーチェ・アルキテートス：イリャベラの住宅

38 Maki Onishi + Yuki Hyakuda: T hut
大西麻貴＋百田有希：T hut

20 Smiljan Radic: Conguillio House
スミリャン・ラディッチ：コンギジオの住宅

84 RICA Studio*: Periscope House
RICA スタジオ*：ペリスコープ・ハウス

89 Hiroshi Sambuichi: SATO
三分一博志：水上の郷

8 selgascano: Sol House
セルガスカーノ：ソル・ハウス

66 Yo Shimada: House in Mukogawa
島田陽：武庫川の住居

170 Fran Silvestre: Zarid House
フラン・シルベストレ：ザリド・ハウス

44 SPBR Arquitetos: House in Sagaponack
SPBR アルキテートス：サガポナックの住宅

140 Studio TonTon: RT House
スタジオ・トントン：RTハウス

178 Peter Stutchbury: Night Sky House
ピーター・スタッチベリー：夜空の家

144 Makoto Tanijiri + Ai Yoshida / Suppose Design Office: House in Karuizawa
谷尻誠＋吉田愛／サポーズデザインオフィス：軽井沢の家

136 Makoto Takei + Chie Nabeshima / TNA: M-Project
武井誠＋鍋島千恵／TNA：M-Project

174 Vo Trong Nghia: Thang House
ヴォ・チョン・ギア：タン・ハウス

182 Wespi de Meuron Romeo: Project New House in Morcote
ウェスピ・ド・ムーロン・ロメオ：モルコテの新しい住宅

41 Akira Yoneda: Boat House (Landing House IV)
米田明：ボート・ハウス（ランディング・ハウスIV）

《世界の住宅》157
発行・編集人：二川由夫
編集スタッフ：斎藤日登美，仲村明代

2018年3月23日発行
エーディーエー・エディタ・トーキョー
東京都渋谷区千駄ヶ谷3-12-14
電話 (03)3403-1581(代)
ファックス (03)3497-0649
E-mail: info@ga-ada.co.jp
http://www.ga-ada.co.jp

ロゴタイプ・デザイン：細谷巖

印刷・製本：図書印刷株式会社

取次店：
トーハン，日販，大阪屋栗田，
西村書店，中央社，鍬谷書店

禁無断転載
ISBN978-4-87140-209-5 C1352

GA HOUSES 157
Publisher/Editor in Chief: Yoshio Futagawa
Editors: Hitomi Saito, Akiyo Nakamura

Published in March 2018
©A.D.A. EDITA Tokyo Co., Ltd.
3-12-14 Sendagaya, Shibuya-ku, Tokyo,
151-0051 Japan
Tel. (03)3403-1581
Fax. (03)3497-0649
E-mail: info@ga-ada.co.jp
http://www.ga-ada.co.jp

Logotype Design: Gan Hosoya

Printed in Japan by
Tosho Printing Co., Ltd.

All rights reserved.
Copyright of Photographs:
©GA photographers
All drawings are provided by
architects except as noted.

Cover: Conguillio House by Smiljan Radic
Title pages:
T hut by Maki Onishi + Yuki Hyakuda
Model photo by Nohara Yamazaki
English translation: Erica Sakai (p.13, p.71,
p.74, p.90, p.96, p.131, p.159, p.178),
Joyce Lam (p.30, p.39, p.41, p.67, p.137,
p.144, pp.154-155), Shingei Katsu (p.54,
p.111, p.117, p.124)
和訳：原田勝之 (p.49, pp.100-101, p.104,
p.143). 小室沙織 (p.11, p.37, p.65, p.110,
p.129, p.151). 前嶋詠子 (p.19, p.59, p.83, p.95,
p.153). 平林祥 (p.24, p.52, p.72, p.79, p.88).
佐藤圭 (p.114, p.134, p.173, pp.176-177).
印牧岳彦 (p.27, p.121, p.164, p.168, p.185)

View from south

Location

Site plan

East elevation

First floor S=1:300

Second floor

This house was designed for a very particular site in Ketchum, Idaho, US. Ketchum is a very cold and sunny place and thats why is the home to the first Ski Resort built in USA, and this very reason is why the house is a secondary residence for skiing.

The low temperature, the snow, the skiing but furthermore the dense vegetation and the close proximity of neighboring houses were the determining factors faced on this project. Specifically, the high density of trees create dense shadows on the terrain and the ugly houses surrounding the house threatened the enjoyment of the occupants.

The response to these parameters was twofold, both material and formal. We molded the house to the negative space left by the trees in the center of the site, trying to maintain and respect the vegetation and cladding the exterior of the house with mirrored steel sheets and wood, so that it would blend into its surrounding. This created both a feeling of fleeting disappearance and an array of light reflections that would brighten the exterior space and move in synchrony with the natural light of the sun.

Primary study

Model

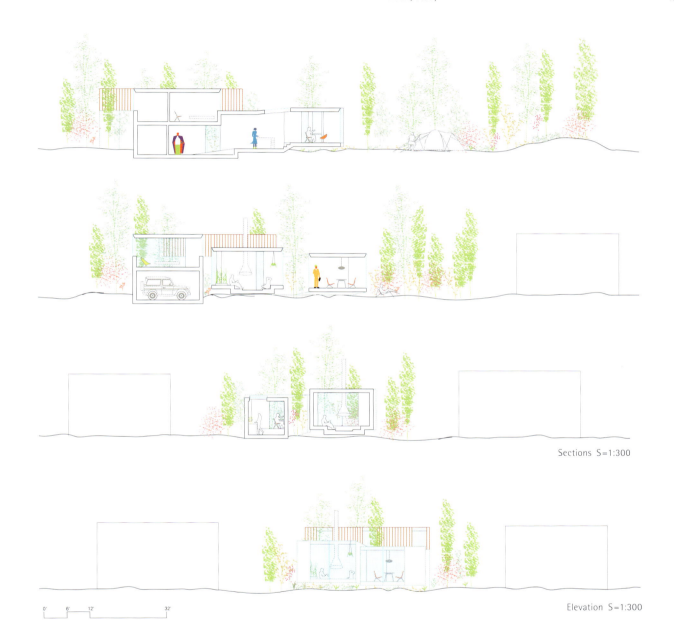
Sections S=1:300

Elevation S=1:300

Model

　この住宅は米国アイダホ州ケチャムにある,非常に特殊な敷地のために設計された。ケチャムは寒さが厳しいが晴れの日が多く,この地で米国初のスキーリゾートが建設されたのも,この住宅がスキー用の別荘であるのも,これが理由となっている。

　この計画が直面した決定的な要素として,気温の低さ,雪,スキーに加え,植生密度の高さや隣接する近隣住宅が挙げられる。とりわけ,樹木が密集しているために地面に落ちる影が深くなり,さらに見苦しい周辺の住宅は居住者の楽しみを脅かす存在であった。

　このようなパラメータに対して私たちは,物質的かつ形態的に対応することとなった。敷地中央の木と木の間に住宅を配置し,植生をそのままの状態で保つよう試みた。さらに,住宅が周囲と溶け込むように外壁を鏡面加工が施されたスティール板や木材で覆った。これによって移ろいゆく消失感と,屋外空間を照らし,自然光と同時に動く一連の光の反射がもたらされた。

West elevation

North elevation

Architects: selgascano—
José Selgas, Lucía Cano, principals-in-charge;
Sara Ouass, Inés Olavarrieta, project team
Consultants: selgascano, landscape
Structural system: steel frame

Major materials: cross laminated timber,
colored mirror steel sheet
Site area: 8,100 sq. ft.
Building area: 1,600 sq. ft.
Total floor area: 2,120 sq. ft.

RYUE NISHIZAWA
I HOUSE

Nagano, Japan
Design: 2016-17
Construction: 2018-

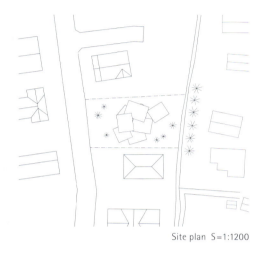
Site plan S=1:1200

This is a new residence currently planned in a quiet housing estate. The neighborhood streets are lined with residences, which each have a large garden.

The clients are a married couple whose requests included a study for their vast private library, a bright and open living room, a classroom for running English classes, a bedroom for the wife on the upper floor, and a sense of connectedness throughout the home. The clients are sensitive to sounds and vibrations, so above all, it was important to create a serene living environment.

This was originally a single-story plan, but we eventually realized that meeting size requirements would result in a building comparatively much larger than neighboring houses. The building would also cover the entire plot, which would give it a claustrophobic feeling.

In response, we felt that by arranging the desired room-functions into distinctly sized living spaces and stacking them like building blocks, the layering would create a compact building with a spacious garden in a scale consistent with neighboring residences. By considering the surrounding structures, gardens and their relationships, we are aiming to create a structure that, while at a glance seems free-standing, is also in harmony with the surrounding environment.

Each spatial volume faces multiple directions so that there is no front or back. Various apertures and the spaces between rooms allow air and light to filter through from the surrounding garden. By stacking volumes of different sizes, we also created a split-level design with floors of various heights layered both internally and externally. As each room faces the open-ceiling living area at the core of the building, the home is an open space that feels connected three-dimensionally.

As for the structural design, reinforced concrete construction creates an interior environment protected from external noise and vibrations, with light, steel-frame box stacked above. This difference in construction is also visible externally. The plan is designed so that proximate rooms will support each other like they are holding hands to sustain a well-balanced composition.

We hope that by freely combining multiple spaces, from the open-plan areas to the rooms protected from external commotion, this residence will become a cozy, nest-like home that inspires new spaces to be born with the changing seasons and environment.
Masahiro Tachi/Office of Ryue Nishizawa

View toward living room from kitchen

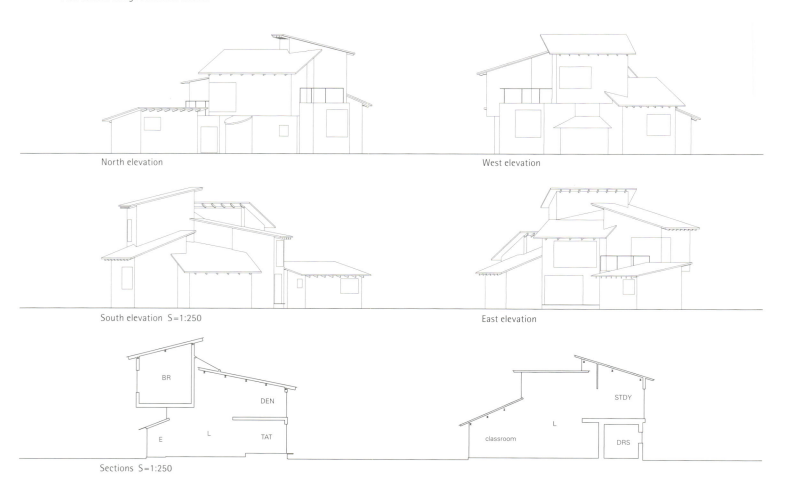

North elevation

West elevation

South elevation S=1:250

East elevation

Sections S=1:250

Architects: Office of Ryue Nishizawa—
Ryue Nishizawa, principal-in-charge;
Takuya Yokoyama, Masahiro Tachi,
Mayumi Kanemaru, project team
Consultants: Komatsu Structural Design,
structural; System Design, mechanical
Structural system: reinforced concrete, steel
frame
Site area: 496.9 m²
Building area: 110.0 m²
Total floor area: 165.2 m²

閑静な分譲住宅地に計画中の住宅である。周辺にはゆったりとした庭を持った住宅が建ち並んでいる。

住まい手はご夫婦二人で、要望としては、たくさんの蔵書を納められる書斎、開放的で明るいリビングルーム、英会話教室を開くためのクラスルーム、上階に奥さんの寝室を設けること、全体としてつながりが感じられる住宅であること、などが望まれ、何より音や振動に敏感な住まい手のために安定した居住環境が必要であった。

当初は平屋の案も検討していたが、必要な大きさを平屋の建物で計画すると周囲に比べてとても大きく、敷地いっぱいに建物が広がることでどこか息苦しさを感じた。

そこで私たちが考えたのは、求められた各機能をヴォリュームに分け、積み木のように積んでいくというもので、積層させることで周辺の住宅同様に広い庭を持つコンパクトな建物とした。周囲の建物や庭との関係を考えながらヴォリュームを配置することで、一見フリースタンディングな建物でありながら環境と調和した住宅をつくろうとしている。

各ヴォリュームはいろいろな方向を向いているので、表裏がなく、開口部や部屋と部屋のすき間を通して周囲の庭から光や風を取り込むことができる。また、大きさの違うヴォリュームを積んでいったので、内外にいろいろな高さの床があるスキップフロアの建物となった。それぞれの部屋は中央の吹き抜けのリビングルームに面しているため、全体として立体的につながりのある空間となっている。

構造計画としては、RC造で外部の音や振動から守られた環境をつくり、その上に鉄骨造の軽い箱を載せる構成としている。また、構造の違いがそのまま外観に現れるようにしている。平面的には隣り合う各部屋が手を繋ぐように支え合うことでより安定した構造となるよう計画している。

開放的な空間から外部の喧騒から守られた空間までいろいろなものが自由に組み合わさり、季節の変化や周辺環境とともに様々な居場所が生まれることで、快適な巣のような住宅になればと思っている。

（舘真弘／西沢立衛建築設計事務所）

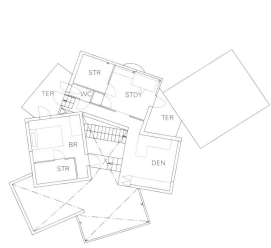

Second floor

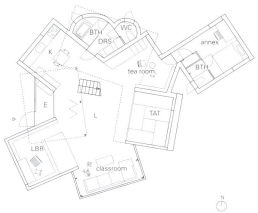

First floor S=1:250

Living room

AIRES MATEUS
HOUSE IN MONSARAZ

Alqueva Lake, Monsaraz, Portugal
Design: 2007-09
Construction: 2010-18

Construction site

Site plan S=1:10000

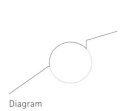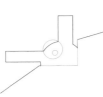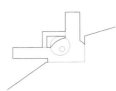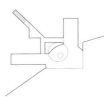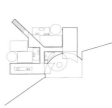
Diagram

Dome

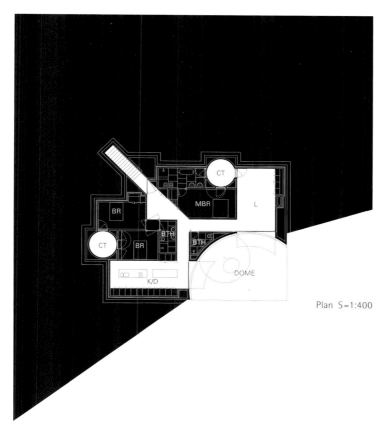

Plan S=1:400

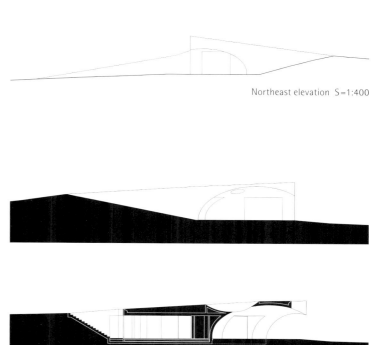

Northeast elevation S=1:400

Sections S=1:400

View toward living room from dome

Entrance

Faced with the boundless extents of the Alqueva Lake, the house requires a centre: a protected courtyard embracing the water. It uses the terrain to cast a dome that covers the social areas and is the life centre of the house. An inverted dome intersects it and creates an opening that lights the space, shaping its precise geometry and limits. The bedrooms open onto circular patios. Amid a wide natural landscape, the scale of the house is that of the patios and superior dome. They are the sole visible elements, painted in radiant white.

広大なアルケヴァ湖に面するこの住宅は、水辺を抱く守られた中庭という、中心となるものを必要としていた。地形を利用し形づくった共有スペースを覆うドームは、住宅における生活の中心となる。そこに交差する逆向きのドームが、空間に光を取り込む開口をつくり出し、明確なジオメトリと境界を形にしている。寝室は円形のパティオに向かって開いている。広々とした自然の風景の中心において、住宅のスケールはパティオや上部のドームのそれである。明るい白色に塗装された構成要素は、唯一目に見えるものである。

Architects: aires mateus e associados—
Manuel Aires Mateus, Francisco Aires Mateus, principals-in-charge; Inês Cordovil,
Helga Constantino, project-in-charge;
André Passos, Humberto Silva,
Susana Rodrigues, Joana Simões, project team
Consultants: AFA consult, structural/mechanical
General contractor: JDS—Mateus Frazão
Structural system: concrete
Major materials: concrete
Site area: 21,100 m²
Building area: 190 m²
Total floor area: 174 m²
Cost of construction: 1 million euros

SMILJAN RADIC
CONGUILLIO HOUSE

Conguillio National Park, Araucania Region, Chile
Design: 2016-17
Construction: 2017-18

Overall view from north

© Gonzalo Puga

PRISM HOUSE + ROOM TERRACE

The gradient of the land passes naturally beneath the feet of the terrace of the house, from which can be seen the dead river of lava, like a haunting ghost, reminding us of the last eruption of the Llaima Volcano.

On this terrace or platform, I have installed the Prism House (1974) by Kazuo Shinohara, or what is left of it, and the Room built in Chiloe in 1997, or what is left of that.

From the Prism House, I have attempted to repeat its air, based on its geometric structural plans, expressed in its side facade with a radial cut at 45 degrees and by the diagonal wooden post: a support that like many others in houses by the Japanese architect, orders the interior space, while appearing to be out of place. I repeated the room proposed in the photographs of the interior space and the side façade, simply because these images are the only ones that appear in the record published by Shinohara himself, which leads to the assumption that for him these views were the Prism House. As far as I know, the bedrooms and the view of the longitudinal façade are not included in these images. Thus, I copied the 7.20 meters structural cross-section at the axis and I calculated the length, maintaining the same measurement, aiming that the cross-section of the volume would accurately represent that of a cube. In addition, I recreated the exquisite idea of lightness in the walls and we prefabricated them.

From the Room, I repeated the last extension carried out on it: a metallic structure that supports a red tent in the middle of the Chiloe forest. We reformed the cross-section into a 7.20 meters isosceles triangle in order to better accompany what is left of its neighbour, the Prism House. We repeated its informal air, the idea of a resting place.

These two prisms built on the black platform do not represent an exercise in interpretation. To interpret is to pretend to do something else with the same, and that does not interest me. This house is actually an exercise in repetition. To repeat is to do something a second time, though the attempt always seems to fail.

The past can become something else while remaining the same.

The past can become something else while remaining the same?

The past can become something else while remaining the same!

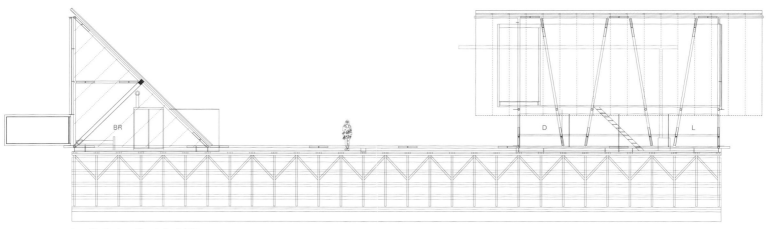

Longitudinal section A S=1:200

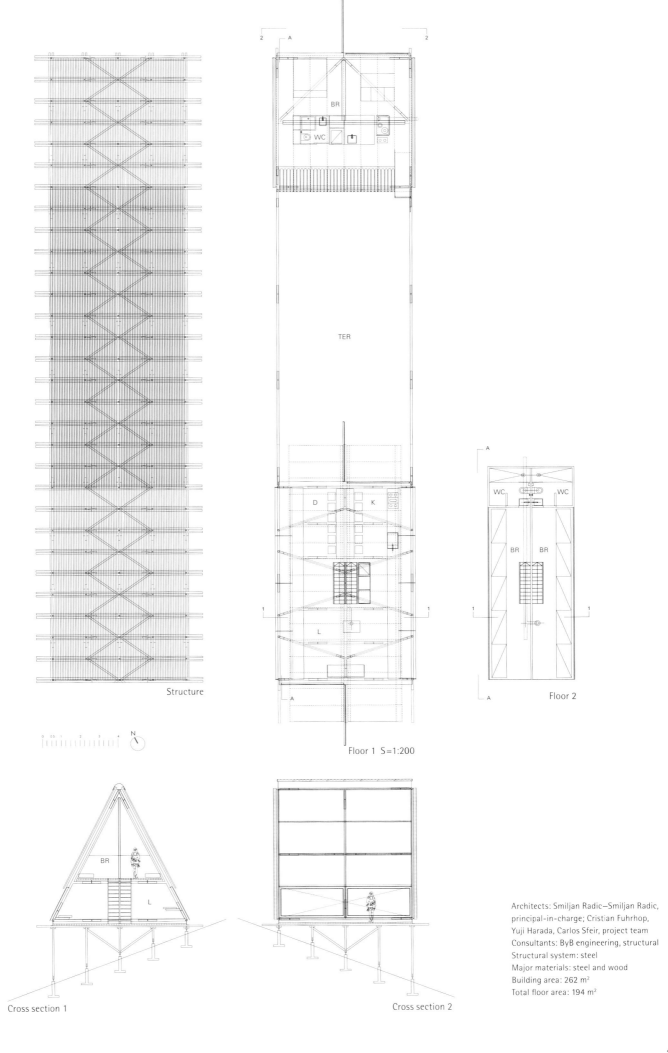

Structure

Floor 2

Floor 1 S=1:200

Cross section 1

Cross section 2

Architects: Smiljan Radic—Smiljan Radic, principal-in-charge; Cristian Fuhrhop, Yuji Harada, Carlos Sfeir, project team
Consultants: ByB engineering, structural
Structural system: steel
Major materials: steel and wood
Building area: 262 m²
Total floor area: 194 m²

Mount view from terrace: looking south

© Gonzalo Puga

プリズム・ハウス＋ルーム・テラス

敷地は，住居のテラスの下で自然に傾斜している。このテラスからは，亡霊のような溶岩が固まった川を望むことができ，見る者に前回のジャイマ山噴火を思い出させる。

このテラス，もしくはプラットフォームを基礎として，篠原一男の「直角三角柱（プリズム・ハウス）」（1974年）とチロエ島に1997年に建てた「ルーム」，それぞれの現存する部分を取り入れたデザインとした。

「直角三角柱」についてはその雰囲気を再現するべく，側面ファサードに取り入れられた45度の急勾配や対角に設けられた木柱に代表される，幾何学的な構造を参考にした。このような木柱は日本人建築家の設計する家屋によく見られるもので，室内空間に秩序をもたらすと同時に，その場から浮いているかのような印象も与える。

また居室の雰囲気を再現するうえでは，屋内空間と側面ファサードをとらえた写真を参考にした。篠原自身が発表した唯一の画像であり，そこに写るものこそが，篠原の考える「直角三角柱」の真の姿だと考えられるからだ。私の知る限り，寝室と正面ファサードをとらえた写真は存在しない。そこで，「直角三角柱」の構造断面の7.2メートルという寸法から長さを計算し，立方体に正確に当てはめて，新たな建造物の構造断面を導き出した。また，軽量な壁という卓抜したアイディアも再現しようと考え，プレハブ式の壁を用いた。

「ルーム」については，最後に実施した増築部を再現した。チロエの森の真ん中に建てられた赤いテントを支える，金属構造部である。断面を7.2メートルの二等辺三角形に改築することで，隣接して再現された「直角3角柱」との一体感を図った。さらに，「ルーム」が持つくつろいだ雰囲気，憩いの場というイメージも再現した。

黒色のプラットフォームに建てられた二つのプリズム（三角柱）は，作品に対する解釈を示すものではない。解釈とは，あるものを用いて別のことを行おうとする活動であり，そのような試みには私は興味がない。この住宅は，再現そのものである。再現とは，失敗に終わる危険を常に伴いつつ，あることを再度行おうとする試みである。

過去は，過去の姿を保持したまま，別の何かになれる。

過去は，過去の姿を保持したまま，別の何かになれるのだろうか？

過去は，過去の姿を保持したまま，別の何かになれるのだ！

GRUPO SP
CIDADE JARDIM HOUSE

São Paulo, SP, Brazil
Design: 2017-18
Construction: 2018-19

View from courtyard

Site plan S=1:4000

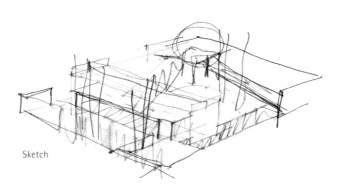
Sketch

This project is the result of a process of direct collaboration with the client that we had never tested before. It was held in four weeks in three weekly meetings, in which the designs were developed, discussed and redesigned with the effective and affective participation of the client. Consequently, traditional design presentations and revisions were avoided, since it was done together with the owner of the house who was aware of each decision made, shortening the time usually spent.

The preservation of existing vegetation was one of the premises of the project. In the original site there is a dense tree occupation, with 32 trees, of which we removed 7 that presented problems. The 3-meter slope of the plot, provided an occupation by half-levels that organizes and articulates the program of the house through a ramp that connects two proposed blocks.

This organization results in a block in the alignment of the street with the more social spaces and a terrace half-covered by a portico on the level above the street. In the other block are the studio and dorms, as well as an uncovered observation deck that overlooks the city of São Paulo. Between the blocks and the ramp, an internal patio promotes the visual connection between all the activities of the house.

Interventions made by the owners of the house, as well as the children's mess and parties with friends will also impregnate the concrete structure that will conform all the spaces of the house.

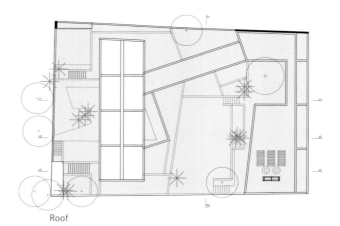
Roof

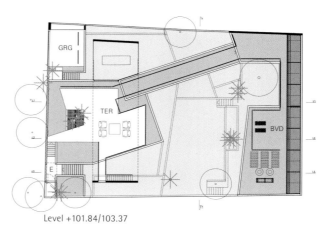
Level +101.84/103.37

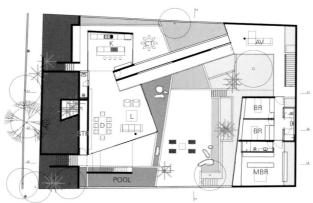
Level +98.78/100.31

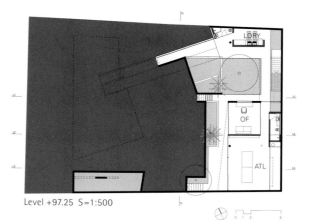
Level +97.25 S=1:500

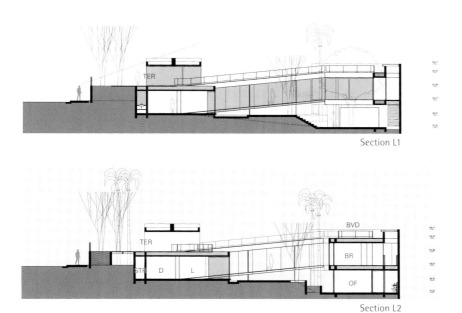

Section L1

Section L2

Section T1 S=1:400

Architects: Grupo SP Arquitetos—
Alvaro Puntoni, João Sodré, principal-in-charge; Ana Mulky, Bruno Satin, Miguel Meister, Otávio Melo, Paola Ornaghi, project team
Consultants: Eduardo Duprat, structural; JPD Projetos, mechanical; Ricardo Heder, lighting; Raul Pereira, landscape
Structural system: reinforced concrete
Major materials: concrete, glass, wood
Site area: 780.00 m²
Total floor area: 500.00 m²

このプロジェクトは，今まで試したことのなかったような，施主との直接的な協働のプロセスの結果である。4週間にわたって週3回のミーティングが開催されるなかで，施主の効果的かつ情緒的な参加のもと，デザインの発展，議論，再検討が行われた。結果として，慣習的なデザイン・プレゼンテーションややり直しは回避された。なぜなら，ともに作業を行った施主は，なされた決定のそれぞれについて把握していたからであり，これによって通常費やされる時間が短縮された。

既存の植栽の保全が，プロジェクトにおける前提の一つであった。もとの敷地には，32本の木が密集した林が存在したが，そのうち問題のある7本は取り除かれた。土地の3メートルの傾斜が半階分を占めており，提案された2棟をつなぐ傾斜路によって，住宅のプログラムを構成，分節している。

この構成によって，より社会的な空間を持った街路と，街路より上のレベルにあるポルティコによって半分覆われたテラスの並びのなかに，棟の一つがつくられている。他方の棟には，スタジオと寝室，そしてサンパウロの都市を見通すことのできる，覆いのない展望デッキが存在する。それらの棟と傾斜路の間では，中庭によって住宅におけるあらゆる活動に視覚的なつながりが導入されている。

施主によってなされた介入に加えて，賑やかな子供達や友人とのパーティーもまた，住宅のあらゆる空間に順応するコンクリートの構造体を活気づけることだろう。

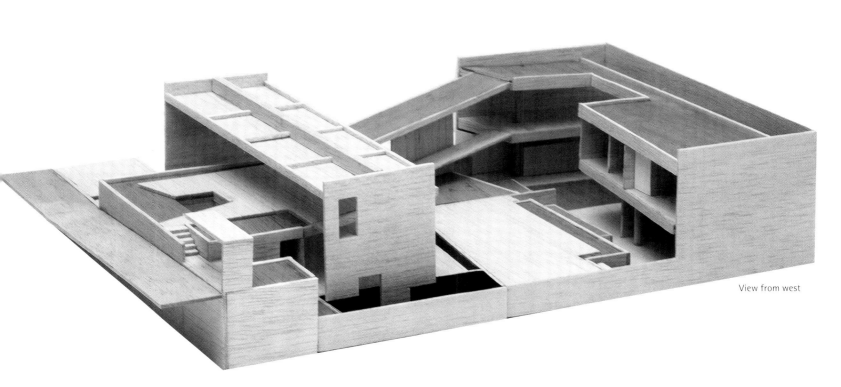

View from west

TAKASHI FUJINO
SCAFFOLD

North Kanto, Japan
Design: 2017-18
Construction: 2018-

Site plan S=1:3000

North view

Roof terrace

Perspective

Living room

View toward dining room

Dining room

Architects: Ikimono Architects—
Takashi Fujino, principal-in-charge;
Naoki Mazawa, project team
Consultants: Structural Design Firm Accurate—Emiko Sukegawa, structural
Structural system: reinforced concrete
Major materials: exposed concrete (wall & roof), exterior; exposed concrete, steel plate, flooring, lauan plywood, interior
Site area: 178.95 m^2
Building area: 61.44 m^2
Total floor area: 152.18 m^2

Model photos: Ayane Hirose

Space is there

A detached residence in the city center. Stand on the vacant plot and look around at the surrounding. The skyline of the buildings in the neighborhood cut the blue sky in a zigzag line. The space existed even before architecture is constructed here. Soon, columns and walls will be built and it will be no different to the neighboring houses that enclose the site or the electrical wires or the mountains far away. The town is part of the architecture. We all live in the environment as a whole.

A little taller

Building a little taller than the surrounding buildings in the town. Faraway buildings and mountains can be seen from the upper floors. At the same time, the lower floors confront with the congestions of the town. By climbing up and descending inside the house, the range of the landscape becomes wider and more narrow. Every day that transverses within this width.

A little separated

It is possible to achieve a smaller footprint of building area by creating multiple floors, higher. By doing so, a set back from the boundary of the site to the window can be composed. The window that only faced the exterior wall of the neighboring house can now have a view of the sky and cats; it is possible to feel many different things. Every day that is cradled by the diversity of the environment.

Mixture of many things

The interior is a mix of many different materials, scales and details. The warm floorboards, mirror-like metal plates, and thick concrete. These are the same as the trees, the cars, and the electrical posts outside. From civil engineering and construction to furniture, from figurative to abstraction, every day that is connected to the surrounding landscape.

Scaffold

The scaffold is a device to take an extensive view of the spread of space. Air and the landscape trespass through the framework. From right beneath my feet to the blue haze far away, we can acknowledge the existence, the location and movement of things that are scattered at multiple distances. It is possible to verify the current location. Orient oneself within the expanse. I aimed to build a residence that is like a scaffold.

Takashi Fujino

Plans S=1:300

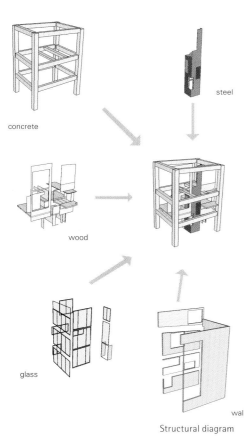

Structural diagram

空間はそこにある

市街地の戸建住宅。まっさらな敷地に立って周りをぐるりと見回す。周辺建物の稜線が青空をジグザグに切り取っている。建築が建つ前からすでに空間はここにある。やがて建ちあがる柱や壁は、敷地を囲む隣家や電線や遠くの山と何も違わない。街は建築の一部だ。私たちは環境全体の中に暮らしている。

ちょっと高く

建て込んだ街中に周辺建物より少し高く建てる。上階からは遠い建物や山が見えるようになる。一方で下階は街の雑踏と向き合っている。家の中を登ったり降りたりすると、風景の射程が広がったり狭まったりする。そんな幅を横断する毎日。

ちょっと離す

高く多層化すれば、建築面積は狭くできる。すると敷地境界線から窓までの引きがとれる。隣家の外壁しか見えなかった窓から空や猫が見え、たくさんのものをいっぺんに感じられるようになる。環境の多様さに包まれる毎日。

いろいろ混ぜる

室内には様々な素材・スケール・ディテールが混在する。暖かい床板、鏡のような鉄板、極太のコンクリート。それらは、外の樹木や、車や、電柱に同じ。土木から家具まで、具象から抽象まで、周りの風景と繋がる毎日。

櫓

櫓は空間の広がりを見渡す装置である。骨組みを空気や風景が通り抜ける。自分のすぐ足下から、青く霞む遠方まで、様々な距離に散らばるものの存在・位置・動きが分かる。今いる場所が確認できる。広がりの中に自らを定位する。目指したのは櫓のような住宅である。

（藤野高志）

Concept sketch

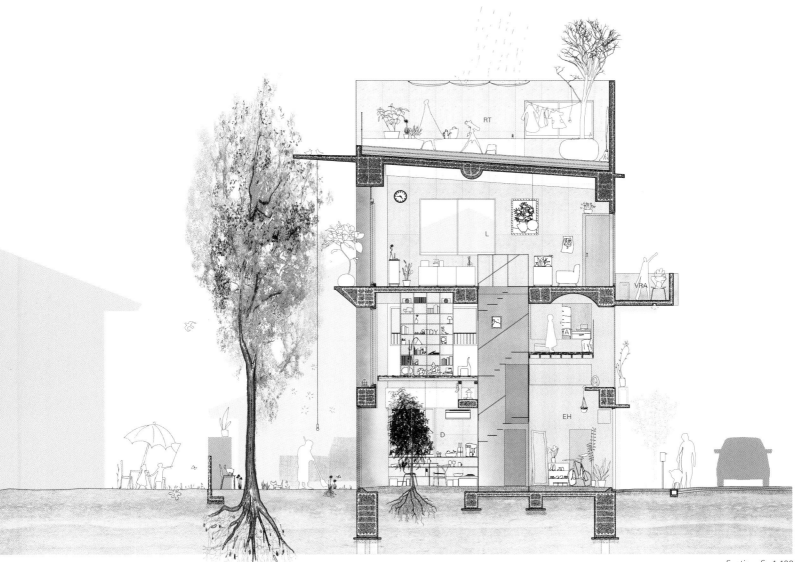

Section S=1:120

TATIANA BILBAO
WAYS OF LIFE

Kassel, Germany
Design: 2017-

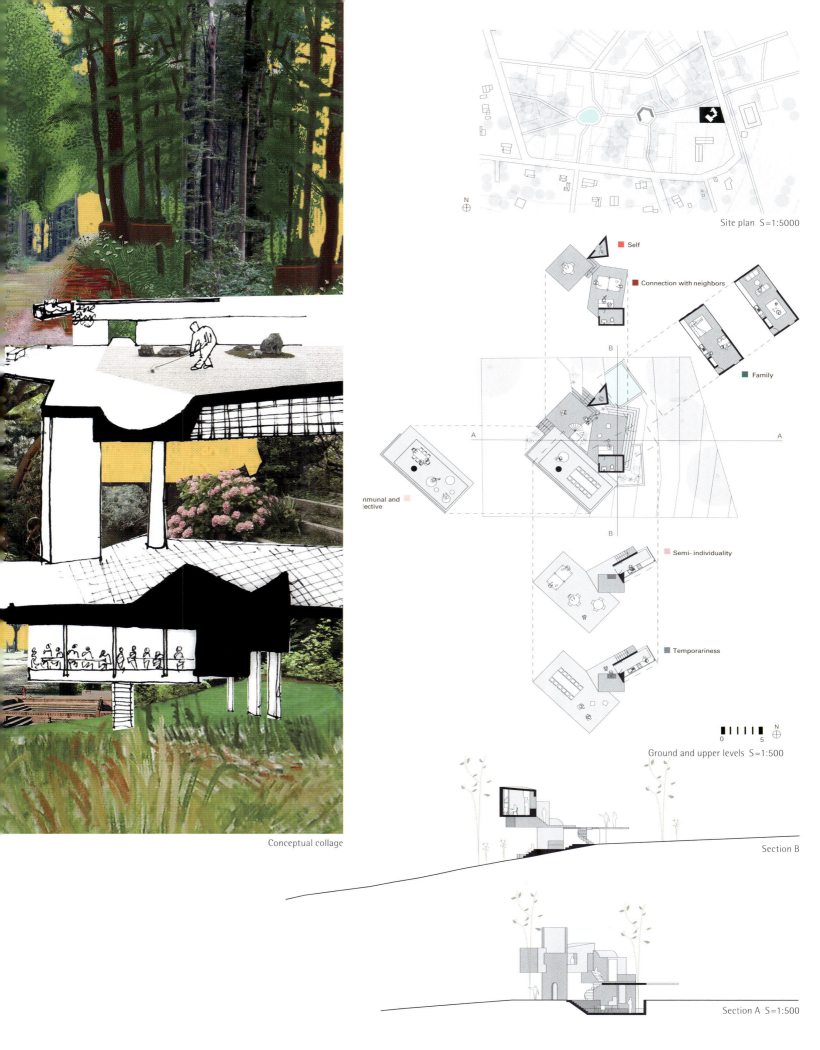

North view

Volumes are arranged in spiral

Architects: Tatiana Bilbao Estudio—
Tatiana Bilbao, principal-in-charge;
Catia Bilbao, Juan Pablo Benlliure, partners;
Sofía Betancur, Shilpa Mevada,
Simona Solorzano, project team
Site area: 500 m²
Building area: 118 m²
Total floor area: 208 m²

Southeast view

Collage

Ground level

Self

Family

Connection and neighbors

Semi-individuality

Six strings of life

Nowadays everyone is connected by internet, thinking together as one organism. But in this process of connecting with each other virtually, we have somewhere forgotten about our physical connection to one another and nature. Hence now it becomes important to connect our virtual life to the physical surroundings and enjoy it to the fullest. As Aristotle said "Human being is by nature a social animal." It is essential to study living through our relationships; individual to family, family to friends and further to the community life. Our 21st century house aims to be flexible to transform itself according to the human necessity of being isolated yet communally connected and part of a larger process in the making of our world.

We understand this making through daily mundane activities that we perform, trying to connect these activities to certain emotions that arise; and then developing a ways of life activity diagram, which further evokes the configuration of 6 strings of life: Connection with neighbors—Self—Communal and Collective—Semiindividuality—Temporariness—Family.

The house is hence a manifestation of various ways of doing the same activity and various emotions arising while performing them. It is a breathing organism which opens out or closes; transforming according to the number of dwellers. The result is a sum of six unique spaces, each of them with spatial characteristics closely linked to the activities happening inside them. The volumes are arranged in a spiral, where the more public of them lays in the ground and the most private is on top. A semi covered communal gathering space is created beneath the suspended volumes.

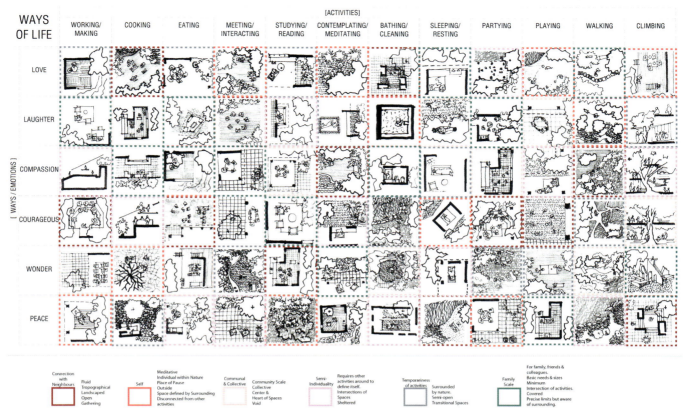

Diagram: strings of life

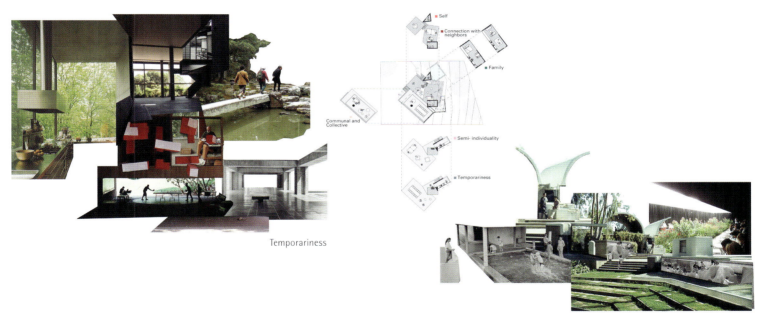

Temporariness

Communal and collective

今日，私たちはインターネットでつながり，一つの有機体として共に思考する。しかし，ヴァーチャルなつながりを構築する過程で私たちは，ある時を境に他人や自然とのつながりを忘れてしまった。このようなわけで，ヴァーチャル・ライフに物理的な環境との関係性を持たせ，それを最大限享受することが今では重要となった。アリストテレスが言ったように「人間は社会的な動物である」。個人と家族，家族と友人やその先にある社会生活といった，私たちが構築する関係性を通して生き方について学ぶことは必須である。21世紀における住宅が目指すもの，それは孤立しつつも人々と繋がったり，世界を構築するより大きなプロセスの一部となるような人間が必要とするものに合わせて，柔軟な変化ができるということである。

私たちが理解しているように，これが現実化する要因となるのは，日常のありふれた活動に他ならない。そして，そのような活動と，それによって湧き上がるある種の感情とを結びつけようと試みると，「近隣住民とのつながり・自身・地域社会と集合体・半個人・一時性・家族」といった，暮らしを構成する六つの要素から成る，暮らし方のアクティビティ・ダイアグラムが展開される。

したがって，この住宅は同じ活動を行なうための様々な方法と，活動を行う中で湧き上がる様々な感情を表明したものとなっている。これは開閉する，息をする有機体であり，居住者数に応じて姿を変える。結果的に六つのユニークな空間が生まれ，各空間は，その空間内で発生する活動と強いつながりのある空間的特性を帯びたものとなる。各ヴォリュームは，公共性の高いものが地面に，最もプライベートなものが頂上にくるように螺旋状に配置される。半分屋根が架かった共同の交流空間が浮遊するヴォリュームの下に設けられる。

Sketch

MAKI ONISHI + YUKI HYAKUDA
T HUT

Maebashi, Gunma, Japan
Design: 2016-

This is an ongoing project of an extremely small residence in Maebashi. The owner is a young man still in his 20s, and a person with the rare experience to have lived in Sou Fujimoto's *T-House* untill now. His father must have wanted his son to gain the same experience of meeting young Fujimoto and building a house just like himself. At the first meeting, when the father and son came, we saw black and white photographs of the old landscapes of Maebashi town; we heard stories about Sakutaro Hagiwara, a poet born and raised in Maebashi; we found out about the son, a photographer commuting to the town and documenting the vanishing sceneries; looking at the site plan of tiny triangle plot facing a large intersection that used to be a stamp shop, we completely fell in love these guys, and we had the feeling that we really want to try designing their house no matter what.

There, we proposed to create a large roof that is almost like a living creature crouching down, or like an enormous skirt floating over the triangular piece of land that sits there as if it was left behind time, concaved by large-scale buildings and roads. With a photo studio and kitchen on the first floor, making the loft on the second floor a bedroom, everything else a semi-outdoor *doma* (earth floor), we wanted to create a space where people can feel that they are basked under the roof. We want to create something special, for people to want to actually touch the roof, to continuously look at it; we are searching for ways to make things by mixing together with the construction done by professional contractors, for example to dye the cement plates by ourselves and adapt handmade construction methods. We expect the project to change and evolve and there are more things undecided than confirmed at the moment, but we are looking to continue to develop our ideas and study ways to make "a roof that leaves an impression" or "an architecture that can be somewhat associated with living creatures".
Maki Onishi + Yuki Hyakuda

View from east

Architects: onishimaki+hyakudayuki / o+h—Maki Onishi, Yuki Hyakuda, principals-in-charge; Kotaro Igo, project team
Structural system: steel, wood
Site area: 60.89 m²
Building area: 52.04 m²
Total floor area: 42.11 m²

Site plan S=1:2000

Bird's eye view　　　　　　　　　　　　　　　　　Model photos: Nohara Yamazaki

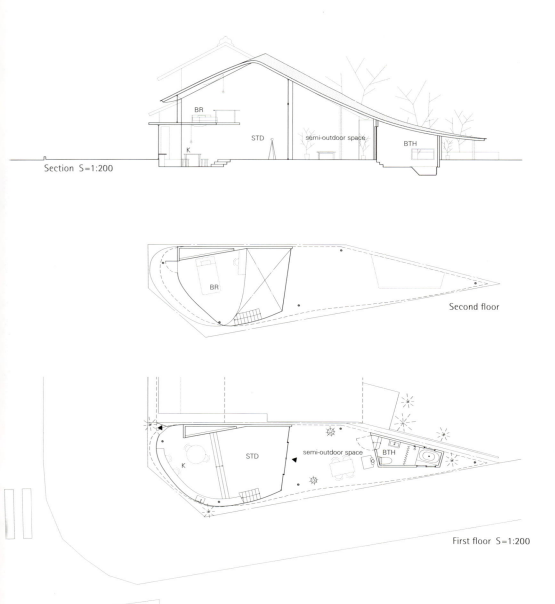
Section S=1:200

Second floor

First floor S=1:200

前橋に計画している，とても小さな住宅である。施主はまだ20代の若い男性で，これまでの人生を藤本壮介さんが設計した「T-house」で暮らして来たという稀有な体験の持ち主であった。お父様が若い頃，若い藤本さんに出会って家を建てたという経験を，息子である彼にも経験してほしいと考えたのだろうか。初めての打合せに親子でいらっしゃって，前橋の町の昔の風景を撮った白黒写真を見たり，前橋で生まれ育った詩人・萩原朔太郎の話を聞いたり，カメラマンである彼が，町の中で消え行く風景を何度も現場に通いながら記録している活動を知ったり，元判子屋さんがあったという，大きな交差点に面した三角形の本当に小さな敷地図を手にしたりするうちに，すっかりお二人を好きになり，何が何でも彼らの家を設計してみたい，という気持ちになっていた。

そこで私たちが考えたのは，巨大なスケールのビルや道路の中に囲まれ，時間の中に取り残されたような三角形の土地に，生き物がちょこんとうずくまっているような，あるいは巨大なスカートが浮かんでいるような，大きな屋根を一つかけるという提案である。1階には写真スタジオとキッチンがあり，2階の屋根裏部屋を寝室としているが，それ以外は半屋外の土間空間となっていて，「屋根に包まれている」という感覚を感じられる空間にしたいと考えている。屋根はそれ自体が触ってみたい，ずっと見ていたい，という気持ちになるような特別なものにしたいと考えていて，例えばセメント板を自分たちで染色するなど，手づくりの施工と，プロの工務店の施工を混ぜ合わせたようなつくり方ができないかなと模索している。まだ決まっていないことの方が多く，これからどんどんプロジェクトが変化して行くのだろうと予想しているが，「印象的な屋根をかける」「建築でありながらどこか生き物を連想させる」，というアイディアをより膨らませるようにスタディしていけるよいなと思っている。

（大西麻貴＋百田有希）

AKIRA YONEDA
BOAT HOUSE (LANDING HOUSE IV)

Chiba, Japan
Design: 2017-18
Construction: 2018-19

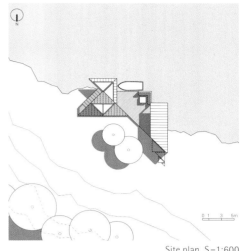

Site plan S=1:600

The site is located in a peaceful countryside, at the banks of a relatively big artificial lake that acts as a regulating reservoir. When viewed from the site, the lake expands towards the southwest direction, and on the opposite side there is a thicket on a gentle slope with limited flat land. The site can be approached after exiting an undulating forest road, and on the other hand it can also be approached by a simple rowing boat from the opposite shore. The plan was to build a weekend residence with priority given to water activities.

Because it is a shallow artificial lake, the condition of the water's edge changes quite drastically depending on the different water levels we experience during the dry and wet seasons. Considering the relation between land and water, the design is primarily composed of a large deck that connects the two. Dining with an excellent view at the large deck that serves as an outdoor living room as well as a place to anchor the boat, and a base for relevant activities with small storage for the boat. Using local cedar and conventional methods of construction, the compact design tries not to use any heavy-duty machines as much as possible.

They contour of the water's edge is typically fractal. Similar shapes of different sizes repetitively appear to make a geometrical structure, and this residence reflects such conditions of the water onto the structural aspects of the architecture, and it is constituted of repeating different sizes of the same right-angled isosceles triangle as a basic motif. Rather than a 2-dimensional profile, I intent to create an architecture where human life infiltrates into the 3-dimensional domain that is interweaved by nature, man-made objects or geometry.
Akira Yoneda

View from lake

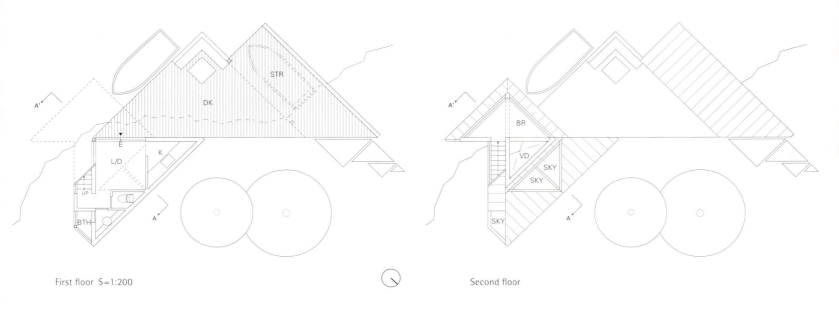

First floor S=1:200

Second floor

Model photos: Nohara Yamazaki

敷地は，のどかな田園地帯の比較的大きな，調整池として機能する人造湖のほとりにある。湖は敷地からみて南西方向に広がっており，反対側はゆるやかな斜面地の雑木林で平坦な部分はわずかである。敷地へは陸路で起伏のある山林道を抜けてアプローチするが，一方で簡易な手漕ぎボートを使って対岸からのアプローチも可能である。そこに水辺でのアクティビティを前提とした週末住宅が計画された。

浅瀬の人造湖であるため，乾季と雨季の水位の違いによって，水際の様相はかなり変化する。そうした陸地との湖水の間にあって，両者を結びつける大きなデッキを中心とした構成をとっている。見晴らしのいい開放的な屋外で食事をし，くつろぐアウトドア・リビングとして機能すると同時にボートの停泊が可能で，ボートを格納する小さな倉庫が併設されていて，ボートによるアクティビテティの基地としても機能する。建屋は地場で採れた杉材を用いた在来工法によって建設され，できるだけ大掛かりな重機にたよらないコンパクトな設計となっている。

一般に水際の輪郭線は，フラクタルなものとされている。大きさの違う相似形が反復して現れる幾何学構造を指すが，この住宅ではそうした水辺の様相を建築の構造的な側面に反映させ，直角二等辺三角形を基本のモチーフとして大小反復する構成をとっている。2次元的なプロフィールというより，むしろ自然と人工物，あるいは幾何学が織りなす3次元的な領域に人間の生活が浸透するような建築を意図した。

（米田明）

Architects: ARCHITECTON—
Akira Yoneda, principal-in-charge
Structural system: wood
Major materials: venner plywood, cedar flooring
Site area: 360.58 m²
Building area: 36.06 m²
Total floor area: 44.88 m²

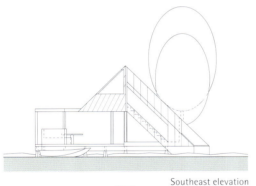

Southeast elevation

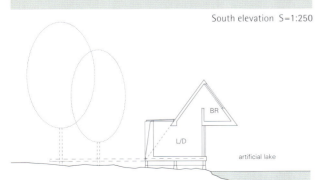

South elevation S=1:250

Section A-A' S=1:250

SPBR ARQUITETOS
HOUSE IN SAGAPONACK

Sagaponack, New York, U.S.A.
Design: 2016-17

South view

I Maestri
In 2015, Neil Radnal, director for the IMaestri, kindly invited us to design one of the houses for Sagaponack Project. Our task was taken as to design a strategy that could accomodate any of those five sizes of house, from 280 to 560 square meters. Among them, following his request, the largest version of house in a 8,400 square meters site placed at East Woods Path, was taken to illustrate this proposition.

Long Island modern tradition
It happaned that I have been in East Hampton before, in 2006, to visit the site in order to design a house in Ocean Avenue with Hook Pond Lane. Although not built, it gave me the opportunity to realize how strongly related Long Island is to the history of the modern architecture and art in United States. Gordon Bunshaft's own house and its remarkable garden by Nogushi. Robert Motherwell's house by Pierre Chareau. Early works by Richard Meier, by Philip Jonhsnon. It was there where Pollock begun to display his canvas on the ground; where De Kooning, Saul Steinberg or Mark Rothko have produced some of their masterpieces.

PROPOSAL
A strategical scheme rather than a specific project
Luigi Snozzi, Celerina, and John Heyduk, Wall Houses, are precedents to be named here.

By explotating the unite of a house into separated rooms it is possible to free its size from the area it covers, as if its footprint area was made by both out and inner spaces No matter its version 280, 350, 420, 490 or 560 sq m, their shape look very similar. It means, even a small house can face and qualify massively a much bigger site.

On the other hand, to detach the house from the ground allows to preserve the soil permeability and existing vegetation. In addition, it enhances the view from the house over landscape on that quite flat topography.

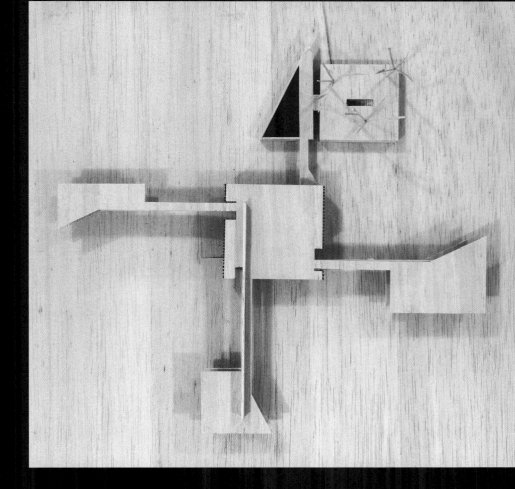

Spread out rooms

A living room plus kitchen in the center, as a square meeting point. Gravitating surround it, displayed as the four cardinal points, are other blocks of program: [1] children/guests bedroom on north; [2] main bedroom on east; [3] office and library on South and [4] swimming pool and garden on west.

Reinforced Concrete Structure

On ground level: as if rocky outcrop bringing 'nature' to the same level of the house, swimming pool and garden are the only volumes which touch the ground. In correspondence to the swimming pool an excentric 9 meter-long concrete wall seems to be the only column supporting the 15 x 15 meter-square of the living room in the center.

On the upper level: starting at the central square, two 34 meter-long beams define a inner 9 x 9 meter-square living space that open to a north and south porch and, on the other side of them, a kitchen on the west and a small living, laundry and a bed and bath wardrobe on the east facade of it. Scaping out in opposite directions toward north and south these beams provide paths and structure respectively to the guest bedrooms and office.

On the rooftop: one more 34 meter-long beam hangs a corridor toward the main bedroom.

Materials

The solid weight of the concrete is counterbalanced by the transparence of the glass panels and the cozy ambience provided by wood panel and floor. Quite thin and flat concrete slabs floating among oak trees.

Dualities

Rational and sensitive, weight and lighness, teluric and tectonic or, as a very first assumption: a closed strategy for a scheme open enough to accomodate multiple possibilities, this proposal tends to consider duality as the best sort of integrity in architectural design.

East view

North view

Architects: spbr arquitetos—
Angelo Bucci, principal-in-charge;
Felipe Barradas, Lucas Roca, Victor Próspero,
Tatiana Ozzetti, Martha Dallari Bucci,
Henrique Castro, Vitor Endo, Paula Dal Maso,
project team
Structural system: reinforced concrete
Major materials: concrete, steel, glass, wood
Site area: 8,400 m²
Building area: 560 m²
Total floor area: 804 m²

Office/library

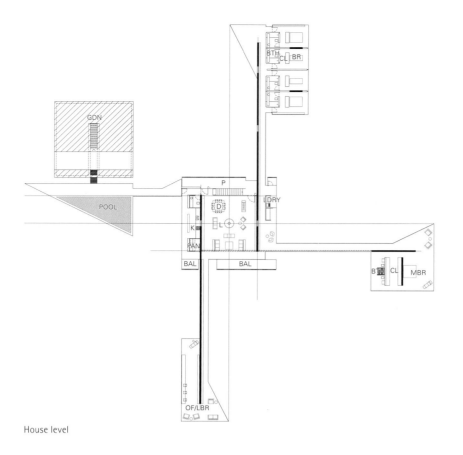

House level

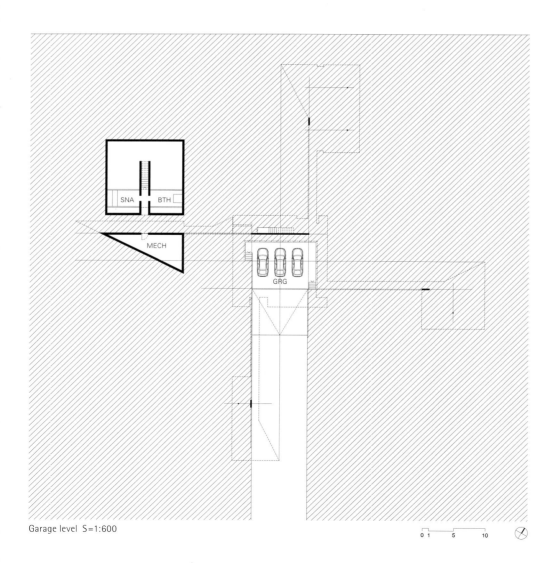

Garage level S=1:600

TYPE A
GROSS INTERNAL AREA 292.14m²
≈ 3,000 sq.ft [278m²]
3 bedrooms w/ bathroom [2+1]

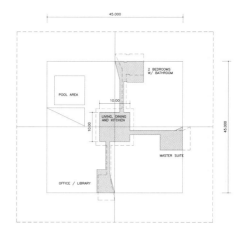

TYPE B
GROSS INTERNAL AREA 359.99m²
≈ 3,750 sq.ft [348m²]
3 bedrooms w/ bathroom [2+1]

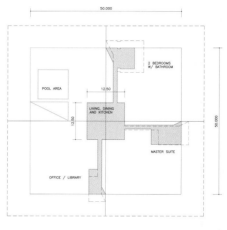

TYPE C
GROSS INTERNAL AREA 422.06m²
≈ 4,500 sq.ft [418m²]
4 bedrooms w/ bathroom [3+1]

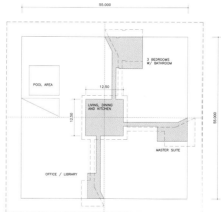

Diagram: variations of size from 280 to 560 m²

TYPE D

GROSS INTERNAL AREA 504.60m²
≈ 5,250 sq.ft [488m²]

4 bedrooms w/ bathroom [3+1]

490

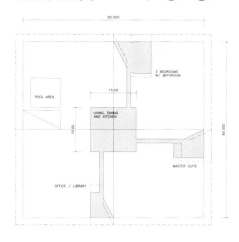

TYPE E

GROSS INTERNAL AREA 568.20m²
≈ 6,000 sq.ft [558m²]

5 bedrooms w/ bathroom [4+1]

560

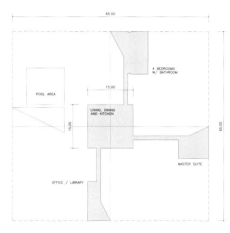

イ・マエストリ

イ・マエストリのディレクター, ニール・ラドナルからサガポナックのプロジェクトの住宅についてオファーされたのは2015年のことである。私たちが依頼されたのは280平米から560平米までの五つの大きさの住宅について, そのいずれにも応えることのできるコンセプトを組み立てることであった。彼の要求に沿って, それらの住宅のうち最大のものをイースト・ウッズ・パスの8,400平米の敷地に提案することが決定された。

ロングアイランドの近代的な伝統

2006年のことになるが, 私はオーシャン・アヴェニューにあるフック・ポンド・レーンで住宅を計画するのに敷地を訪れるため, イースト・ハンプトンに滞在したことがあった。当時この住宅は建てられなかったが, その時の出来事はロングアイランドがアメリカ合衆国において, 近代建築と美術の歴史にいかに強く結びついているかを知る良い経験となった。ゴードン・バンシャフトの自邸とイサム・ノグチによる素晴らしい庭。ピエール・シャローのロバート・マザーウェル邸。リチャード・マイヤーやフィリップ・ジョンソンの初期の作品。ポロックがカンヴァスを地面に広げ, デ・クーニングやソール・スタインバーグ, あるいはマーク・ロスコが傑作の数々を生み出したのもこの土地であった。

プロポーザル ─ 特定のプロジェクトではなく設計のスキームとして

ルイジ・スノッツィの「セレリナ」やジョン・ヘイダックの「壁の家」といった住宅は, よく名の知られた作品である。住宅という結束を複数の部屋に分解することで, 住宅の規模を敷地から自由に解き放つことが可能となる。住宅が必要とする面積は, 内外部の空間の双方によって定義されるのだ。280, 350, 420, 490, 560平米のいずれの住宅も, 非常に類似した形態を持っている。たとえ小さな住宅であったとしても, 広大な敷地と向き合い, それにふさわしい存在となることができる。

その一方で, 住宅を地面から切り離したことが, 土壌の通気性を維持し, 自生する植物を守ることを可能にしてくれる。さらに住宅からは, 起伏のない広大な地形からなる自然を一層よく眺めることができる。

拡散する部屋

正方形の交流地点としての居間と台所。その周囲には次に掲げるその他のプログラムが四つの中枢機能として引き寄せられる。すなわち, [1]北面の子供用/来客用の寝室, [2]東面の主寝室, [3]南面の書斎・書庫, [4]西面のスイミングプールと庭である。

鉄筋コンクリートの構造

1階：露出した岩肌は, 住宅と同じレベルに「自然」を引き込んでくるかのように見える。スイミングプールと庭は地面に接する唯一のヴォリュームである。スイミングプールに対して偏心した9メートルのコンクリートの壁は, 中央に置かれた15メートル角の正方形の居間を支持する唯一の柱であるかのように見える。

上階：中央には正方形が置かれ, 2本の34メートルの梁が内部にある9メートル角の居間を定義する。リビングの南北方向はポーチに向かって開かれ, これらの反対側では西面に対して台所, 東側のファサードに対しては小さな生活空間, 洗面室, 寝室, 浴室とワードローブが続く。南北の反対方向に向かって飛び出したこれらの梁は, 各々, 来客用の寝室と書斎への動線と構造の役割を果たしている。

屋上：ここでも主寝室に向かう渡り廊下が34メートルの梁から吊り下げられている。

素材

コンクリートの堅牢な重厚感は, ガラスの透明性や木の壁と床のもたらす居心地の良い雰囲気とは対照的である。非常に薄く平らなコンクリートスラブがオークの木々の間に浮遊している。

二元性

理性と感性, 重厚かつ軽快であること, 地球的かつ構造的であること, あるいは当初の想定のように複数の可能性を満たす上で十分に開放的なスキームを提供する閉じた設計として, このプロポーザルは建築デザインにおける統合の極致としての二元性について考察を試みたものである。

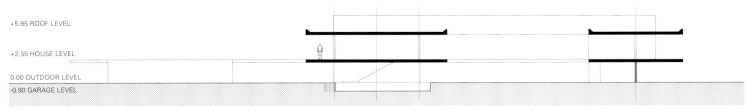

Section S=1:400

GRUPO ARANEA
CASA MUCHAVISTA

Playa Muchavista, El Campello, Alicante, Spain
Design: 2017-18
Construction: 2018-19

Sketches

50

Diagram

They wanted to live on the heights of Alicante, overlooking the Playa Muchavista, with the Mediterranean heat as background of their intimacy.

A house offering a view in the East, on the sea... This landscape is completed by the Sierra de Aitana, the Puig Campana and the Sierra Helada in the North and with the Cabo de las Huertas in the South.

We proposed to convert the ascension to this private watchtower into a rich daily experience, full of variations: concatenation of staggered terraces, hanging gardens, resting areas, exposed to the sun, flooded by the sea.

We proposed an infrastructure facilitating moments of pleasure in this privileged location. This will offer infinite, immersive experiences as changing as the sea itself. Amplifying reverberations of the waves, privileging awakenings by the sea (sunrise by the sea), protecting oneself from torments and occasionally exposing oneself to saltpeter bath.

Built on the sea front of the Playa Muchavista borough, with vacation buildings on both sides, identical repetitions of terraces and striped awnings, we renounced building something that would drastically interrupt the sea breeze and went instead for a more open volume where crawling vegetation and water sheets are protagonists.

Before the imposing presence of the sea, mirror of the overwhelming celestial vault, our forms leave everyone in awe, and then begins the game of catching the horizon.

A set of horizontal platforms connect the gardens and make them ascend. Multiple diagonal spaces then appear to link the distinct levels. The vertical structure is concentrated. The three support elements are respectively: the vertical access core, the chimney and an enclosure/compound of various services. From them emerge the different parts of the building, composed of gardens with swimming pools, terraces with lounges...

This ascending labyrinth unveils secret places...

Hanging orchards, vegetal filters, edible walls, irrigation ditches that will generate several waterfalls, will interlace interiors and exteriors spaces. A thermodynamic system designed for the climatic comfort of each room.

A wide program, a huge house.

How many projects can fit inside this one project?

The project could be described as a series of islands that would give birth to a magnificent archipelago.

These autonomous and interconnected universes make it necessary to set some rules of coexistence between the different inhabitants.

Although the lower zone is accessible to a lot of different persons, the higher you get in the building, the more private will become the rooms. The second floor marks an inflection point in the ascension. A succession of gardened spaces, leisure and relax zones still much connected to the gardens of the lower levels, serve as buffer for the higher private levels. The rampant garden ends here. But not everything...

In the more private zone, a concatenation of horizontal spaces gently descending to the South drawing you to the sea.

On the highest level, the master bedroom, literally above the sea, is the culmination point of this series of atmospheric hugs.

Model photo

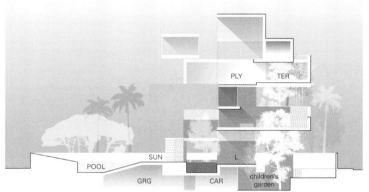
Cross section

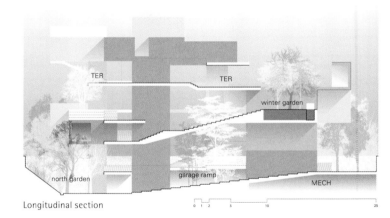
Longitudinal section

　プラヤ・ムチャビスタの浜辺を見下ろすアリカンテの高台，地中海の熱気を身近に感じられる場所に住みたいと彼らは考えた。
　東に海を臨む家である。その景色を完成させているのが，西に広がるアイタナ山やブイグ・カンパナの山並み，北のシエラ・エラダ自然公園，そして南に伸びるカボ・デ・ラス・ウェルタスの岬である。
　このプライベートな「灯台」までの上りの道のりを，多彩に変化する日々の体験として楽しめるようなプランを提案した。灯台までの道のりに，ひな壇や空中庭園，東屋を設け，陽射しを浴びながら，あるいは海に抱かれながら，上っていけるようなプランである。
　私たちの提案は，この特別な場所で過ごす一瞬一瞬を存分に味わうための家だ。刻々と姿を変えていく海のように目まぐるしく変化する体験に，どこまでも浸りきってもらうのが狙いである。この家で，波の残響を楽しみ，海がもたらす目覚め（海の向こうに広がる朝焼け）というこの地だけの恩恵を享受し，日々の苦難から身を守り，時には硝酸カリウムを入れた浴槽に身を浸してもらいたいと考えた。
　敷地はプラヤ・ムチャビスタ村の海に面しており，リゾート施設が左右に建ち，まったく同じデザインのテラスや縞模様の日よけがずらりと並ぶという周辺環境である。これらの条件を考慮し，海風を存分に浴びられる家というアイデアは断念。豊かな植生と青い海を主役とした，より解放感のあるデザインを目指した。
　堂々たる蒼穹を鏡のように映す大海原を前に建つ家を見て，誰もが圧倒され，やがて，水平線を見つけようと視界を広げるはずだ。
　水平に連なるプラットフォームは庭と庭をつないで，訪れた人を上り坂へと導いていく。ほどなくして，各階を結ぶ，対角に並んだ複数の空間が現れる。ここに，垂直構造をまとめた。建造物を支える三つの要素はそれぞれ，上下のアクセスを提供するコア，煙突，各種の設備をまとめたエリアとなっている。ここからさらに，プール付きの庭やラウンジ付きのテラスなど，建物のさまざまなエリアに移動することができる。
　この上り坂の迷路が，隠された空間を徐々に明らかにしていく。
　たとえば，たわわに実のなる果樹園，植物のフィルター，食べられる壁，何本もの滝をつくる灌漑用水路などが，屋内外のスペースに交錯するように設けられている。また各部屋には，快適な暮らしを約束するために，熱力学を利用した空調システムを導入した。

幅広いプログラム，広大な邸宅。
　この一つのプロジェクトに，いくつのプロジェクトを組み込むことができるだろうか？
　このプロジェクトは，いくつもの島が連なってできた一つの巨大な群島と言えるかもしれない。
　それぞれに自律的でありながら相互につながった宇宙では，そこに住む人たちが共存していくためのルールが必要である。
　たとえば建物のなかでも低いほうのゾーンにはいろいろな人がアクセスできるが，高いゾーンへと進むにつれ，各室のプライベート度は高くなる。2階では，上り坂に変化が表れる。庭園や娯楽スペース，リラックス空間が連なり，それらが低層の庭へとつながって，上層のプライベート空間とのバッファーとして機能している。緑生い茂る庭園空間はここで終わるが，居住空間はさらに先まで続いている……。
　プライベート空間では，水平に連なるスペースを南に移動して徐々に下層に降りていくと，海が見える仕組みだ。
　そして，文字通り海の上に位置する主寝室を設けた最上階が，自然に抱かれたいくつもの空間の連なりの，最高点に達する場所である。

Fourth floor

Third floor

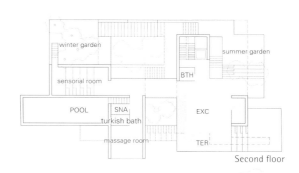
Second floor

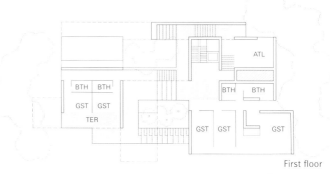
First floor

Architects: Grupo Aranea—
Francisco Leiva Ivorra, principal-in-charge;
Artur Rodrigues, Juan Luis Gallego, project-in-charge; Alessio Lo Vullo, Lorena Gebran, José Luis Carratalá Rico, Agnieszka Chromiec, Andrés Llopis Pérez, Konstatina Pagalou, project team
Consultants: David Gallardo Llopis, structural; Ángel Cremades, interior design; Marta Garcia Chico, landscape;
Luis de Diego Fort, José Luis Carratalá Rico, quantity surveyors; Quatre Caps, infographics
Structural system: reinforced exposed concrete
Major materials: concrete, glass
Site area: 2,108 m²
Building area: 3,198 m²
Total floor area: 1,752 m² (indoor spaces), 2,464 m² (outdoor spaces)

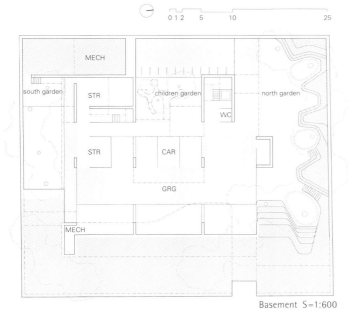
Basement S=1:600

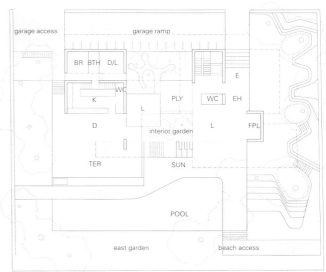
Ground floor

53

This is a project to build a house on a tiny plot of land along the rail road.

Since both the area of the site and the maximum building envelope are not enough for a family of five, we thought it is necessary to make it more open and connected with the city to extend its space, and fold and pile the spaces up vertically on the small footprint.

Will such a house be able to figure out a specific form of mathematics, or develop a sort of new grid, which is modest but universal?

We first focused on its stairs which is essential for connecting the area above the retaining walls with the street level, or connecting upstairs and downstairs in the interior space. Since the footprint is so small that it is almost occupied by the staircase, we added multiple functions and meanings to the staircase and made it a space spiraling up to the air, just like a wind whirling up the city.

This spiral is an approach connecting the interior and the exterior, also a staircase, a void to link the places, a rationally compressed space containing both interior spaces and exterior spaces, a window to let the light and the wind in, and a main structural element.

By thinking of this architecture as a connection between the vast city and the skies, we can imagine a house in a broad extent, and such imagination is exactly a spacial framework in which spaces can be folded plastically.
Tomohiro Hata

Architects: Tomohiro Hata Architect and Associates—Tomohiro Hata, principal-in-charge; Minami Sakaue, project team
Consultants: Takashi Manda Structural Design—Takashi Manda, structural
Structural system: steel
Major materials: galvanized steel, exterior; steel plate, structure and interior
Site area: 70.36 m²
Building area: 41.87 m²
Total floor area: 98.53 m²

TOMOHIRO HATA
HOUSE IN GOSHIKIYAMA

Hyogo, Japan
Design: 2017-18
Construction: 2018-

Model photos: Ayane Hirose

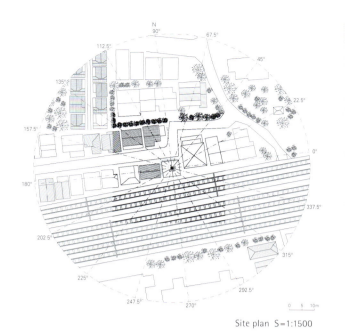
Site plan S=1:1500

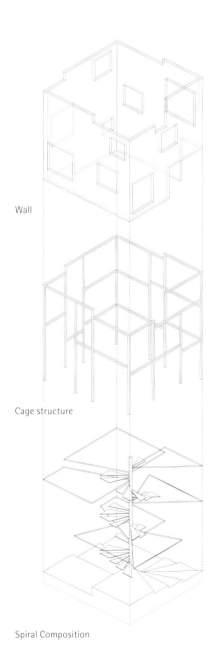
Floors continue in spiral

Wall

Cage structure

Spiral Composition

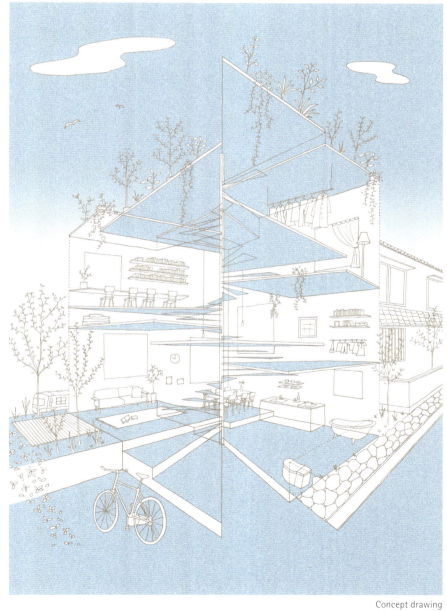
Concept drawing

55

五色山の家

鉄道沿いのとても小さな敷地に立つ住宅の計画。

この場所に家族五人のための住まいを計画するにあたり，平面的にも立体的にも小さな気積の中で計画する必要があることから，物理的にこの場所に閉じず，街とつながることで拡がりを生み出すような住まいのあり方と，住まいとしてのそれぞれの居場所を，小さなフットプリントの上に立体的にコンパクトに折りたたむことが必要であるように思えた。

そのような住まいが背負う背景から，言うなれば固有の数学的な形式を導き，新しいグリッドのような，ささやかながらも普遍性を持った空間的な枠組みとして展開することはできないだろうか。

初めに，擁壁上の敷地と街路のレベル差をつなぐ，或いは内部で上下階をつなぐ要素として不可欠な階段に着目した。階段を配置するとそれだけで一杯になってしまいそうなフットプリントであるからこそ，この階段に多層的な機能や意味を重ねていくことを試み，街から空までをぐるぐると巻き付けるような，螺旋階段をそのまま空間化したような形式に至った。

この螺旋は，内外をつなぐアプローチであり，階段であり，場をつなぐ吹き抜けであり，内外の居場所を合理的に折りたたんだ空間であり，内部に光や風を導く窓であり，構造における大黒柱でもある。

圧倒的な拡がりを持った街と空をつなぐものとして建築を位置づけることで，大きな拡がりの中にある住まいのイメージが浮かび上がり，それは伸びやかに空間を折りたたんでいく，空間的な枠組みのあり様そのものである。
　　　　　　　　　　　　　　　　　　　　（畑友洋）

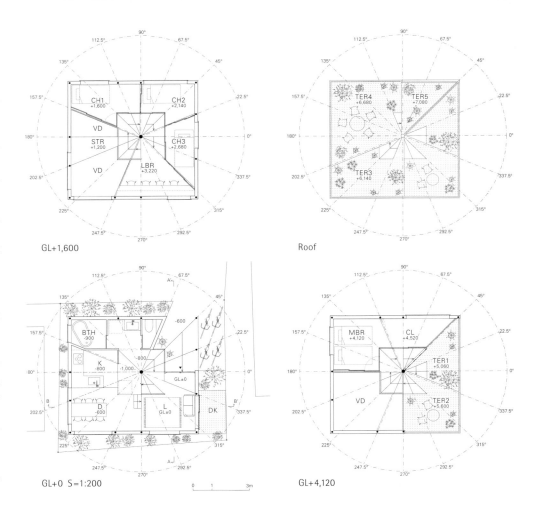

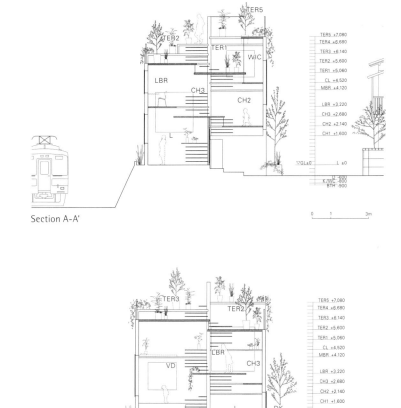

Main wing

MATHIAS KLOTZ
HITES HOUSE

Lo Curro, Santiago, Chile
Design: 2017
Construction: 2018-

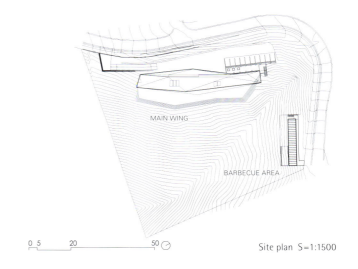

Site plan S=1:1500

View toward main wing from barbecue area

View toward barbecue area from main wing

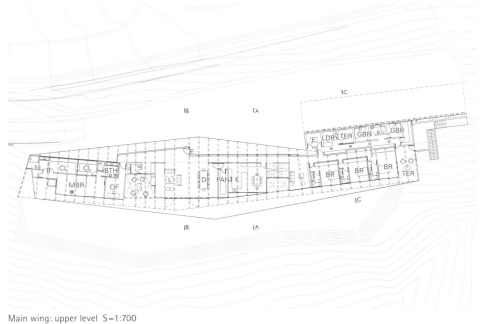

Main wing: upper level S=1:700

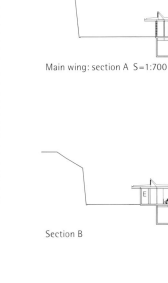

Main wing: section A S=1:700

Section B

Section C

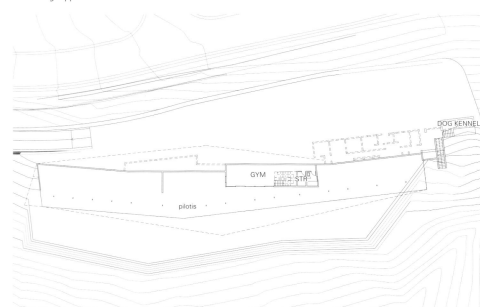

Main wing: lower level

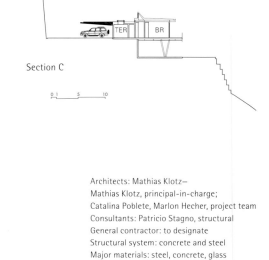

Architects: Mathias Klotz—
Mathias Klotz, principal-in-charge;
Catalina Poblete, Marlon Hecher, project team
Consultants: Patricio Stagno, structural
General contractor: to designate
Structural system: concrete and steel
Major materials: steel, concrete, glass
Site area: 12,240 m²
Total floor area: 670 m²

The work is about a detached house, approximately 700 square meters, located in the hills sector of Lo Curro, Vitacura commune in Santiago. The land has an area of 1,200 square meters and an average slope of 50%.

These topographical conditions make it look for a horizontal volume, which does not exceed 8.50 meters, which follows the same elevation. In this way, the whole house always has a continuous view from the same height towards the city. The way to structure this body is to support it on its west side, and leave it with only punctual metal supports leaving the eastern side free that has the best views towards the mountain range. This type of structure generates the sensation of a volume that floats on the hill.

The program of the house is developed throughout this volume, leaving towards the ends the bedrooms and towards the center the most public areas. All the enclosures privilege a transparent closure towards the east and opaque towards the west.

On the baseboard, the volume of the gym against the ground appears, which seeks a more direct relationship with the immediate exterior and the gardens. This level is connected by a linear route with the area of the barbecue and the pool.

The materials used are reinforced concrete, metal pillars and wood.

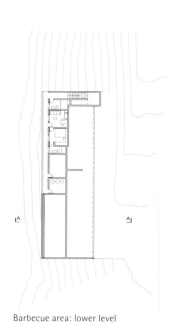

Barbecue area: lower level

View toward dining room from living room

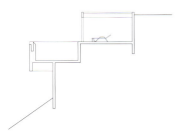

Barbecue area: section　S=1:350

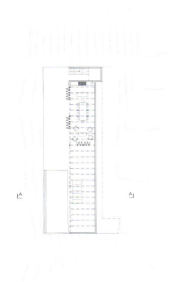

Barbecue area: upper level　S=1:700

この計画は，サンティアゴのビタクラにあるロ・クロの丘に位置する約700平米の戸建住宅である。敷地は1,200平米の広さで，平均して50％の傾斜地になっている。

これらの地形条件により，同じ高さで続く，8.50メートルを超えない水平なヴォリュームが求められた。この方法で，住宅全体から常に，均一の高さからの連続した景色を望むことができる。この主要部のストラクチュアは，西側で支持され，山脈に向かう最も素晴らしい景色のある東側を解放するようにして，規則的な金属の支柱のみで支えている。この種のストラクチュアは，ヴォリュームが丘に浮いているような感覚を引き起こす。

住宅のプログラムは，このヴォリュームを通して展開し，端側に寝室を，中央には最もパブリックなスペースを配置している。外皮は全て，東側に向かって透明，西側に向かって不透明なものとしている。

地下には，間近の外部や庭とのより直接的な関係を必要とする，ジムを備えるヴォリュームが大地を背にして現れる。このレベルでは，バーベキューやプールのスペースと，直線的な通路で接続されている。

使用される材は，RC，金属の支柱と木である。

Living/dining room

ENSAMBLE STUDIO
CA'N TERRA

Menorca, Spain
Design: 2017-18
Construction: 2018-

Ca'n Terra is the house of the earth. The fruit that nature gives us, as a found space; which requires tillage and cultivation to imbue the received offering with domesticity. If the history of civilization has greatly evolved transforming ideas into built work, in *Ca'n Terra*, the process is inverted and history interpreted to transform it into architecture.

The transfer from drawing to built mass gives way to the translation of given matter to digital data through the architectural reading of a geological discovery. The discovered space has industrial logic as former Mares stone quarry, artistic potential as sublime cavern carved by hand, and mineral nature as extract of the stony landscape on the island of Menorca. Finding this excavated space in the guts of the earth and reinventing its use implies writing a new story that can rescue it from its abandonment. As first contact we enter the space like explorers would do, equipped with the technology that expands our vision in the dark; throwing millions of laser points on the wrinkles of the continuous stone surface we register with millimetric precision the solid structure that was built for us and is now ready to be polished and inhabited. Behind the scan, the architect's eye, directing, interpreting, creating the space again. That's why the discovery is considered a new work, destined this time to become a room to contemplate nature.

In lieu of an imposing action that many times architecture exerts on the environment, we propose a trip to the interior being of matter, and recognize the freedom with which it gives us spaces to live.

*Débora Mesa & Antón García-Abril/
Ensamble Studio*

Axonometric

EXISTING PLAN

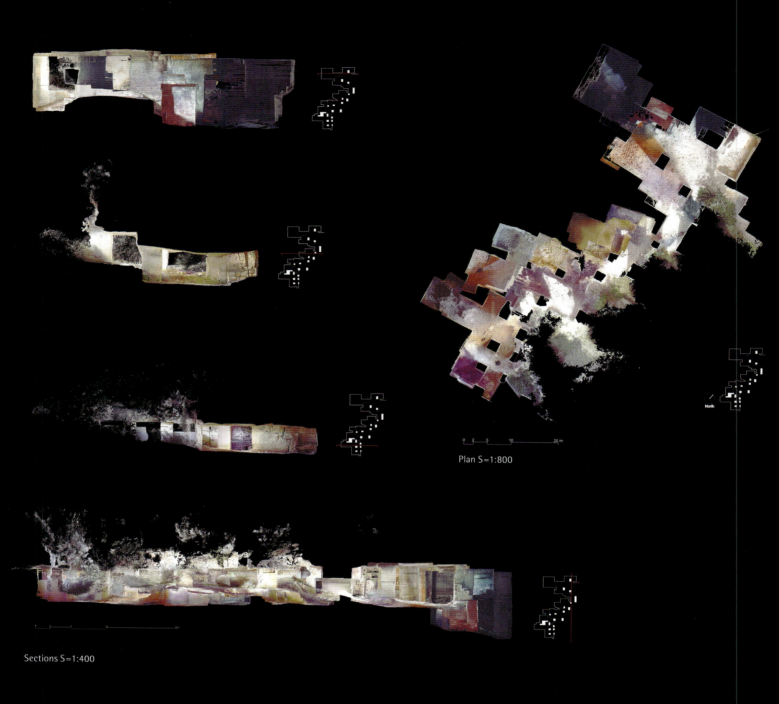

Plan S=1:800

Sections S=1:400

Existing states

PROJECT PLAN

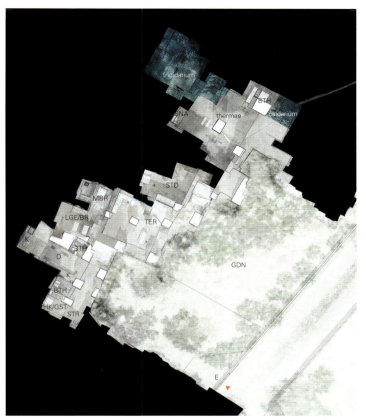

Plan S=1:800

Roof

Architects: ENSAMBLE STUDIO—
Antón García-Abril & Debora Mesa, principals-in-charge; Javier Cuesta, Borja Soriano, Massimo Loia, Gabriele Marinello, project team
Consultants: Jesús Huerga, structural
General contractor: Materia Inorgánica S.L.
Major materials: stainless steel and acrylic
Site area: 10,000 m²
Building area: 700 m²
Total floor area: 1,300 m²

Northeast elevation

Terrace

Master bedroom

Thermae

Studio

View toward kitchen from dining room

　カンテラは大地の家だ。それは発見された，自然の恵みとしての空間であり，その恩恵を家庭生活に浸透させるために耕作や開拓が求められる。アイディアを建造物にすることで文明史が大きな発展を遂げたならば，カンテラではそのプロセスが反転し，歴史を解釈することで建築が生まれる。

　ドローイングから建ち上がったマッスへの変位は，地学的発見の建築的解釈を通して，物質からデジタルデータへの変換に取って代わられる。発見された空間は，旧マレス採石場としての工業的ロジック，人力で彫られた壮大な洞窟がもつアーティスティックな可能性と，メノルカ島の石だらけのランドスケープを抜き出したような鉱物性の自然を有している。大地の中からこの空間を発見し，新しい空間の使い方を見つけ出すことは，この場所が放棄から救うことのできる新しい物語を紡ぐことだ。初めて足を踏み入れる時は，暗闇でも視界が確保できるテクノロジーを身に付けて探検者のように空間へ進入し，連綿と続く石肌に走る襞をめがけてミリ単位の精度で無数のレーザーポイントを投げる。私たちのためにつくられた堅牢な空間に，今，仕上げが施され，人々が住まおうとしている。スキャニングの裏では，建築家の見解をもとに演出と解釈を加え，空間が再生されたのだ。発見とは一つの新しい作品であり，この計画は自然について熟考する機会となるべくしてなった。

　幾度に渡り建築が環境に対して課してきた行為に代わり，私たちは物質の内部空間へと進み，そこが住空間となる自由を評価したい。

（デボラ・メサ&アントン・ガルシア＝アブリル／アンサンブル・スタジオ）

YO SHIMADA
HOUSE IN MUKOGAWA

Amagasaki, Hyogo, Japan
Design: 2017-18
Construction: 2018-

Diagram: spatial sequence

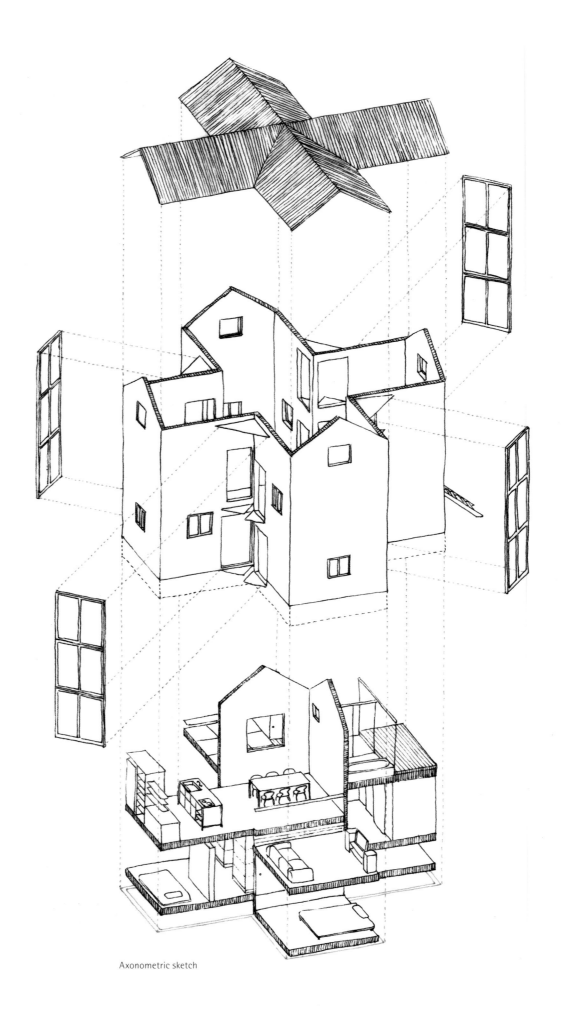

Axonometric sketch

66

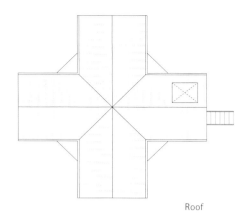

Roof

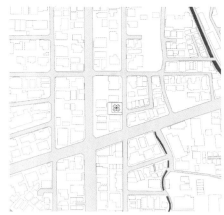

Site plan S=1:5000

First floor S=1:200

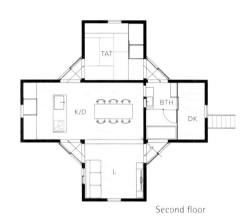

Second floor

Northeast elevation

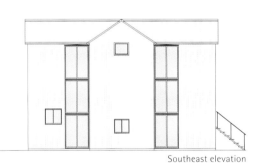

Southeast elevation

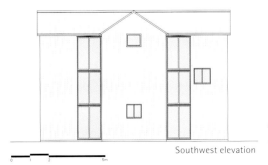

Southwest elevation

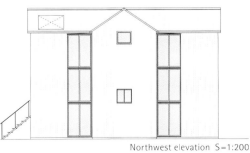

Northwest elevation S=1:200

A residence for a family of four. On the south of the site along the major road, it is an area with buildings that are built at a substantial height. The north side of the site, including the site itself, is determined by law a low-rise residential area, resulting lighting in the house to be an issue. There, I created a cross plan by connecting five squares, and by placing them diagonally on the site to make several vacant lots. A triangular room for the staircase was arranged in the corner that faces the vacant lot, with openings on all sides to ensure lighting in the room. The spiraling skip floors connect the space as one, and by having each floor exiting to the staircase, making one to have to climb up a few steps before entering the room next door, I tried to create an relationship that is nearby but far away at the same time. By placing the entrance porch at 1.5th floor, it creates a suitable distance with the surrounding and becomes a semi-outdoor space where the living/dining room/kitchen that guests would come in to is above, and bedrooms for family use only is below. The simple composition allows a diversity of experience inside and we can expect simplicity like a storage but also sublimity on the external form that consists of crossing volumes of the house.

Yo Shimada

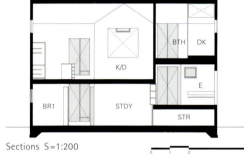

Looking inside through window   Model photos (*): Ayane Hirose

Sections S=1:200

Architects: Tato Architects—Yo Shimada, principal-in-charge; Nobuhiko Sato, project team
Consultants: Takashi Manda Strutural Design—Takashi Manda, Sou Dou, structural
Structural system: wooden
Major materials: Red Cedar plank, glass, exterior; Moiss (Vermiculite plate), plywood, pure oak flooring, interior
Site area: 166.43 m²
Building area: 57.88 m²
Total floor area: 112.00 m²

家族四人のための住宅。敷地南側は幹線道路沿いの，ある程度高さのある建物が建てられる地域，敷地を含む北側は低層住宅地と定められた地域で，どのように採光を確保するのかが一つの課題だった。そこで正方形が五つ連結した十字形平面とし，敷地に斜めに配置することで周囲にいくつかの空地をつくり出した。それらの空地に面する入隅に三角形の階段室を用意し，全面開口として採光を確保した。全体を螺旋状のスキップフロアとしてひとつながりの空間としつつ，それぞれの床から一旦外部のような階段室に出て，数段階段を登って隣の部屋に入るような構成によって，近くて遠い関係をつくり出そうとしている。玄関ポーチを1.5階程度の場所に用意することにより，周囲と適度に距離を取る半外部空間とし，そこから上をLDK等来客も体験する空間，そこから下を個室など家族のみが使う空間と切り分けた。単純な構成により複雑な内部体験をつくり出し，家型のヴォリュームが交差したような外形に，倉庫のような素朴さと崇高さが宿ることを期待している。

（島田陽）

Structure installed between existing house and forest

SHINGO MASUDA + KATSUHISA OTSUBO
MARK THE LAND

Tokyo, Japan
Design: 2017–
Construction: 2018–

View toward terrace

Architects:
Shingo Masuda+Katsuhisa Otsubo architects—Shingo Masuda, Katsuhisa Otsubo, principals-in-charge
Consultants: HSC—Yoshiyuki Hiraiwa, structural
General contractor: BEANS LTD.
Structural system:
timber (building), RC (landmark)
Major materials: RC
Site area: 72.21 m²
Building area: 37.82 m²
Total floor area: 72.19 m²

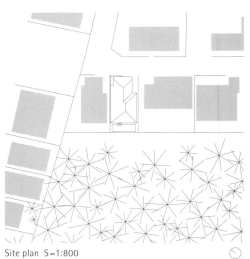
Site plan S=1:800

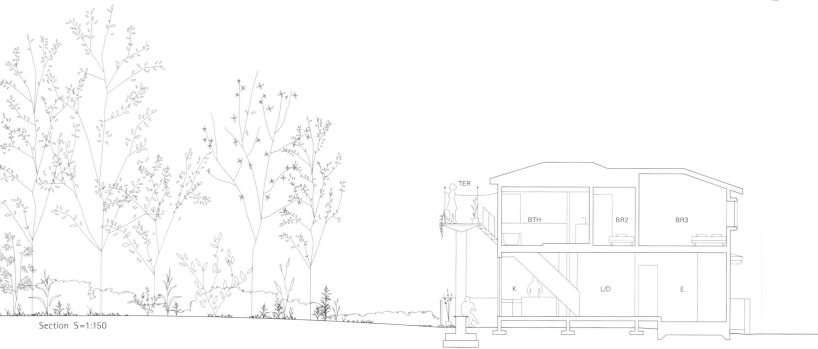
Section S=1:150

This is a renovation project for a two-story house with a small yard located along a park with a lush, expansive forest. To take advantage of such a rich natural environment, the house was designed with large openings towards the forest on both first and second floors, with a deck that stretched as widely as possible on the second floor. Presumably, the original concept of this house was to rid any "distance" between the park, home and its yard to aim for a kind of unity with nature.

However, there was a municipal green-colored fence at the park border, and the house suffered from humidity, bugs, cold winter climate and various other challenges posed by the adjacent forest. Despite original intentions, this had caused its large openings and second-floor deck to remain completely closed, and even become obstacles to receiving light, which inevitably promoted further separation from the forest. Thus, we began the design process from a point of fully accepting such inevitable things and phenomena, and to create a sense of adequate "distance" for the house.

The plan included relocating the staircase near the entrance towards the yard-side living room, and extending and straightening the access from the entrance to the second-floor bedroom as much as possible, so that the experience of the home can feel free and open despite its size.

Extending this circulation further, we removed the barely functioning deck and built a floating slab-like structure as close to the park as possible. To prevent the structure from falling, its foundations were laid from one end of the site to the other, firmly drawing a line of separation between the forest and the house. This large structure, which belongs neither to the forest nor the house, temporarily enforces a clear division, creating a "gap" between the two regions. The idea was that, if this structure become the mediator of this "gap," then we can perhaps create a more concrete relationship between the house and the forest.

Although the size of the original openings of the house have been properly reduced, the newly created space between the house and the structure filter more sunlight; the temporary cut-off from the surrounding environment has introduced new ways to recapture them and appreciate them as distant scenery. Intensifying, rather than obscuring, the presence of different elements; keeping proper "distance"; and establishing practical relationship between front and back—this is how the project was designed to create a sense of expansion and depth, and foster a life of ease and grace in this location.
Shingo Masuda + Katsuhisa Otsubo

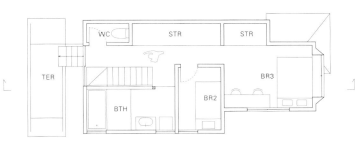

First floor S=1:150

Second floor

豊かな森が広がる公園沿いの敷地に建つ，小さな庭付きの2階建住宅の改修．こんなにも豊かな周辺環境であるため，そこに向けて1階も2階もなるべく大きく開口部が設けられ，2階には目一杯の長さでベランダがついている．つまり家と庭と公園の「距離」をなくし，一体的にすることがこの住まいの一つの全体像なのだろう．

しかし，公園との境界には市が設けた緑色のフェンスが備えられ，また湿気や虫，冬場の寒さといった森の厳しい側面から，その大きな開口部や2階のベランダは想いとは裏腹に，閉じきられ，差し込む光の邪魔となり，むしろ森と断絶する方向を促していた．だからまずは，そういったどうしようもなく存在するモノや事象をしっかりと受け止めた上で，むしろ適切な「距離」を与えることを設計のスタートとした．

プランとしては，玄関近くにあった階段を庭側のリビングに移し，玄関から2階の寝室までの距離を折り返しを含め直線的になるべく長くし，とても小さな住宅でも家の体験としては伸びやかに感じられるようにした．

その折り返しの動線の延長上に，あまり機能していないベランダを取り外し，敷地のなるべく公園側の空中にスラブとなるような構造体を新築する．構造体の転倒を防ぐため，その基礎は敷地の端から端まで渡し，森と家の間にしっかりと一線を引いている．家の一部でもなく森の一部でもない，大きな構造体が一旦その場所を分断して明確化することで，家と森に"間"をつくる．構造体がその"間"を取り持つ存在になれば，家と森に具体的な関係性がつくれるのではないか．

家の開口は以前より適度なサイズに小さくしているが，構造物との隙間があるから前よりも光がたくさん入るようになったり，森をはじめとした周辺環境と一旦切れることで，それらを遠くの"景色"として取り込めたり．それぞれの存在を曖昧にせず，むしろ強め，「距離」を取り，前後の関係性をリアリティーをもって築いていく．そうすることで，広がりや奥行きのある豊かな生活が，ここで繰り広げられるよう計画している．

（増田信吾＋大坪克亘）

The site for this 're-visioning' and addition to a modest 350 sq. ft. 1950's concrete masonry guesthouse is a 65'x 360' long urban/suburban. Equipped with 'flood irrigation' the parcel served as a tree farm for more than five decades. Within its borders are 307 mature palm trees. Commissioned by an owner-builder professional information technology engineer, the program is to create a one bedroom and great room vertical 'tree house' on the masonry foundation walls of the original structure along with a roof level viewing perch/nest/porch in the canopy of palms that offers views across the urban landscape beyond.

Simple in plan strategy and sculptural in section, the new home grows to 992 sq. ft. The design locates the bedroom and bath on level one. An angular cantilever staircase with a small desk alcove at the base landing leads to the loft above. A small kitchen-dining island sits at the west edge of a tall living space and adjoins an east facing sunrise balcony. Access to the roof deck above is via an exterior steel lamprey ship's ladder.

The exterior skin is crafted of corrugated and flat seamed galvanized and bonderized unpainted steel siding with scrims of perforated metal. The overall effect will be that of a silver vessel almost disappearing in rusticated forest of palm tree trunks and dappled shade of the palm frond canopy.

Custom metal window apertures optimize daylight and views. Floors are exposed concrete and OSB natural finish board panels with walls of exposed concrete block and naturally finished MDF sheeting. These materials will create a visually unexpected, texturally rich palette to compliment the owner's life style and sophisticated tastes in music, art and furnishings.

都市と郊外の中間に位置する65×360フィートの敷地で、1950年代に建てられた総面積350平方フィートのこぢんまりとしたコンクリートとれんがのゲストハウスを増改築するプロジェクトである。この敷地は「湛水灌漑」を導入することで、50年以上にわたって林業地として活用されてきた。境界線内には現在、307本の成長したヤシの木が植わっている。ITエンジニアとして活躍するオーナービルダーの依頼は、寝室が一つと広間で構成された縦型の「ツリーハウス」で、元の家のれんがの構造壁を生かすこと、止まり木あるいは巣箱とも呼ぶべき、ヤシの木を天蓋としたポーチを屋根の高さに設けることが条件だった。またこのポーチからは、はるか遠くの都市の風景が見渡せるようにしなければならなかった。

シンプルなプランと一部に彫刻的な装飾を組み合わせた新しい住宅は、総面積992平方フィートとなった。寝室と浴室は1階に設けた。1階の踊り場に小さなアルコーブ・デスクをしつらえた角度のある片持ち階段は、階上のロフトへと続いている。天井高のある居間には、西端にアイランド式の小ぶりなダイニングキッチンを配し、東に面して朝焼けを望むバルコニーを設けた。上層のポーチへは、屋外に設置したスティール製の船はしごを使う。

外装は、亜鉛メッキ加工とリン酸塩処理を施した、未塗装の波形平葺きスティールサイディングと、パンチングメタルのカバーという組み合わせである。ヤシの木の生い茂るのどかな森と、ヤシの葉の天蓋が生むまだらな影に、銀色の邸宅が溶け込むような効果を狙った。

メタル製の窓開口部は、陽射しと眺望を存分に堪能できるよう特注したものだ。床は打放しコンクリートと無垢のOSBパネル、壁は打放しコンクリートブロックと無垢のMDFシートをそれぞれ組み合わせた。これらの素材の組み合わせが、オーナーのライフスタイルや、音楽、アート、調度品の洗練されたセンスにマッチした、見た目の意外性と触感の多彩性を生み出すだろう。

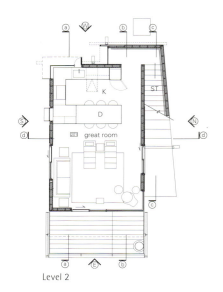

Level 2

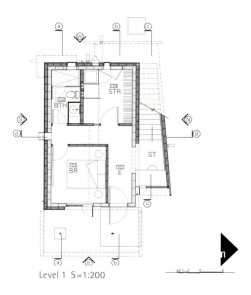

Level 1 S=1:200

WILL BRUDER
PALMSTREE HOUSE

Phoenix, Arizona, U.S.A.
Design: 2016
Construction: 2017-18

Northeast elevation

Architects: Will Bruder Architects—
Will Bruder, principal-in-charge
Consultants: Rudow & Berry, Inc., structural;
Will Bruder Architects, interior design
General contractor: Jonathan Atkins
Structural system: wood stud framing on existing concrete masonry
Major materials: corrugated and flat seamed galvanized, bonderized unpainted steel siding with scrims of perforated metal, exterior; OSB natural finish board, exposed concrete block, naturally finished MDF sheeting, interior
Site area: 21,253 sq. ft.
Building area: 435 sq. ft.
Total floor area: 992 sq. ft.

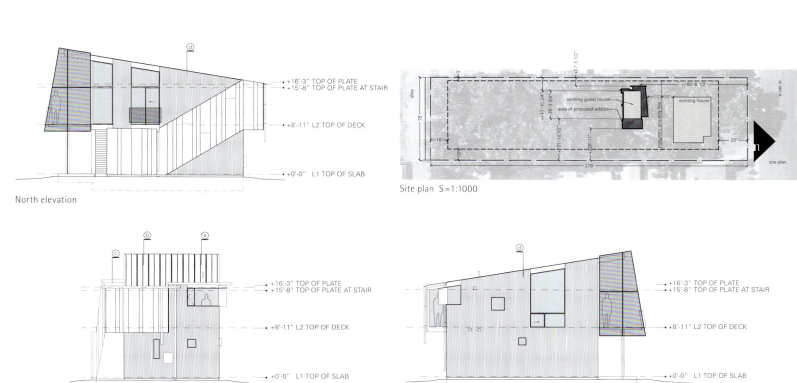

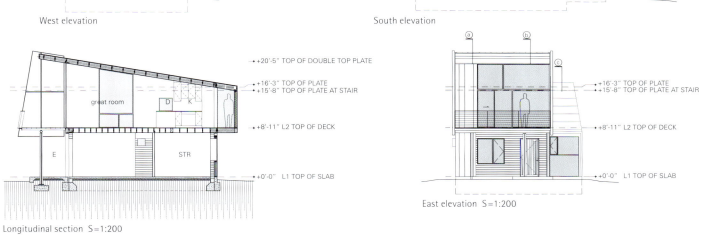

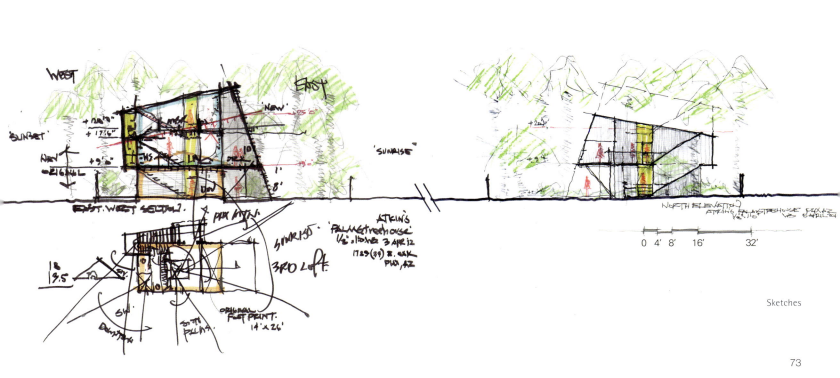

Sketches

ERIKA NAKAGAWA
TOWER AND ONOMATOPOEIA

Tokyo, Japan
Design: 2017-18
Construction: 2018-19

This project is a tall and narrow apartment complex built on a small 28 square meters site with a frontage of 3.4 meters. The building will span over five floors and one underground level in a total of six floors; there will be five different units including a single duplex. While the capacity of the project is tight and smothering, it actually faces a large street that runs 33 meters wide, calling for a building that would act as a bridge between the narrow human scale of the building and the expansive scale of the environment.

The limiting conditions of this incredibly small site affect the building size in various ways. Construction methods, regulation compliance, facility, and plumbing etc., directly influence the way the building is designed. In order to consider a building that transcends the surrounding environment, human body, and structure at once, we imagined that all of these elements need to be simultaneously considered and combined from the very beginning stages of the design process, resulting in a raw, dynamic force propelled by its smallness. This would then become part of a diversely intertwined assembly in which each element also fulfills multiple roles.

We made use of the models as the most important design tool, building first a 1/50 model of the environment to study the building size as it relates to other urban elements. Then, we explored various structural compositions including the construction method by building a 1/20 framework model, and then built a 1/15 model to study spatial quality, usage, and how objects and areas will emerge on a human body scale. We finally built various parts models in from 1/10 to 1/1 to study how objects will organize and manifest in the spaces.

In this tall, tower-like building, its relationship with the environment changes both vertically and horizontally on each floor at different moments in time; the building fosters diverse, emotional and onomatopoeic communication between the body and space in a way that is difficult to express in words. Furthermore, because the building is so small, its inner functionalities and designs for comfort directly affect its outer appearance; it is fascinating how, like clothing, aspects of the interior manifest themselves directly on the outer elevation. My belief is that, once this concept transcends the human body and building to ultimately associate with the larger environment, we can achieve a completeness far more vast and universal.
Erika Nakagawa

Location S=1:5000

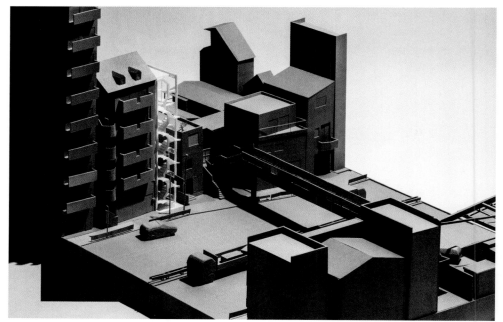
Site model

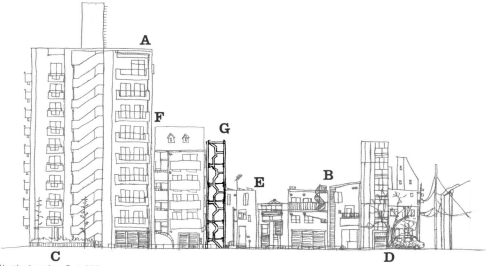
North elevation S=1:600

間口3.4メートル，面積28平米の狭小敷地に，地下1F地上5Fの6層，メゾネット1戸フラット4戸の5住戸という細高い共同住宅をつくる計画。この身体にまとわりつくようなスケールの一方で前面道路は33メートルと広く，環境スケールと身体スケールを横断する建築が求められた。

小さい敷地ゆえ，そのサイズが建築のサイズにもたらす影響がとてもたくさんあり，施工方法・法規解釈・設備配管経路などがすべて建築の建ち現れ方にダイレクトに結実してしまう。周辺環境と身体と構造が横断的に展開していく建築を考えるためには，設計序盤からそれらすべてを同時に考慮し合体させながら組み立てていく，小ささが生み出す生々しい動的な迫力と，各エレメントが一人何役も担わなければならない多様に絡み合った集合性が予想された。

設計の最重要ツールとして模型を活用し，はじめに50分の1の環境模型にて周辺スケールや都市エレメントに対しての建築サイズを把握した上で，20分の1の架構スタディ模型で施工方法をふくめて建築の組み立て方を模索し，15分の1の本体模型をつくって場の質や使われ方，身体スケールでモノや領域がどう現れてくるかの検討をし，10分の1から1分の1のたくさんの部分模型により実際のモノの納まり方・現れ方を検討していく，という進め方をしている。

細高い塔状の建物では，1層ごと時間ごとに，断面的にも平面的にも周辺環境との関係性が刻々と変わり，言葉では言い表しにくい，オノマトペのように多種多様で感情的な，場と身体のコミュニケーションが繰り広げられる。そして，洋服のように小さいからこそ，内側の機能性や快適性・素敵さが，そのまま外に現れてくるという，内部の様相が立面に直結するおもしろさがある。このおもしろさが，身体スケールや建築スケールにとどまらず，最終的に環境スケールでのおもしろさにもまたつながっていくと，より大きな全体性を獲得できるのではないかと考えている。

(中川エリカ)

Architects: Erika Nakagawa Office−
Erika Nakagawa, principal-in-charge;
Kirin Tago, Hibiki Saitoh, project team
Consultants: Konishi Structural Engineers, structural
Structural system: steel
Major materials: steel, glass, concrete, wood
Site area: 28.56 m²
Building area: 21.75 m²
Total floor area: 163.64 m²

Plans S=1:200
Street elevation S=1:200
West elevation S=1:600

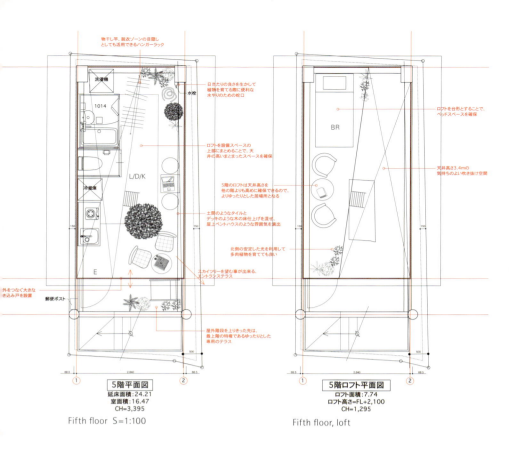

5階平面図
延床面積:24.21
室面積:16.47
CH=3,395

Fifth floor S=1:100

5階ロフト平面図
ロフト面積:7.74
ロフト高さ=FL+2,100
CH=1,295

Fifth floor, loft

Fifth and fourth floor

Fifth and fourth floor

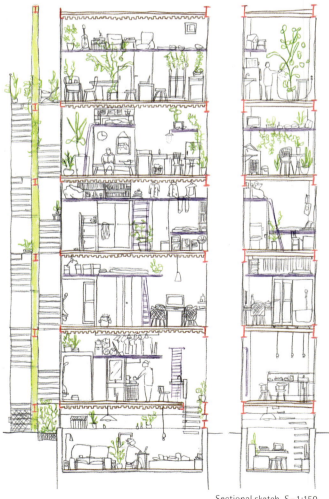

Sectional sketch S=1:150

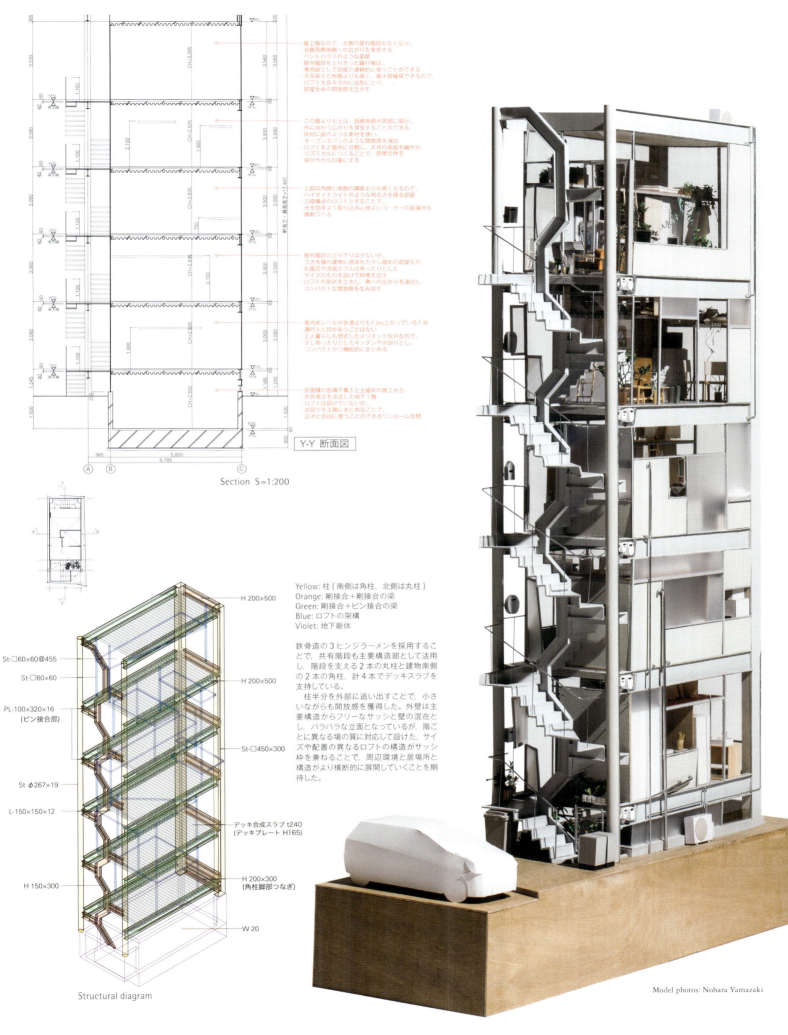

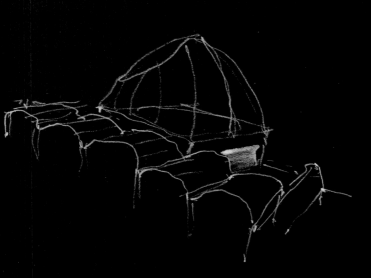

Rarely is a project more considerate of night than day. Night sky is a residence for an astronomer who has qualifications in aeronautic engineering and architecture—he also holds amateur rocket altitude records—in a nutshell; a gentleman who understands sky.

The site is located on the uppermost contour of the west-facing segment of the Great Dividing Range at an altitude of 1,100 meters.

The land is a series of folds that move intriguingly along a north-west axis. Their creases forming small gullies that water it's adjoining sunken valley.

Unpretentious, the site is at the lead waters of these creeks. The building rises off the rock plateau anchored and reaching. Formed in masonry it labours a horizontal serenity that captures the finite qualities of the immediate land. The vertical room alone reaches for the sky and beyond—both metaphysically and evocatively. The colonnade single corridor at once disturbed by the seduction of a parabolic volume—penetrating the reaches of this room in a single offset penetration directed by both location and surround toward the most memorable of night skies—the Milky Way—from this room and through a crisp evening atmosphere the stories of the universe are told. This little building lives for the stories and accumulates time as an expression of the patterns it entertains.

The palate is tight, the plan is self-evident, the section is not without subtlety...eventually it turns to one room and one opening toward the sky for credence of the unknown for connection to places that only exist in the minds of outrageous thinkers and great explorers.

This building sits connected to land and sky with fragile rigidity. Night Sky come inside and become the poet.
Peter Stutchbury

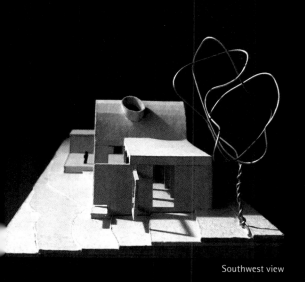
Southwest view

このプロジェクト以上に，昼よりも夜のことを考えたプロジェクトはまずない。「ナイトスカイ・ハウス」は，ある天文学者のための住まいだ。航空工学と建築に造詣が深く，ロケット飛行距離のアマチュア記録保持者であり，端的に言って，空をよく知っている紳士だ。

敷地はオーストラリア東部グレート・ディヴァイディング山脈の西側，標高1,100メートルの最高地点に位置する。

北西に褶曲（しゅうきょく）と呼ばれる波上の美しい地層が広がる土地で，この褶曲が小さな峡谷を形成し，隣接する深い谷へと山水を注いでいる。

敷地は，それらの谷川の起点に慎み深く広がっている。岩の台地に建つ「ナイトスカイ・ハウス」は，はるか遠くを見渡している。れんが造りの建物に，フラットで落ち着いたフォルムを取り入れることにより，この土地の限りある自然との調和を図った。背の高い観測部屋だけが，形而上的に，あるいは一つのイメージとして，空へ，さらにその先の高みへとそびえている。1本の柱廊に足を踏み入れると，放物線を描くヴォリュームにただちに魅了される。放物線は，この場所と周囲の環境によって導かれるかのように部屋全体を満たし，夜空で最も深く人びとの記憶に刻まれる「天の川」へと広がっている。この部屋と，すがすがしい夜気を通して聞こえてくるのは，宇宙の物語だ。「ナイトスカイ・ハウス」は物語を伝えるための小さな家であり，時を蓄積し，時が織りなすパターンを見せてくれる。

確固たる嗜好，明確なプラン，それでもなお残る，名状しがたい何か……そうして完成したのが，一つの部屋と，空を見上げる一つの天窓でできた家。未知のものを確かなものとして信じ，奇抜な思想家と偉大なる探検家の心にのみ存在する場所につながるための家だ。

「ナイトスカイ・ハウス」は，たおやかだが力強く，大地と空につながっている。夜空（ナイトスカイ）は住む人の心に入り込み，やがて詩人となるのだ。

（ピーター・スタッチベリー）

West view

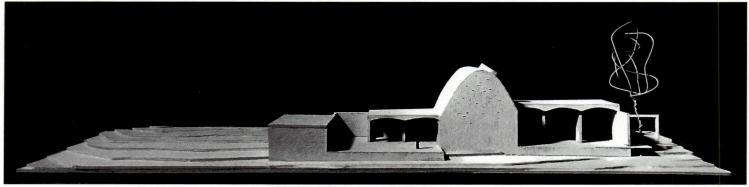
West view

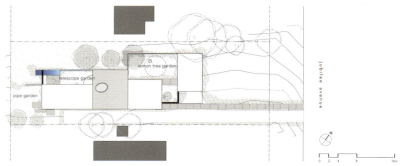
Site plan S=1:800

Architects: Peter Stutchbury Architecture—
Peter Stutchbury, principal-in-charge;
Fernanda Cabral, project team
Consultants: ROC Engineering Design, structural; Peter Stutchbury Architecture, interior design
Structural system: brick cavity
Major materials: brick, concrete, glass
Site area: 1,003 m²
Building area: 190 m²
Total floor area: 128 m²

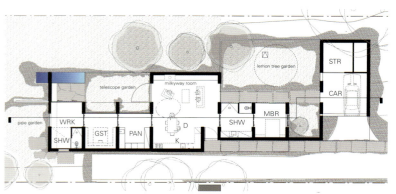
Plan S=1:400

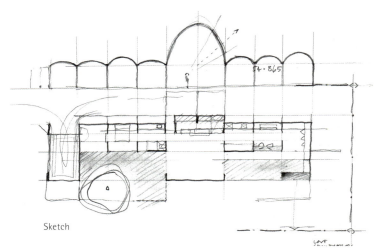
Sketch

Section S=1:400

North elevation S=1:400

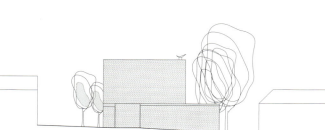
East elevation

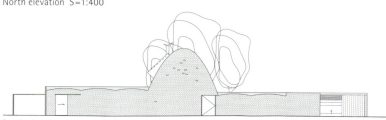
South elevation

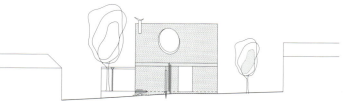
West elevation

GURJIT SINGH MATHAROO
SOUND ARCHITECTURE

Ahmedabad, Gujarat, India
Design: 2015-16
Construction: in pipeline

The typical Indian city development involves ever widening roads where plot margins are encroached upon, and where domestic use is perpetually converted to commercial to allow for increasing Floor Area Ratio. With the city becoming less congenial to live in, people move further away from dense centres into trending remote suburbs. The three generations of this family however chose to build a new home at their ancestral property in the heart of the city, that would now accommodate the changing demands of the growing family, while offering privacy and independence in the traditional joint family setup.

Property acquired cumulatively over the years resulted in an irregular L shaped plot with its long side along the noisy road and other sides overlooked by high structures. Adding to this, the house was to be compliant to Vaastu—the strict ancient guidelines that govern the placement of spaces within the house. Besides, there was a self imposed restriction to retain the few but large trees on site. The challenge was to make living with nature possible within the contradictory conditions of its context and program.

The building itself was conceptualized as a noise barrier and lined along the road on the North, with linear double height living and dining areas having low openings of heavy pivotting doors of Red sandstone. They are protected by a second layer of high compound wall—the mandatory 18' margin between the two layers forming an enclosed front garden. The entire length of the block opens into a large green area on the rear side, through a deep verandah that cuts visibility from the high surrounding structures.

The shorter east side of the block is occupied by the entrance vestibule, temple, formal living and kitchen—cocooned spaces that open into an arrival garden and water body; their carefully positioned openings that do not allow the bottle neck of the L site to be felt from inside. Along with the toilets, these occasionally used spaces flank the East and West to form an additional buffer against noise and insulation from the intense heat, making for a bookend composition.

Bedrooms are placed over the low verandah bay with generous views to the rear garden, while the connecting passage and the swimming pool accessed from the second floor entertainment zone are placed over the living bay to achieve suitable scales. These staggered and interlocking floor plates have ensured low overall heights and compact structure where levels are bound together in a single volume of space.

Openings of the bedroom and the entertainment zone are screened by a system of Burma Teak louvers modulated to cut off the outsiders gaze while allowing for ample light, ventilation and views of the garden and sky as requried. They serve to add a new dimension of transparency when set against the massive red stone walls and seemingly closed concrete boxes—surfaces that come alive when bathed in tropical sunlight.

The resultant space is an attempt to replace the chaos outside with the shade of neem trees, brimming lily ponds and the sound of chirping birds, to be one resonating with nature.
*Trisha Patel & Krishna Mistry/
Matharoo Associates*

Diagram

Entrance view

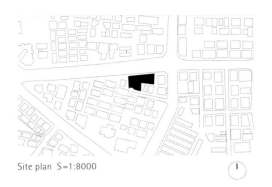
Site plan S=1:8000

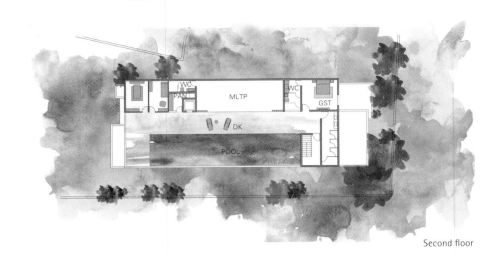
Second floor

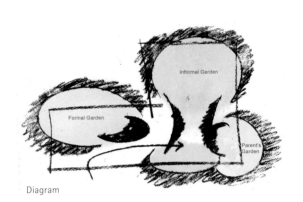
Diagram

Ground floor S=1:500

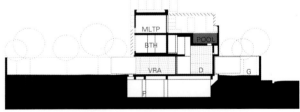
Section AA S=1:500

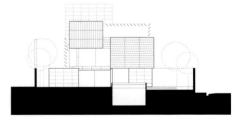
Section BB

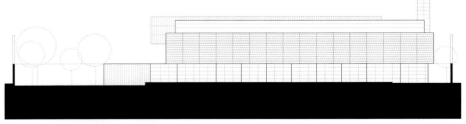
East elevation

North elevation S=1:500

Architects: Matharoo Associates—
Gurjit Singh Matharoo, principal-in-charge;
Sandip Bind, Arvind Krishna, project team
Consultants: Rusabh Consultants, structural; Pankaj Dharkar Associates, mechanical; Matharoo Associates, interior design/landscape
Structural system: reinforced concrete cement
Major materials: red sandstone and reinforced concrete
Site area: 1,466 m²
Building area: 416 m²
Total floor area: 1,445 m²

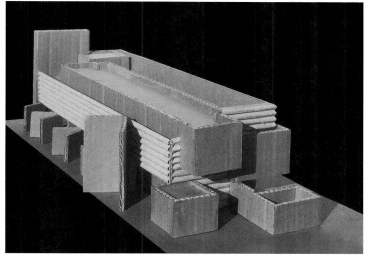
Southeast view

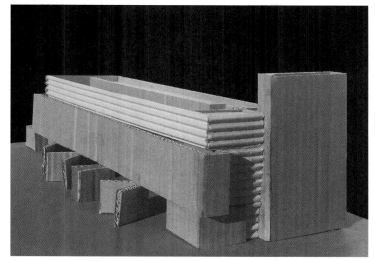
Northwest view

典型的なインドの都市開発は，道路幅を広げることを常に伴い，そこでは，土地の余白は侵食され，住居利用されていたものは，容積率を高くするために絶えず商業利用化されている。都市が住居に適したものでなくなるにつれ，人々は密集した中心地から遠く離れた流行りの郊外に移住する。しかしながら，この3世代の家族は都市の中心地にある祖先から受け継いだ土地において，伝統的な家族構成の中でプライバシーや独立性を保つ一方で，家族が増えることで変化する要求に応える新たな住宅を建築することを選択した。

何年もかけて累積的に得た結果として，土地は長手側が賑やかな道路に，もう一方が高層建築に見下ろされるようにして面する不規則なL字の形となった。それに加えて，この住宅は，住宅内のスペースの配置を厳しく取り決める古来の指標であるヴァーストゥ（インド風水）に対応する必要があった。さらに，自身で課した制約として，敷地内の少ないながらも巨大な木々を保護することがあった。コンテクストとプログラムにおける矛盾した状況の中で，自然との共生を可能にすることが，最大の挑戦であった。

建物自体を，騒音に対するバリアとして考え，低い位置に赤色砂岩の重厚な回転扉がある，直線的で2層吹き抜けの居間，食堂空間を北側の道路に沿って配置した。これらは，第2の層となる高い塀により保護され，2層間には規制で決められた18フィートの余白があり，囲まれた前庭がつくられる。ブロックの長手側全体は，周囲の高層建築からの視線を遮るための奥行きのあるベランダを通して，後方の広々とした緑地に開いている。

ブロックの短手である東側には，玄関ホール，礼拝室，正式な居室と台所を備え，前庭と池に向かって開きながらも取り囲まれた空間となっている。それらの開口はL字型の敷地のボトルネックが室内より感じられないように慎重に配置されている。騒音をさらに緩和し，厳しい暑さを遮断するために，トイレのように時々使用されるスペースは東と西に沿って置くことにより，ブックエンドのような構成をつくり出す。

寝室は，ベランダ部の上方に配置され，裏庭の豊かな景色を望む。その一方で，2階の娯楽スペースに通じる渡り廊下とスイミングプールは，適したスケールとなるように，リビング部の上方に配置している。これらの互い違いに配置された連動的な床プレートにより，全体の高さを低く抑え，単一ヴォリュームの空間において複数のレベルが繋がりを持つコンパクトなストラクチャーを確保している。

寝室と娯楽スペースの開口は，必要に応じ，十分な自然光や風通し，庭や空への景色を与える一方で，屋外の熱を遮断するために調節可能なブルーマチークのルーバーシステムにより保護されている。熱帯の日光を浴びることで生きいきとした表情を持つ面である。重厚な赤石の壁や一見閉じたように見えるコンクリートの箱と対照的に，それらは，透明性における新たな側面を提供する。

結果として生じる空間は，外部のカオスを，ニームの木や満ち溢れる睡蓮の池や小鳥のさえずりに変え，自然に共鳴するものとなるための試みである。

Pool

Garden level

Street level: approach

Bedrooms on lower level,
living/dining room on upper level

RICA STUDIO*
PERISCOPE HOUSE

Torrelodones, Madrid, Spain
Design: 2017
Construction: 2018-

Site plan S=1:600

The area in Torrelodones where the house is located is characterised by a rough topography. A very steep slope facing the skyline of the city is what makes the site unique. The house is split in three volumes in order to negotiate with the topography, create as much inhabitable exterior space as possible and maximize the west views towards the city. Two of these three parts are embebed in the ground, anchoring the construction and minimizing the visual impact of the house in the landscape, but the third one rises rominently, like a periscope, in order to capture as much horizon as posible, floating over the green ocean of olive trees. The perception of the extreme slope preceding the view of the skyline of Madrid are framed and transformed by a sequence of concrete surfaces, glass walls and water reflections that enlarge, focus and enhance the natural beauty of the area.

The house is composed by 3 distinctive volumes that define three different datums. From the street only one is visible, discovering when crossing the bridge a hidden garden in the level below. The lowest part is not visible from outside, an excavated space facing the views. The three pieces are moved apart horizontally and vertically, so each of them could accomplish different functions. The back pavilion anchors the house to the terrain, acting as a retaining wall. It's roof which is at the level of the access street creates a platform for arking. It contains the space for production, a home office that is separated from the residence by an open space, a garden and a swimming pool that are in intimate connection with the office. The residence is also split in two parts, physically separated by a void that allows the garden to be in connection with the best views and that creates a compressed covered area that emphasises the scale of the landscape. The lower volume, integrated in the topography contains the most private spaces of the house, the three bedrooms and the bathrooms. This excavated space, is also fully open to the views and the western light. The upper volume, goes forward into the slope, and higher than any other construction around, hoovering above the landscape. This pavilion becomes a device to capture the view, a periscope that transforms its perception. It contains the public programs, living room and an open kitchen.

The periscope cantilevers, as a floating concrete shell just supported by an eccentric core that contains the vertical communication, minimising its footprint, to maximise the dimension of the landscape,. The inbetween exterior space result of splitting the house vertically and horizontally in three pavilions becomes a trapped piece of nature, a domesticated landscape that frames the far views of the city.

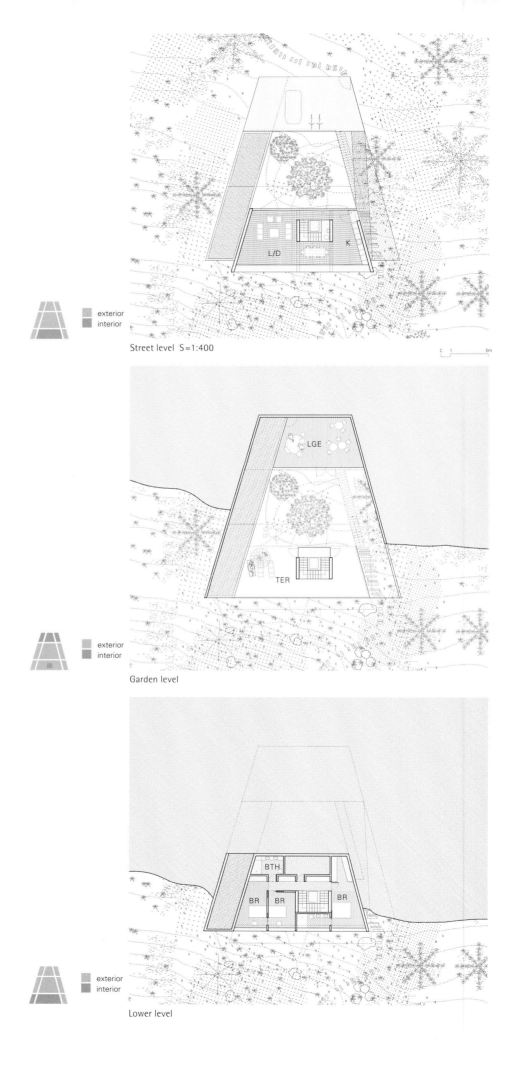

Street level S=1:400

Garden level

Lower level

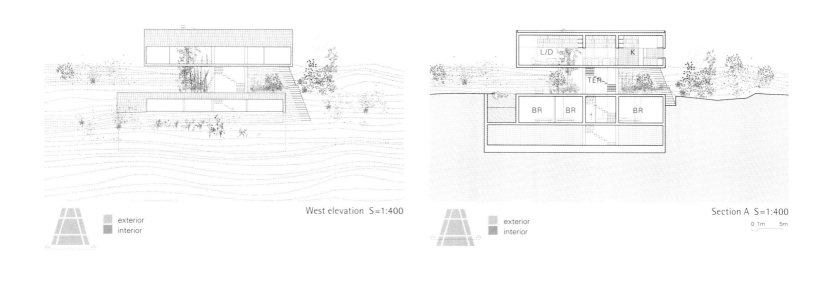

West elevation S=1:400

Section A S=1:400

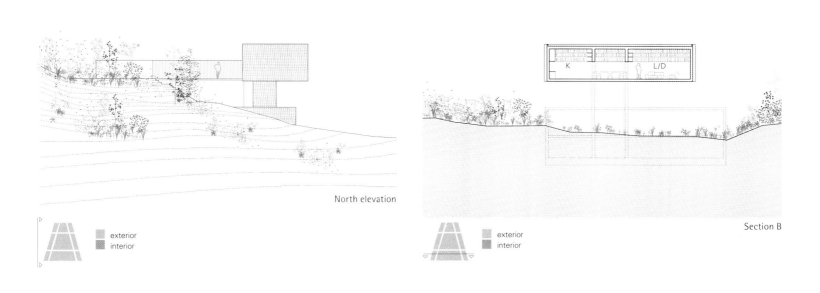

North elevation

Section B

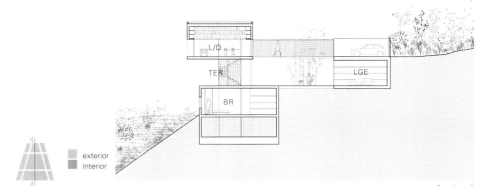

Section C

Overall view

Architects: RICA STUDIO*—
Iñaqui Carnicero, Lorena Del Rio, principals-in-charge;
Ihowa Choi, Takuma Johnson, Angela Posse, project team
Structural system: concrete walls
Major materials: concrete
Site area: 1,000 m²
Building area: 200 m²
Total floor area: 350 m²
Cost of construction: 550,000 euro

「ペリスコープ・ハウス」が建つスペイン中部のトレロドネスは，荒々しい地勢を特徴とする土地だ。街のスカイラインを正面に見わたす急峻な勾配が，敷地に個性を生み出している。このプロジェクトでは住宅を三つのヴォリュームに区分けすることで地勢との調和を図り，住居にふさわしい屋外空間を可能な限り広く設けると同時に，街に面した西の眺望を最大限に生かせるよう工夫した。三区画のうち二区画は，地面に対してフラットなデザインとすることで建造物の安定を図り，家が景観に与える影響を極力なくした。残る一区画は，ペリスコープ（展望鏡）のように高くそびえるフォルムを採用しており，広々とした地平線を見わたすことができる。その様子は，オリーブの木々が織りなす緑の海にペリスコープが浮かんでいるかのようだ。マドリードのスカイラインを見わたす急峻な勾配，というイメージを切り取り，コンクリートの平面やガラスの壁，水面の反射によって変容させ，当地の自然の美しさを拡大し，一つにまとめ，さらに高めている。

住宅を構成する三つの異なるヴォリュームは，高さも異なっている。通りから見えるのは一つだけで，橋をわたると，一段下に広がる庭が見えてくる仕組みだ。最も低い部分は窪地にあり，通りからは見えないが，眺望が楽しめる。これらの三つのヴォリュームが水平方向と垂直方向に分けられ，それぞれの機能を果たしている。裏手に位置する棟は一種の擁壁として，住居全体を地面に固定する役割を果たしている。この棟については，屋根を通りと同じ高さに設けることで，駐車スペースとして利用できるようにした。さらにこの棟には，オープンスペースで居住エリアと区切った作業場兼オフィスエリアを配置したほか，オフィスと隣接するかたちで庭とプールも設けた。居住エリアも二つに分割。ヴォイドによって物理的に分けることで，庭と最高の見晴らしに連続性を生み出すと同時に，周囲の広大さを強調するような閉じた空間をつくった。地勢に溶け込むかのような低いほうのヴォリュームには，プライベート空間である三つの寝室と浴室をまとめている。こちらのヴォリュームからは，開けた眺望と西陽も楽しめる。一方，高いほうのヴォリュームは傾斜を上がるようなデザインで，周辺の建物よりも高い位置にあり，景観を見下ろすことができる。この棟は風景をとらえ，さらにそのイメージを変容させるペリスコープだ。ここには居間やオープンキッチンといった共有スペースを設けた。

ペリスコープの張り出し部分は，個性的なフォルムのコアで支えられた，中空に浮かぶコンクリートシェルである。このようなデザインにすることにより，縦方向の対話を図りつつ，基底部を最小限に抑えながら，最大限の眺望が得られるようにした。間に設けた外部空間が，垂直方向と水平方向に住居を三つの棟に分割し，周囲の自然を閉じ込め，はるか遠くに望む街を額縁のように切り取って見せている。

Living/dining room

Looking southeast

HIROSHI SAMBUICHI
SATO

Kyushu, Japan
Design: 2016-18
Construction: 2018-

View from northeast

An established company with four generations of history began to plan for a facility that opens up to its neighborhood. On a site that expands to 1.8 hectares, a marketplace, assembly hall, theater stage, office, residences (dormitory and apartments), public bath, cafe, lounge, gallery, warehouse, farmlands, pond and garden will be developed with the cooperation of surrounding farms.

These facilities are connected with hallways that run over the water, and by making one section of the site open to the local public, the project becomes part of the community traffic flow, creating a "village (sato) over the water." Here, we will focus on the residential areas of the project.

The site is located in a valley dotted with villages, temples and shrines around farmlands and fields. There are three rivers and water canals that run from east to west, parallel to the Jori allotments. Since the Yayoi period, people have continually grown rice on this fertile land which is fed by a rich water system; as such, numerous ancient tombs can be found in the surrounding area. There is an underground water vein that have been used until recently to supply the residents of the region with 630 cubic meters of water a day, and this entire area is historically known for its high quality water, rice and sake-making. This place was also home to the oldest sake brewery of western Japan, which recently closed business due to the economic decline of the area.

Back during the Edo period, however, this place was a post town with flourishing commerce. Small theater stages and martial art gymnasiums still exist, as well as festivals and shishimai lion-mask dances taking place in shrines and temples to celebrate the autumnal harvests and yields. Culture that merge the elements of wind, water and sun with farming and trade continue to be deeply ingrained in the region today.

Centering our focus on "water," which seems to be the source of this area's history, industry, and culture, we began to work on a plan to revive the region, continuing our research of close to two years.

Against an expansive backdrop, the position, direction, and shape of each facility will be determined based on the hours of use and the relationships between wind, water, and sun.

For the dormitory, we designed the plan by focusing on the time spent outside of working hours, concentrating on the morning sunlight, early morning and night wind rose and wind speed, and distances between the public bath and lounge from the central well which is the project's source of water.

Residents will wake up to the morning sun, eat breakfast in the east-facing lounge, and depart to their north-facing offices with southern light on their backs.

After work, they will visit the public bath and cafe, and entertain at the marketplace, assembly hall and theater stage, taking part in the local events.

A local company that had been fostered by the beautiful landscape and economy of this place is, after lamenting its decline, working to revive the rich culture and landscape with the people of the region.
Hiroshi Sambuichi

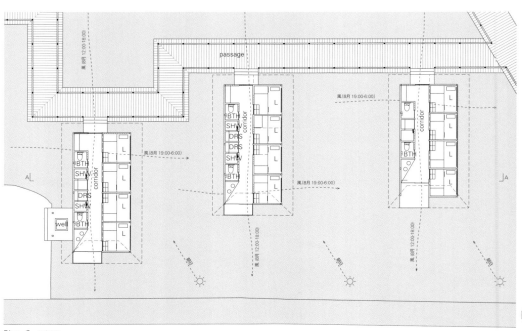

Plan S=1:300

東側に居室，西側にコアを配置することで，朝日が居室内に差し込む。
夏場の風は，就業時間中においてウィンドパスを北から南へ吹き抜ける

Architects: Sambuichi Architects—
Hiroshi Sambuichi, principal-in-charge;
Tsubasa Komura, project team
Consultants: IKEZAKI design Co., Ltd., structural
Structural system: wooden
Major materials: wood
Site area: 17,733 m²
Building area: 142.00 m²
Total floor area: 142.00 m²

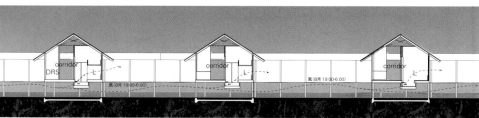

Section S=1:300

夏場の風は，夜間において床下の水盤で冷やされて居室内を西から東へ吹き抜ける

Model photos: Ayane Hirose　　　　　　　　　　　　　　　　　　　　　　View from southeast

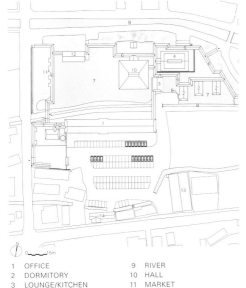

1　OFFICE
2　DORMITORY
3　LOUNGE/KITCHEN
4　PUBLIC BATH/LAUNDRY
5　WELL
6　CORRIDOR
7　POND
8　WATERWAY
9　RIVER
10　HALL
11　MARKET
12　CAFE
13　STOREHOUSE
14　GALLERY/VISITOR CENTER

Site plan　S=1:3000

地元で四代続く老舗企業が地域開放型の施設の構想を始めた。約1.8ヘクタールの敷地内に市場・集会所・舞台・オフィス・居住部(寮・アパート)・銭湯・カフェ・ラウンジ・ギャラリー・蔵等が，農地や池・庭園とともに周辺農家の協力のもと一体となって展開される。

それら施設は水上にて廻廊でつながり，敷地内を地域住民に開放することで周辺の地域動線の一部に取り込まれた「水上の郷」が完成する。本提案は，そのなかの居住部を取り上げる。

計画地は田園を中心に集落，社寺が点在する盆地に位置し，敷地には条里の地割と平行に3本の川や水路が東西に流れている。本水系の肥沃な土地では，弥生時代より稲作が盛んに行われ，周辺各地に古墳が点在する。敷地の地下水脈は，近年まで630立方メートル/日の給水能力を有する地域住民の生活用水としても利用され，一帯は美しい水と米や酒の産地としても知られている。つい最近まで西日本最古級の酒造所が存在していたが地域衰退とともに消えていった。

江戸期には豊かな地域を背景に，宿場が形成され商人文化も繁栄する。舞台小屋や武道場も現存しており，社寺では現在も秋の豊穣の収穫や商いを祝う祭りや獅子舞などの行事が盛んに行われ，風・水・太陽と農・商一体となった文化が今も根付いている。

我々はこの地域の歴史・産業・文化の源と考えられる「水」を中心に既に2年近いリサーチを継続しながら再生の計画に取り掛かった。

各施設の配置や向き，形は，広大なエリアを背景に利用時間と風・水・太陽の関係から適切に導かれる。

寮においては就業外の時間に着目し，朝日の太陽光や早朝・夜間の風配・風速，水源となる井戸を中心とした銭湯やラウンジとの距離に重点をおいて計画している。

入居者は朝日を浴びて起床し，東向きのラウンジで朝食をとり，南光を背にした北向きのオフィスへと向かう。就業後には一般開放された銭湯やカフェ，余暇には市場・集会所・舞台などを行き来し，そこで行なわれる地域のイベントと共に過ごす。

美しい地形と地域に育てられた地場企業がその地域衰退を憂い，地域とともに豊かな文化・風景を取り戻そうとしている。

（三分一博志）

The Unfolding House is located on a long sloping block overlooking a bay on Sydney Harbour. The site is situated between two public areas: a small park on the north and a beautiful reserve on the long southern boundary. The client required a new house for a family of six with some inner reflective courtyards; imagining this as a house to retreat to after retirement. Somehow this house exists not merely as a private dwelling but also gives a chance to create a backdrop for the public spaces surrounding it.

The idea of the house is to create a series of fragmented volumes unfolding along the slope, creating courtyards and voids. The fragmented volumes enable each room to be strategically located to capture the most favourable views and orientation. The resulting form is always variable and continuous. From the northern park, this house recalls an image of a village rather than a single house, while from the southern reserve it appears to be two forms stepping along the slope. The fragmented form also creates a series of inner courtyards and voids open to the interior spaces on each level. Such interior spaces strive to give people an impression of being outside: a feeling of the natural features of the site and the inner courtyards. The house is materialized in light-coloured, reinforced concrete. The subtle reflection of the green with the sunlight creates a strong atmosphere of private space.

The openings of the house strategically follow a chessboard pattern (diagonal) not only for sake of a more animated elevation but also as a strategy for interior space. An angled concrete awning shades each opening from the harsh Australian sunlight. Some low windows are used to frame and focus views towards the bay, reserve or courtyards; and the high windows introduce light without compromising the privacy of the room. A series of stairs along the south connect the levels with a meandering path and offer changing views to the reserve and courtyard within framed openings.

Entering from the discrete entrance at the southeast corner, the winding staircase leads down to a spacious and light formal living room with water views to the front, garden views to the rear, and views toward the sky on the sides. The bedrooms are arranged on top of the second volume. Each captures the impressive views, either to the courtyards or the bay. These rooms also shape a triangular void, which introduces sculptured light to the more dimly lit family and dining room level below.

This house has a mixed character as it unfolds down the site; at once a fragmented whole, a public dwelling, and a home framing nature.

Axonometric

CHENCHOW LITTLE
UNFOLDING HOUSE

Sydney, Australia
Design: 2016-17
Construction: 2019

View from northwest

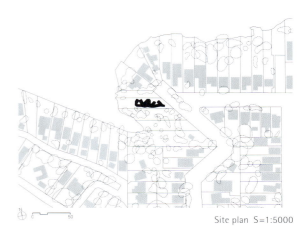
Site plan S=1:5000

South elevation S=1:500

View from west

Staircase

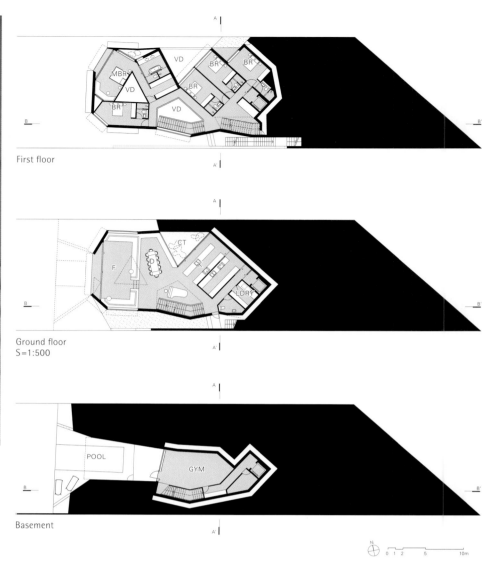

First floor

Ground floor
S=1:500

Basement

Section A-A' S=1:500

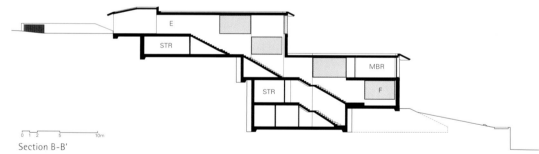

Section B-B'

Living room

Family room/dining room

94

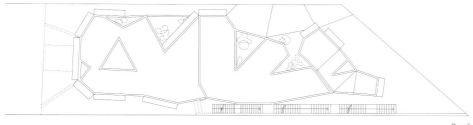

Roof

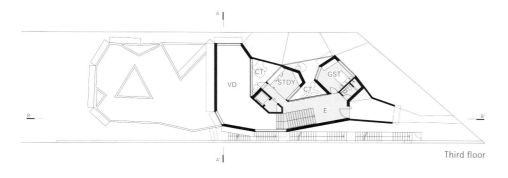

Third floor

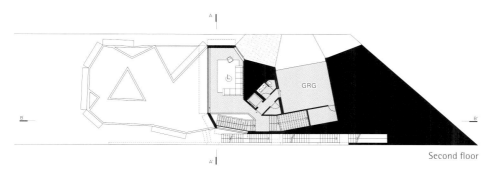

Second floor

Entrance

「展開する家」は，シドニー港の入江を見晴らす，細長い傾斜地にある。この敷地は，北側に小さな公園，長手の南側境界に美しい保護地，という二つの公共区域の間に位置する。クライアントの要望は，黙想的な中庭のある，六人家族のための新たな住宅で，引退後に静養するための住宅としても想定していた。この住宅は，単にプライベートな家として存在するだけでなく，住宅を取り囲む公共スペースの背景となる可能性を持つ。

この住宅の構想は，傾斜に沿って展開する断片的なヴォリュームの連続をつくることにより，中庭とヴォイドをつくり出すことである。断片化したヴォリュームにより，各室が最も好ましい景色と方角を捕えるように考慮した配置となっている。結果としての形態は，常に変化する連続的なものである。北側の公園から見た住宅は，単一の住宅というより，集落をイメージさせるものである。その一方で，南側の保護地からは傾斜に沿って二つの形のものが段々に見える。また，この断片化した形態は，各レベルにおいて，室内空間に開かれる中庭とヴォイドの連続をつくり出す。このような室内空間は，住人が外にいるような感覚を持つこと，つまり中庭や敷地内の自然的要素を感じられることを目指している。この住宅は，明るい色のRC造である。自然光による緑の微妙な反射は，プライベートな空間に力強い雰囲気をつくり出す。

住宅の開口は，表情豊かな立面のためだけではなく，室内空間を考慮した上で，意図的にチェス盤のパターン（対角線状）を踏襲している。角度のついたコンクリートの日除けが，各開口部において厳しいオーストラリアの日光を遮る。いくつかの低い位置にある開口は，湾，保護地，もしくは中庭の景色に焦点をあて，縁取る。そして，高い位置にある開口は，室内におけるプライバシーを侵すことなく，光を取り込む。南側に沿って連続する階段は，曲がりくねった通路で各階を接続し，縁取られた開口を通して，保護地や中庭の移り変わる景色を提供している。

南東の角に位置する別の入口を入ると，下階に続く曲がりくねった階段が，前方に水辺の景色 後方に庭の景色，横には空に向かう景色を望む，広々として明るい居室へと導く。寝室は，二つ目のヴォリュームの最上部に配置されている。各室からは，中庭か入江かどちらかへの印象的な景色を捕らえられる。さらに，これらの部屋は三角形のヴォイドを形づくり，その下の階にある，ぼんやりと照らされた家族の食堂に，彫刻的な光を取り込む。

この住宅は，断片的な全体であると同時に，パブリックな住居，そして自然を縁取る住宅であるという，いろいろな側面が混ざり合った特徴を持つ。

Architects: Chenchow Little—
Tony Chenchow, Stephanie Little principals-in-charge; Jie Xie, project team
Consultants: SDA Structures, structural;
Chenchow Little, interior design
Structural system: concrete walls, concrete floor slabs, concrete roof slabs
Major materials: insitu concrete walls, floors and roof, timber window frames
Site area: 992 m²
Building area: 338 m²
Total floor area: 497 m²

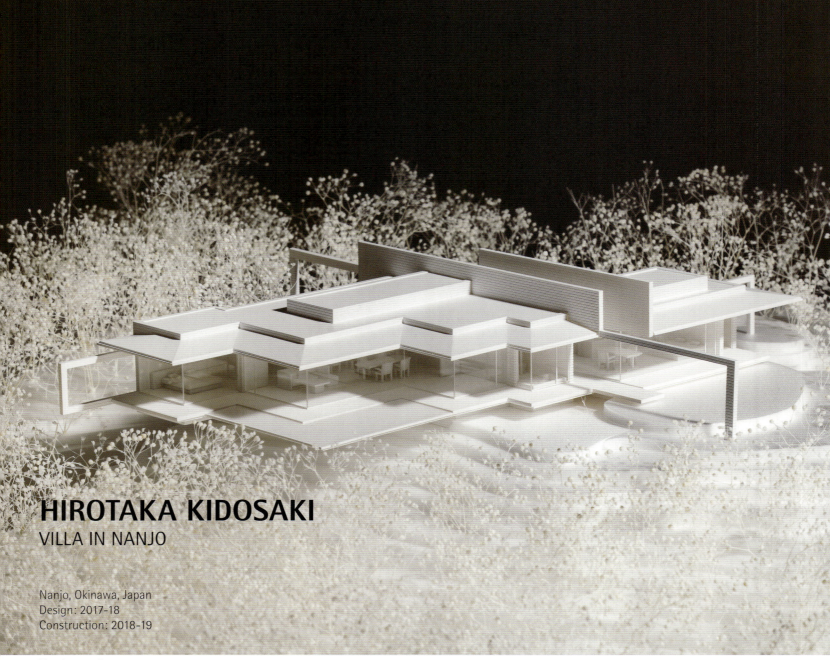

View from south

Model photos: Nohara Yamazaki

HIROTAKA KIDOSAKI
VILLA IN NANJO

Nanjo, Okinawa, Japan
Design: 2017-18
Construction: 2018-19

The site is located along the coastline of Nanjo city in Okinawa, on top of a small hill overlooking the Pacific Ocean.

Its highest parts are taller than the surrounding hills, surrounded by thick trees which hide the houses below. Attention is naturally drawn towards the infinitely expansive sky and ocean, and the horizon that divide them. In the east is the Kudakajima Island, which has long been recognized as a sacred island. The panoramic view awards a sight that can be enjoyed throughout the day, from sunrise behind the Kudakajima Island to sunset into the western sea.

The client wanted to build a second house that would maximize the potential of this land.

Except for the adjacent lot on the eastern side, the site is surrounded by a cliff in all areas that connect with the street. We secured site access by paving a sloping driveway on the western side where the incline was most gentle. Cutting through masses of Okinawa limestone, the driveway exudes a sense of openness that propels one into the vastness of the blue sky.

A slice of the sky and sea is cropped off and captured vertically by a wall made of two slabs of reinforced concrete which extend dynamically from the northwest to southeast.

The design of the approach to the house is such that the view is intentionally interrupted by a narrow construction, creating a sense of anticipation leading inside to the panoramic view of the horizon.

The plan is a simple echelon formation that maximizes the view that spreads from the interior spaces to the outside world. The deck and deep eaves create an in-between area, giving the house a sense of continuation and rhythm. The picturesque panorama further enhances the feeling of freedom and ease. The geometric flying buttress made of the wall pillar and beam constructed over the axis line becomes a frame which impressively crops the vast and wild natural environment. The unique characteristics of the site is manifested on the plane and in three-dimensional reality through the expansive echelon formation and the flying buttress. The design is an experiment in creating a house that responds to and integrates with the surrounding environment.

The horizon over Okinawa's unique sky and sea, and the Kudakajima Island which is also a symbol of local identity... Each moment of this panoramic scenery is captured inside the architectural frame, ceaselessly entertaining the eye by transforming into a view which no one has ever seen before.

Hirotaka Kidosaki

Plan S=1:500

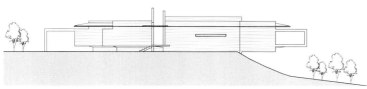

Northwest elevation

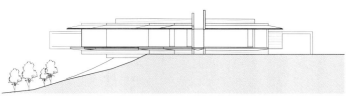

Southeast elevation

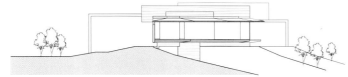

Southwest elevation S=1:500

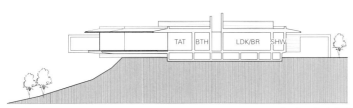

Section S=1:500

Architects: Kidosaki Architects Studio—
Hirotaka Kidosaki, principal-in-charge;
Kazuaki Mori, project team
Consultants: Toyohito Shibamura, structural;
Tasuku Miyagi, development

Structural system: reinforced concrete
Site area: 2,666.00 m²
Building area: 201.86 m²
Total floor area: 155.02 m²

沖縄県南城市の海岸線に沿って連なる，太平洋を一望できる小高い丘の上に本計画の敷地がある。

周辺の丘よりもさらに一段と高い頂上部分は，生い茂った木々に囲まれており，眼下の家屋を視界から消し去っている。身体と視線は，果てしなく広がる空と海とを分かつ水平線へと向けられる。東の方角には，古くから神の島と呼ばれてきた久高島を望むことができる。開かれたパノラマによって，久高島越しに昇る日の出から西の海へと沈む日の入りに至るまで，1日を通して堪能することができる。

建主は，この土地のポテンシャルを最大限に享受できるセカンドハウスを望まれた。

周囲は東側隣地を除き，接道部分は全て崖となっている。高低差の最も少ない西側に斜路を設け，敷地へのアクセスを確保した。沖縄石灰岩の岩塊を切通した斜路は，沖縄特有の抜け感のある青空へと引き込まれてゆくかのような高揚感を醸し出している。

北西から南東に向かってダイナミックに伸びる二枚のRC打放しの壁によって，空と海とがバーティカルなシーンとして切り取られる。

アプローチの計画においては敢えて視界を遮り，絞り込む構成とすることで，水平線を見渡すことができる室内へと至る演出の序章としている。

平面構成はシンプルな雁行配置とし，室内から外界へと広がっていく眺望を最大限に確保している。深い庇とデッキの創り出す中間領域が連続感とリズム感を生み，絵画のようなパノラマビューによって，一層の伸びやかさを付加している。軸線上に設けた壁柱と梁から構成される幾何学のフライング・バットレスは，広大で野性味溢れる豊かな自然を，印象的に切り取る額縁としての役割を担っている。伸びやかな雁行配置とフライング・バットレスによって，敷地がもつ特徴を平面的にも立体的にも顕在化させつつ，周辺環境との呼応と融合を試みている。

沖縄ならではの空と海とが描き出す水平線，そして地域のアイデンティティの象徴でもある久高島。それらの光景は建築がもたらすフレームによって刻一刻と切り取られ，これまで誰も見たことのない風景へと変幻し，見るものを魅了してやまないであろう。

（城戸崎博孝）

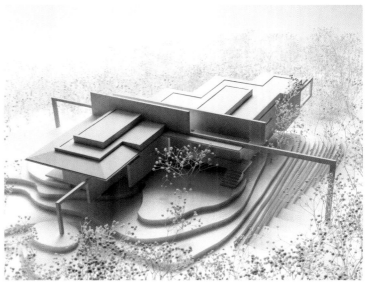

Bird's eye view from north

ALBERO KALACH
CASA EN MONTERREY

Monterrey, Mexico
Design: 2017-18
Construction: 2018-19

Monterrey is a city in northeast Mexico nestled between five mountains. The house is located in the southern part of the city, in the municipality of San Pedro Garza Garcia, which has the Sierra Madre Oriental running from one end to the other.

The house is located at the end of a cul-de-sac in a neighborhood close to the base of the mountain. It has been designed as a sort of "floating" house, having only 2 supports on the ground floor plan, allowing this level to be practically open and letting the garden unfold beneath the enclosed spaces. Walking beside the vertical volume, which contains a single

Sketch

Garden view

Approach

vertical circulation node for the house, and next to a triangular reflecting pool, one can either access the garden or take the stairs to the next level. In the 457 square meters garden there are several water features that will help refresh the atmosphere as the southeastern winds blow. There are also two large walnut trees and one jacaranda on the site that help compose the landscape design, taking into account retreats of shadow and light complemented by native species.

Going up the stairs one will walk through the floating volume of the house, a long nave running transversally along the site, which holds the kitchen and guest bathroom. Further ahead there is a large glass pavilion, which houses the dining and living room, overlooking the garden and at eye level with the tree canopies.

From this point on, only the volume containing the stairs and the long nave continue upwards. The second level, 5m above street level, hosts two mirrored bedrooms and another glass pavilion which holds a small study. The master bedroom is located in the uppermost level with one side of the nave being used as a leisure room and the other end as the sleeping quarters. The dressing room and bathroom separate these ends.

At the very bottom of the house, below the garden level, are all the service areas. The service bedroom has a small sunken patio contained by a mound of plants, which allows a glimpse of the garden and trees.

The openings and orientation of the house respond directly to the prevailing winds and grand views of the mountains. The distribution of the house in its vertical manner allows the user to discover and experience it in different ways as they move through it, bringing the mountains further into the home at each level.

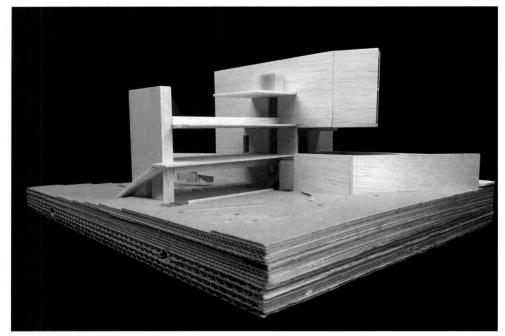

South view

モンテレイは五つの山のあいだに抱かれたメキシコ北東の都市である。住宅は東シエラ・マドレ山脈が町を縦断するように走るこの都市南部のサン・ペドロ・ガルサ・ガルシア市に位置している。

この住宅は山脈の山裾近くにある地区のクルドサックの終端に置かれている。住宅は「浮遊する」ように計画され, 地上階ではわずか2本の支持材で支えられている。その結果, 地上レベルを実際に開放して, 閉ざされた空間の下に庭が広がるようにしている。住宅で唯一の縦動線を包み込む垂直のヴォリュームの側を通り過ぎて行くと, 三角形のリフレクティング・プールの隣から庭に入ったり, 上階へと続く階段を上ることができる。457平米の庭には数種類の水景が用意され, 南東からの風が吹き抜けると爽快な気分を味わうことができる。また, 敷地に植わる2本のウォルナットの大木とジャカランダの木はランドスケープデザインの一部を構成し, 自生する植物によって補われる光と影の隠れ家となるように計算されている。

階段を上ってゆくと, 台所と来客用の浴室を備え, 敷地を縦断する細長い身廊のような浮遊するヴォリューム

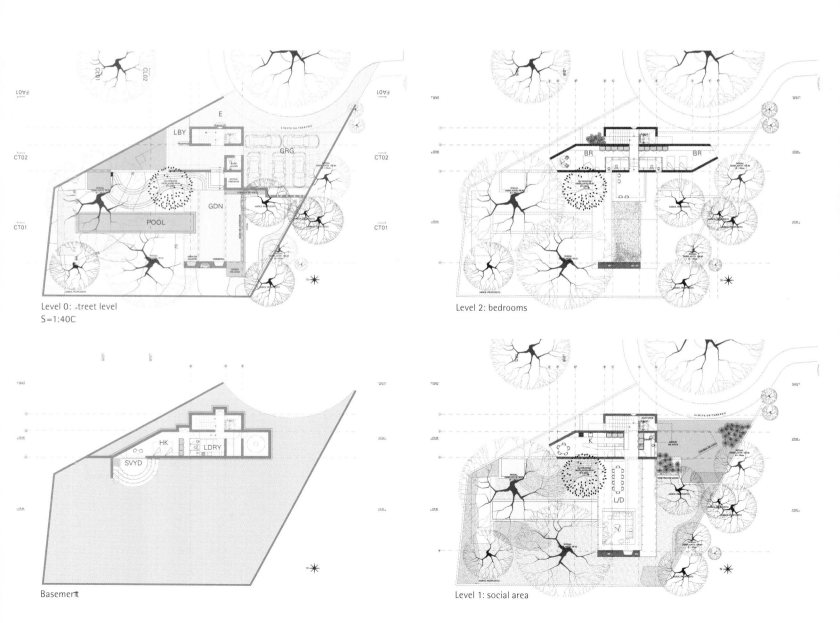

Level 0: street level
S=1:400

Level 2: bedrooms

Basement

Level 1: social area

の中を歩くことができる。さらに進むと庭を見わたし，視線の高さに木々の梢が広がる食堂と居間を収めた巨大なガラスのパヴィリオンへと続く。

このポイントからは，階段室を収めるヴォリュームと細長い身廊のみが上方へと続く。道路面から5メートルの高さに位置する2階には，左右対称の寝室と小さな書斎を収めたもう一つのガラスのパヴィリオンがある。主寝室は最上階に置かれ，身廊の片側は娯楽室に，もう一方の側は寝室になっている。化粧室と浴室はこれらを隔離するように配置されている。

庭よりも低い位置にある住宅の最下部は，全てサービスのための区画となっている。サービス用の寝室には数多くの植物の植わる小さなサンクンガーデンが設けられ，わずかに庭と木々の様子を眺めることができる。

住宅の開口部と方位は，卓越風と山々への壮大な眺望との関係からダイレクトに決定された。住宅を垂直に配置し，山々を家の中の各々の階へと引き込んでくることによって，住まい手は内部を動きながら様々な方法でそれを発見し，経験することができるようになっている。

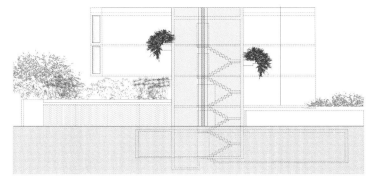

Section FA01 S=1:300

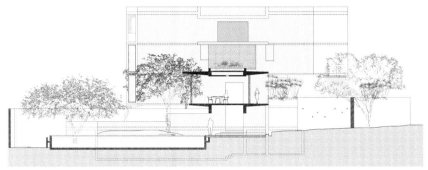

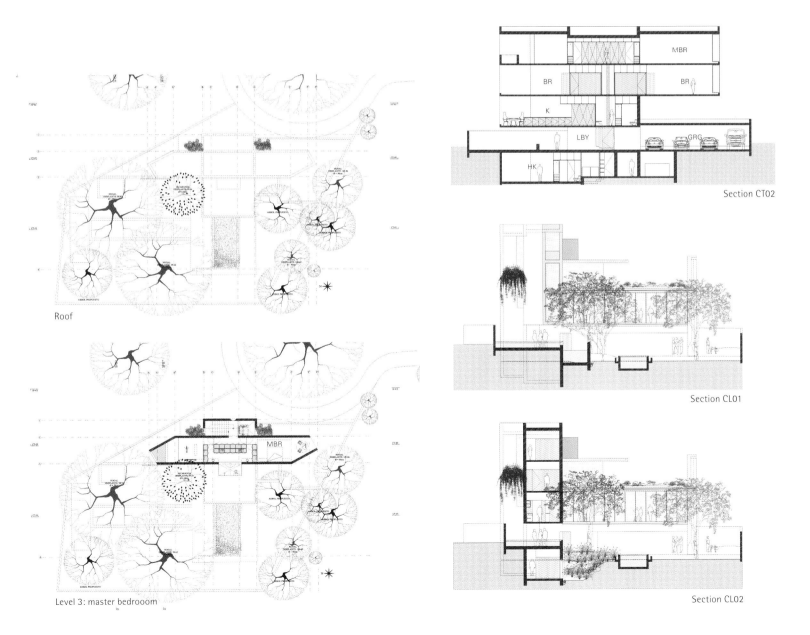

101

Living/dining room

Master bedroom

Architects: Taller de Arquitectura 'X'—
Albero Kalach, principal-in-charge;
Xavier Gonzalez, project team
Structural system: structural concrete
Major materials: concrete, marble and hard-
wood floors, steel columns
Site area: 734 m^2
Building area: 276 m^2
Total floor area: 699 m^2

ALBERO KALACH
CASA BRISAS

Acapulco, Guerrero, Mexico
Design: 2017-18
Construction: 2018-19

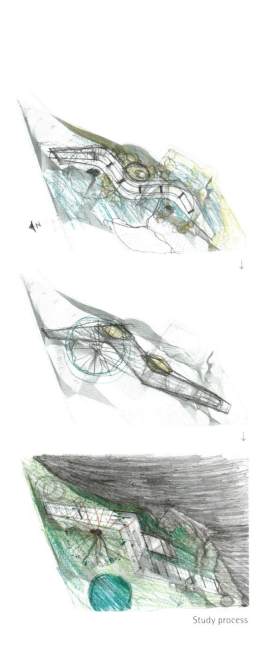

Study process

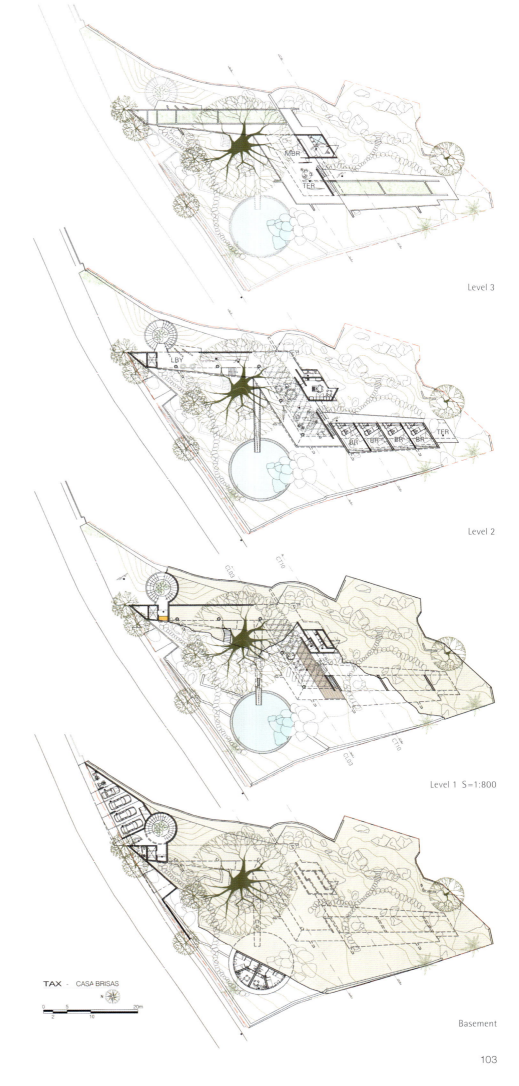

Level 3

Level 2

Level 1 S=1:800

Basement

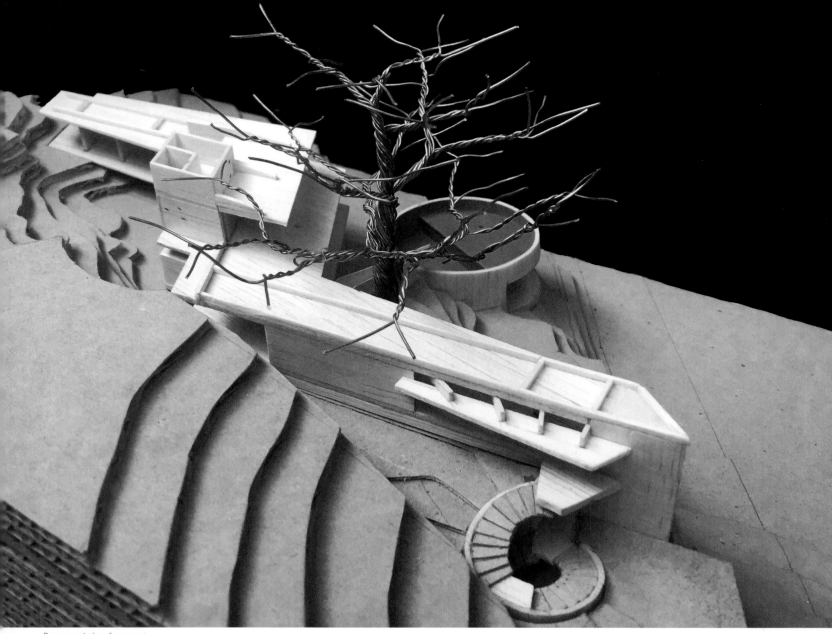

Downward view from east

The house is located on a rocky hill overlooking the bay of Acapulco and the island of La Roqueta on the Mexican Pacific coast. Its structure consists of few walls and concrete columns that make minimal contact with the ground—allowing visitors to walk underneath the house and explore the gardens freely—while supporting the concrete slabs that extend along the land and blend with the topography. The main axis of the project is the large Cuban laurel tree on the property.

In response to the location's warm, sub-humid climate, the house is open horizontally along public and private spaces to allow continuous interaction with the terraces, the landscape, the fresh air and the sea breeze, thus eliminating the need for air conditioning.

住宅はメキシコの太平洋岸に面したアカプルコ湾とラ・ロケタ島を見晴らす岩の多い丘陵に位置している。構造は地面との接点を最小限に抑えるため、— 住まい手は家の下を歩いて庭を自由に散策することができる — 地形と一体化するように地面に沿って伸びるコンクリートスラブを支持しつつも、限られた壁とコンクリートの柱によって構成されている。計画の軸線は敷地に植わるキューバ産の月桂樹の大木から決められている。

温暖湿潤気候の土地柄ゆえ、住宅はパブリックスペースとプライベートスペースの双方で水平方向に開かれる。そのため、テラスや自然、新鮮な外気や海風と常に交わることができるので、機械空調は不要なものとなった。

Architects: Taller de Arquitectura 'X'—
Albero Kalach, principal-in-charge;
Adolfo Romero, project team
Structural system: structural concrete
Major materials: concrete, marble floors, wood
Site area: 2,312.058 m²
Building area: 833.25 m²
Total floor area: 1,304.08 m²

West view

North view

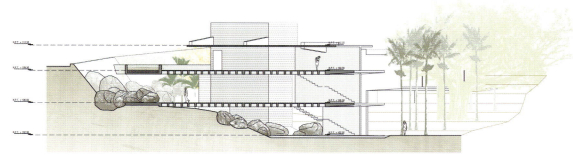

Section CL03 S=1:400

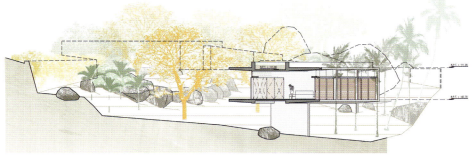

Section CT10

KENGO KUMA
SUSPENDED FOREST

Montricher, Switzerland
Design: 2016-17
Construction: 2017-18

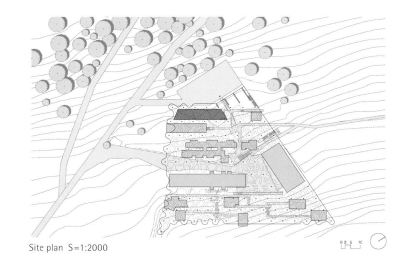

Site plan S=1:2000

North wing on right

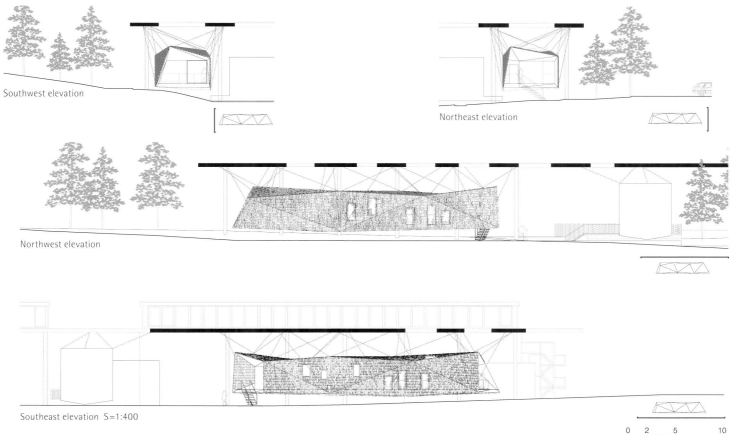

Southwest elevation

Northeast elevation

Northwest elevation

Southeast elevation S=1:400

West view

Exterior wooden filter

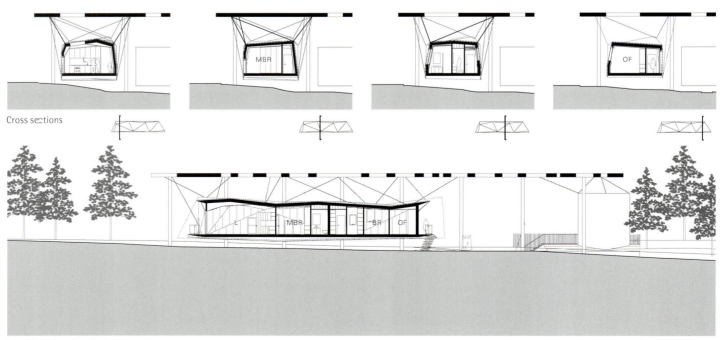
Cross sections

Longitudinal section S=1:400

Living room

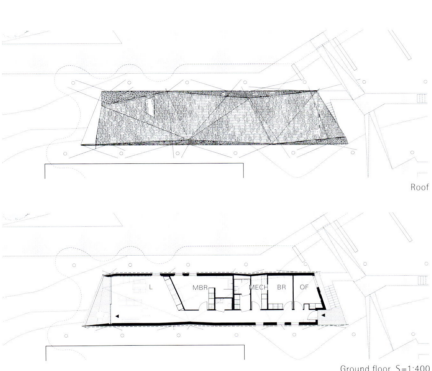
Roof

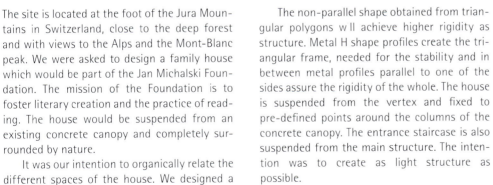
Ground floor S=1:400

Bedroom

The site is located at the foot of the Jura Mountains in Switzerland, close to the deep forest and with views to the Alps and the Mont-Blanc peak. We were asked to design a family house which would be part of the Jan Michalski Foundation. The mission of the Foundation is to foster literary creation and the practice of reading. The house would be suspended from an existing concrete canopy and completely surrounded by nature.

It was our intention to organically relate the different spaces of the house. We designed a cocoon-like, gradual and continuous space containing all the functionalities. A corridor runs from the entrance to the main living space, where the floating balcony connects the interior with the surrounding environment. Then lateral apertures let the light and nature come into the house.

The non-parallel shape obtained from triangular polygons will achieve higher rigidity as structure. Metal H shape profiles create the triangular frame, needed for the stability and in between metal profiles parallel to one of the sides assure the rigidity of the whole. The house is suspended from the vertex and fixed to pre-defined points around the columns of the concrete canopy. The entrance staircase is also suspended from the main structure. The intention was to create as light structure as possible.

To reinforce the idea of a wrapping space, plywood panels in larch are coating the interior walls and ceilings, as a negative of the exterior wooden facade. The inner envelope is not following the exterior but gradually expanding depending on each space.

For the exterior skin we decided to do a re-interpretation of the traditional wooden roof and facade system to cover the house. Working together with a local craftsman to bring off a contemporary expression of this traditional technique, we transformed this covering wooden system widely used in this region into a filter system. The waterproofing is made by white steel plates covering the main structure. Each one of the wooden pieces is manually cut and comes from local forests. We worked with two different species and two different dimensions, 120 x 300 mm for the oak and 120 x 500 mm for the larch, placed in checkered pattern which is altered in a random and organic way by creating a variation of the rhythm to achieve a more vibrant expression. We chose to not treat the wood so it will age with the house, generating a greater diversity of nuances in the facade depending on the sun and rain exposure.

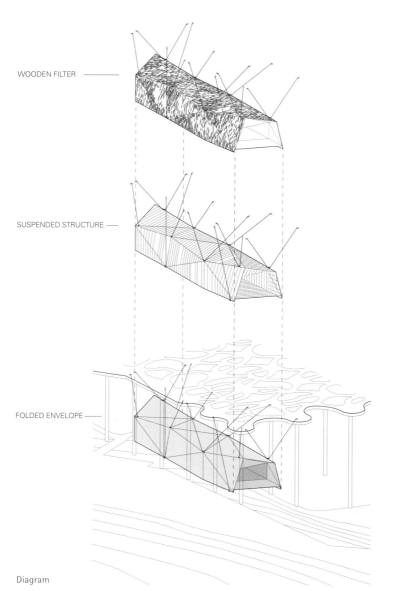

Diagram

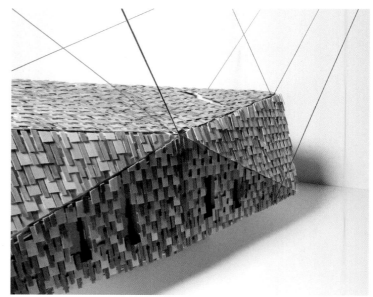

Exterior wooden filter

Front view: living room

スイス，ジュラ山脈の麓にある敷地はうっそうとした森に隣接し，敷地からはアルプスやモンブランの山頂が望める。施主からの依頼は，ジャン・ミシャルスキ財団の一部となる家族用住居を設計するというものであった。この財団は，文芸創作や読書習慣の促進をミッションとして掲げている。住宅は，既存のコンクリートキャノピーから吊るされ，完全に自然に取り囲まれたものとなる。

住宅のさまざまな空間に有機的な関係性をもたらすことを目指し，全ての機能を搭載したコクーンのような，ゆるやかで連続的な空間を設計した。廊下が玄関から居間へと走り，居間にある空に浮かんだバルコニーが室内と周囲の屋外空間をつなげる。横方向に伸びた隙間から室内に光と自然がもたらされる。

三角形ポリゴンから得られた非平行形状によって，より高い構造の剛性が得られる。H型鋼で安定性に必要な三角形のフレームをつくり，フレーム間にフレームの一辺と平行になるよう鋼材を配置して構造全体の剛性を確保している。住宅は頂点から吊るされ，コンクリートキャノピーの柱周囲のあらかじめ定められた点に固定される。玄関の階段もまた，メインとなる構造から吊るされている。このようにして，可能な限り軽い構造を生み出している。

空間を包むというアイディアをさらに高めるように，屋外の木のファサードと反対に，内壁と天井をカラマツ材の合板仕上げとした。内装は屋外空間との連続性はなく，それぞれの空間に左右されながら緩やかに拡張している。

屋外のスキンについては，伝統的な木の屋根や住宅を覆うファサードシステムに再解釈を加えた。現地の職人と協力しながら伝統的な手法を現代的な表現に発展させるべく，この地域で一般的に用いられている木の被覆システムをフィルターシステムに変換させた。メインの構造を白のスティールプレートで覆い防水加工を施し，現地の森から採取した木材は一つひとつ手作業で裁断された。2種類の木と寸法（120×300ミリのオーク材と120×500ミリのカラマツ材）を用意し，躍動感あふれる表現をもたらすようリズムのバリエーションをつくり，ランダムで有機的な格子模様を描くように仕上げられた。無垢材を用いているので，木材は家とともに経年変化を重ね，日光や雨に晒されながらファサードがより豊かな表情を見せてくれるだろう。

Architects: Kengo Kuma & Associates—Kengo Kuma, principal-in-charge; Matthieu Wotling, Silvia Fernandez, project team
Consultants: Muttoni & Fernandez Ingénieurs Conseils, structural; Sorane, HVAC; Louis Richard Ingénieurs Conseils, electrical
General contractor: Losinger Marazzi
Structural system: suspended metal structure
Major materials: wooden tiles, metal
Site area: 21,590 m²
Building area: 132 m²
Total floor area: 132 m²
Cost of construction: 1,455.000 euro (1.7 M CHF)

ALPHAVILLE
NISHI–OJI TOWN HOUSE

Kyoto, Japan
Design: 2016-18
Construction: 2018-

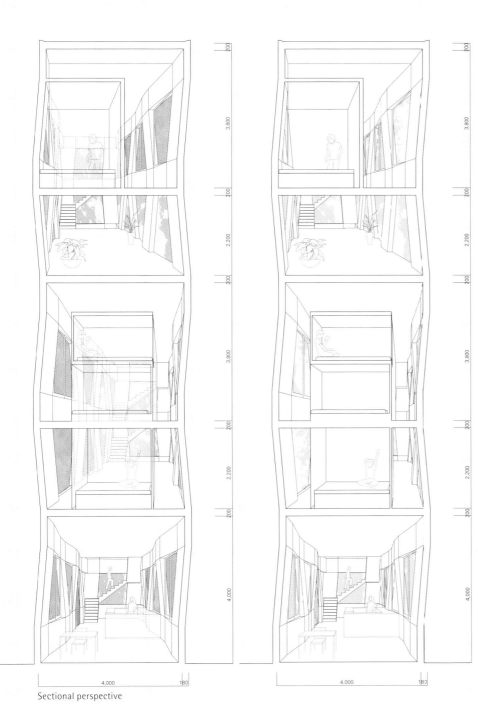

Sectional perspective

This is a five-storied housing complex facing a main street in the west part of Kyoto City. Since the restriction of the height is relaxed along the four-lane road, old *Machiya* buildings have been replaced by medium/high-rise buildings. We were also requested to design a building of four or five stories high on a site where is five minutes' walk from the rail station for economic reasons, but a plot of 4 meters wide and 16 meters long was too narrow to meet such requirement. Except the restaurant on the first floor and owner's residence on the fifth floor, the uses of floors are expected to be flexible— for instance, possible to be changed from a studio apartment to a family apartment, then to a guesthouse and to be reconstructed in the end—to respond to future situations of surroundings. Therefore we decided to use 1-by-1-meter and 2-by-1-meter precast concrete panels for its structure, and each edges of the panels is worked to have different projections on each stories, so that they form a 2-by-2-meter grid structure with wavering openings and five slabs. The spaces can be divided by both interior and exterior partitions—which make it possible to incorporate the surrounding atmosphere in three-dimensionally—so that programs on each floors can be organized flexibly. Precast concrete panels work as thin walls and beams, as well as a wavering wall as a whole. Such wavering walls support the required programs as a minimum structure, and offer diverse and three-dimensional perspectives from the interior to the outside, while make this dense grid-planned city more alive by the ripple-like facades. What we proposed here is a soft infrastructure—which can be used as a private housing, public work place, or a mix of two just like a wooden *Machiya* building, and which can respond to the surroundings yet keep its urban framework.
Kentaro Takeguchi + Asako Yamamoto

Site plan S=1:3000

西大路タウンハウス

京都市西部の大通り沿いに建つ5階建ての複合住宅。4車線の道路沿いだけ高さ制限が緩和されているので、かつて並んでいた町家のほとんどは中層から高層のビルに建て替わってしまった。鉄道駅から歩いて5分の、この場所を建て替えるにあたっても、経済的な要請から4〜5層とすることが求められたが、敷地は4×16メートルと短冊状でかなり小さい。またフロアの使い道も、1階を飲食店舗、5階をオーナー住居とする以外、この街をとりまく状況によって、ワンルームマンションから家族向け賃貸、ゲストハウスそしてまた建て替えと変化していくことが予想された。そこで、1×1そして2×1メートルのPCコンクリートパネル造とし、各パネルの端部を加工して面外へのゆらぎを各階にもたらすことで、2×2メートルで等間隔にならび、四方八方にゆらぐ開口と五つのスラブからなる構造体を考えた。各フロアのプログラムはオープンであり、内外の仕切り方によって、立体的に環境を取り入れることができる。PCパネルは薄い柱・梁であると同時に全体としてゆらぐ壁であり、ゆらぐ壁はそのような必要とされるプログラムを最低限の構造として支え、内部から外部への多様で立体的な視点をもたらすと同時に、さざ波のような外観が高密なグリッド・シティのいきいきとした動きになる。私たちが考えたのは、木造の町家がそうであったような、プライベートな住宅にもパブリックな仕事場にもあるいはその混合体にも使える、周辺状況に応じて変化することのできる、それでいて都市の骨格を維持するような、柔らかなインフラストラクチャーをつくることであった。

（竹口健太郎＋山本麻子）

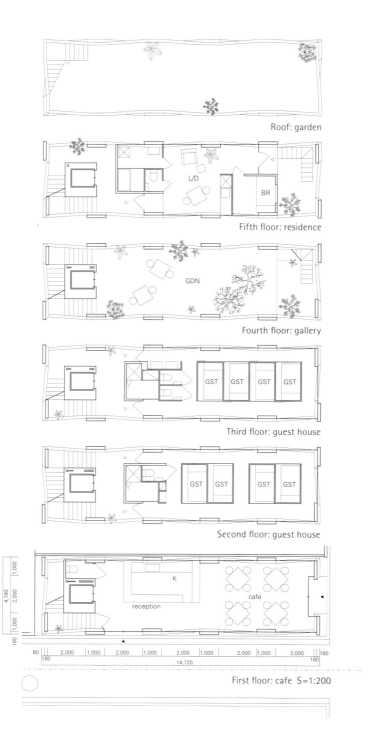

Roof: garden

Fifth floor: residence

Fourth floor: gallery

Third floor: guest house

Second floor: guest house

First floor: cafe S=1:200

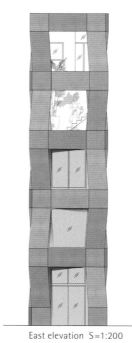

East elevation S=1:200

Section

Southeast view

Model photo: Nohara Yamazaki

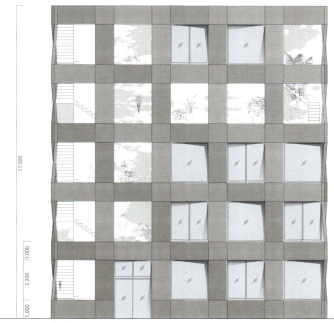

South elevation

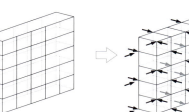 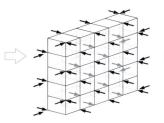 

Diagram

Architects: ALPHAVILLE—
Kentaro Takeguchi, Asako Yamamoto, principals-in-charge; Tomohisa Koike, project team
Consultants: Takashi Manda, structural; pivoto, furniture
Structural system: wall type reinforced concrete structure
Major materials: concrete, glass, steel, wood, alminium sash
Site area: 66.77 m^2
Building area: 55.06 m^2
Total floor area: 275.30 m^2

Upward view

Future Shack

My favourite Thunderbird was Thunderbird 2. Every Saturday morning as a child in the 1960's I would watch enthralled as International Rescue despatched the Thunderbirds across the globe and into space. (After Thunderbirds the next show was the Japanese TV series The Samurai, which I also enjoyed very much)

I loved the way Thunderbird 2 could take off and land vertically and deposit and pick up a variety of pods that contained different rescue equipment for all types of disasters. It has only occurred to me recently how much this deep seated childhood memory has influenced my work. The hydraulic legs of Thunderbird 2 appeared in Future Shack (designed in 1985 and built in 1996) That project used shipping containers as a base module for emergency housing but the idea was influenced in part by Thunderbird 2. Four decades later drones have become a part of everyday life. Their role in wartime is what they are best known for however they have many other possible applications. Imagine being able to transport a house, not by land or sea as was the case with Future Shack, but by air, landing the drone-house by remote control wherever it is required and then taking off again once the need for shelter had passed. The UN could stockpile the houses and air force drone 'pilots' could use their skills for peaceful purposes wherever the need arises. Architecture and technology have always been passionate bed fellows and this project is a case in point.
Sean Godsell, 2018

自分にとって最高のサンダーバードは、「サンダーバード2号」だ。1960年代、子供だった私は毎週土曜日の朝、地球上の何処へでも、そして宇宙にさえも派遣されるこの国際救助隊の姿を見て、魅了された。(サンダーバードの次の番組は日本のテレビシリーズである「ザ・サムライ」で、私はこの番組も非常に楽しんだものだ。)

私はサンダーバード2号が離陸する方法や、垂直に着陸して積荷を降ろしたり、いかなる種類の災害にも備えるためにさまざまな救難装備を載せた多彩な格納庫を積み込む方法が大好きだった。最近になって初めて、心の奥底に根づいたこの子供の頃の記憶がいかに自分の仕事に影響を与えているか、という点に気づいた。サンダーバード2号の油圧式の脚は、「未来の掘立小屋」(1985年に設計され、1996年に建てられた)で表現されている。このプロジェクトでは輸送用コンテナを緊急時の住宅のためのベースモジュールとして用いているが、アイディアの一部はサンダーバード2号に影響を受けている。40年が経ち、「ドローン」は今や日常生活の一部となりつつある。ドローンの戦争時における役割はよく知られていることだが、そのほかにも多くの利用可能性があるだろう。「未来の掘立小屋」の時のように海上輸送したり、陸上輸送するのではない、空輸による住宅の輸送方法を想像してみてほしい──「ドローン・ハウス」は必要とされる場所があればどこへでも遠隔操作で着陸し、このシェルターが必要な期間が過ぎれば再び離陸する。国連はこの住宅を大量に備蓄し、空軍のドローン"パイロット達"は必要になればいつでも彼らの技術を平和目的のために用いることができる。建築と技術は常に情熱を秘めた「仲間」同士の関係にあり、このプロジェクトはある意味、そうした事例の一つなのである。
(ショーン・ゴッドセル、2018年)

SEAN GODSELL
DRONE HOUSE

No fixed address
Design: 2015-17

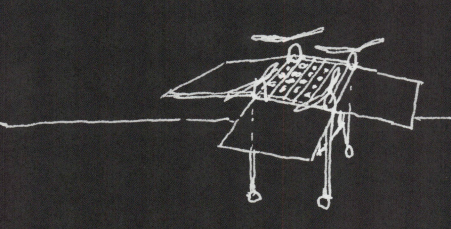

Sketch

Architects: Sean Godsell Architects—
Sean Godsell, principal-in-charge;
Hayley Franklin, project team
Consultants: Sean Godsell Architects, interior design
Program: emergency shelter
Structural system: steel frame
Major materials: steel, glass
Building area: 65 m²
Total floor area: 30 m²

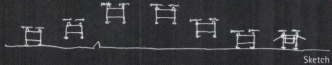
Sketch

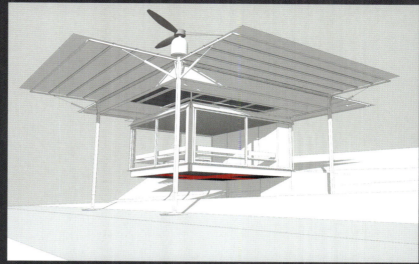
Drone House: open

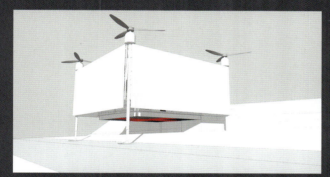
Drone House: closed

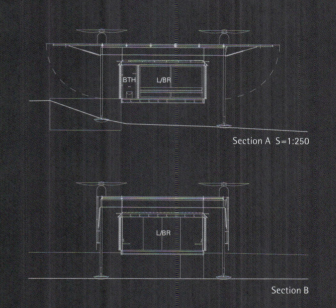
Section A S=1:250

Section B

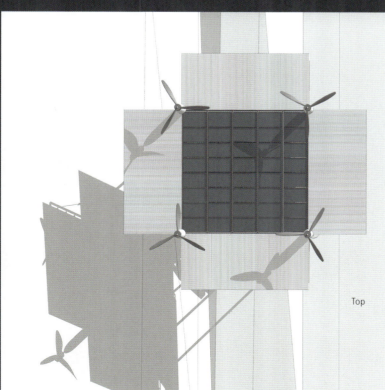
Top

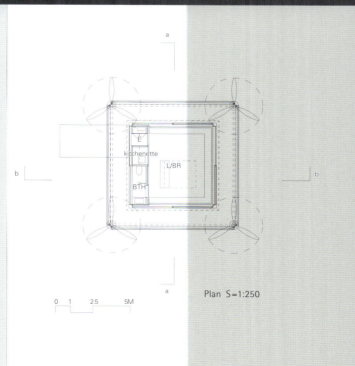
Plan S=1:250

SOU FUJIMOTO
TREE HOUSE TOKYO

Tokyo, Japan
Design: 2017–

Aerial view

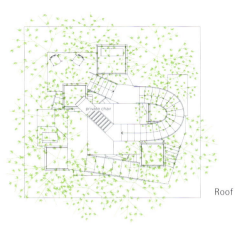
Roof

Level +7,700

Level +4,700

Level +0 S=1:150

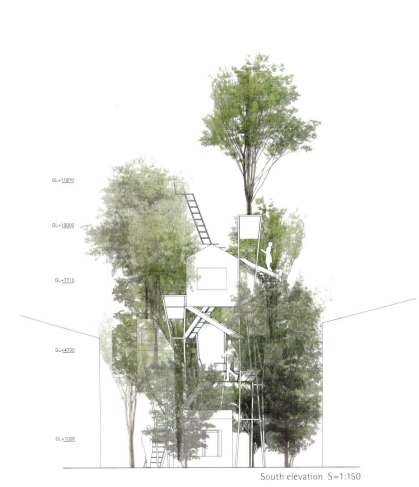
South elevation S=1:150

Making a small tree house in the middle of Tokyo as an architect's own residence.

Here I am proposing a new prototype of a house—towards the future and through requestioning the meaning of living inside the city—which is rather to design a small three-dimensional forest as a living environment than to build a house. Not only functional interior spaces but also various furniture float among the trees, to make this three-dimensional and small forest a place for living. Thousands of trees grow from both the ground and its structure and huts, so that they form an semi-artificial/semi-natural forest with floating trees. Therefore this architecture itself is an extension of the ground where is full of trees and lives, that is to say, the embodiment and architecturization of the earth. Rooms on the ground level are planned to be open and have public programs in the future.

This is an attempt to create a small paradise inside the enormous city of Tokyo, but it is not a closed one, rather a super-urban paradise on the bases of the city. This is a challenge to realize his small ideal by an architect—to create a place, worth and mind, which are small but long-lasting for more than 100 years as a certain existence—in Tokyo where everything changes with the time, and where no one raises questions.
Sou Fujimoto

建築家の自邸として，東京の都心に小さなツリーハウスをつくる。

　都市に住むということの意味を問い直し，未来へ向けて新しくも原型的な「家」のあり方を提案する。それは家をつくるというよりも，居住環境としての小さな立体的な森を設計することである。いわゆる機能的な内部空間だけではなく，木々の間に浮遊するようにさまざまな家具が点在し，この立体的な小さな森全体が住むための場所となっている。無数の樹木は地面から直接生えているものだけではなく，建築的な構造体や小屋の上に生えているものも多く，それゆえに浮遊しながら林立する半人工一半自然の森が形づくられている。それゆえこの建築自体が，樹木と生命を湛えた地面の延長，あるいは地球の身体化，建築化であるということもできるのである。1階部分の居室は，将来的にはより公共的なプログラムへと開いていきたいと考えている。

　これは東京という巨大な都市の中に小さな楽園をつくり出す試みであるが，それは外界から閉じた楽園ではなく，むしろ都市の中であればこそ成り立つ超都市的な楽園となるだろう。そして東京という，全てが変化し移り変わっていくしかない都市の只中において，そこに誰も何の疑問も抱かないような状況の只中にあって，小さいながらも，100年後も変わらずそこにあり続ける場所と価値と意思というものを，確かな存在としてつくることができないだろうか，という一人の建築家の小さな理想への挑戦なのである。

（藤本壮介）

Private terrace

Private chair

Diagram

Architects: Sou Fujimoto Architects—
Sou Fujimoto, principal-in-charge;
Masaki Iwata, Kei Sasaki, Hiroki Nakagawa, project team
Structural system: steel
Major materials: wood, steel
Site area: 49 m²
Building area: 16.2 m²
Total floor area: 19.1 m²

Model photo (p.119): Ayane Hirose

BERCY CHEN STUDIO
ARROWHEAD HOUSE

Austin, Texas, U.S.A.
Design: 2017-18
Construction: 2018-19

Perspective: hillside view

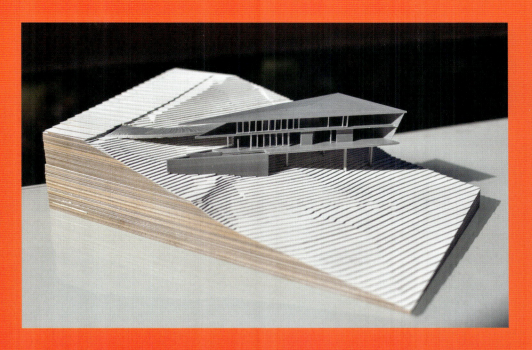

Perched on a steep, heavily wooded slope in West Austin, *the Arrowhead House* points toward the downtown skyline eight miles to the southeast through the valleys carved by the Colorado River and its spring-fed tributary, Bull Creek. The prismatic triangular shape evokes an ancient Native American arrowhead discovered in the landscape. Comanche and Tonkawa hunting arrowheads are common in the area and this archetypal shape gives the house its sharp-edged, iconic form. Like an elevated lookout platform, the house hovers on slender columns above the forest canopy to maximize panoramic vistas and minimize site disturbances of the flood-prone, hydrologically sensitive karst landscape of the Texas Hill Country.

While the triangular plan was primarily driven by the layered history of the site, the shape was also a result of dynamic site forces, view corridor easements, and dramatic topography. Accessed by a roadway tracing the spine of the hill, the site was the last available lot in the neighborhood and previously considered unbuildable due to the steep 45 degree slope. From the street, the house is rotated and positioned below the crest of the hill and the dark material palette merges with the dappled oak branches; however from the downhill side, planes of glass project dynamically over the ravine embracing the view beyond.

Saul Jerome E. San Juan & Colin Simmer/ Bercy Chen Studio

西オースティンの，急勾配で樹木が鬱蒼と茂った傾斜地の上に建つ「アローヘッド・ハウス」は，コロラド川とその湧水支流であるブル・クリークによって形づくられた峡谷の先，南東に8マイル離れた街のスカイラインを指し示している。プリズム状の三角形をした形は，その土地で発見された古代のネイティブ・アメリカンの矢じりを思わせる。コマンチ族やトンカワ族の狩猟用の矢じりはこの地域においてはありふれたものであり，その原型的な形に基づいて，この住宅の鋭く切り立ったアイコニックな形態が与えられた。高所の見晴らし台のように，この住宅は細い柱に載って林冠の上に浮かんでおり，それによってパノラミックな眺望を最大化すると同時に，テキサス・ヒル・カントリーの洪水が多く，水文学的に不安定なカルスト地形による敷地の変動を最小限に抑えている。

三角形の平面がおもに敷地の持つ重層的な歴史によって決定された一方で，住宅の形はダイナミックな敷地の力，ビュー・コリドーの地役権，ドラマティックな地勢にもまた由来している。丘陵の背をなぞる道路からつながっているこの敷地は，近隣のなかでも最も利用しづらい場所であり，その45度の急勾配の傾斜のせいで以前は建設不可能と考えられていた。道路側から見ると，この住宅は丘の頂点の下に回転して位置しており，素材の持つ暗い色彩がまだらになったオークの枝に溶け込んでいる。他方で，下り坂の側から見るとガラスでできた水平面がダイナミックに峡谷に突出し，向こう側の景観をも取り込んでいる。

（サウル・ジェローム・E・サン・ジュアン&コリン・シマー/ベイシー・チェン・スタジオ）

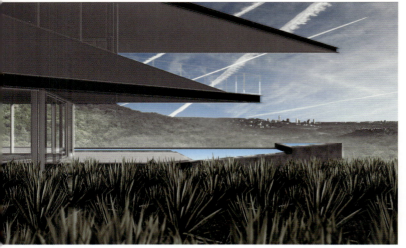
Pool on south end

Kitchen, dining and living room

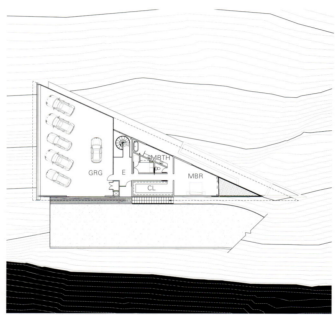
Upper floor S=1:600

Southeast elevation S=1:600

West elevation

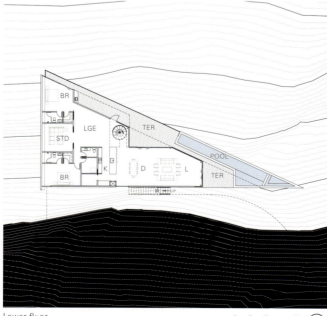
Lower floor

Section S=1:300

Architects: Bercy Chen Studio LP—
Calvin Chen, principal-in-charge;
Colin Simmer, Joshua Mackley,
Saul Jerome E. San Juan, project team
Consultants: MJ Structures, structural
Structural system: steel frame

Major materials: steel, glass, concrete, wood, zinc roof
Site area: 30,270 x sq. ft.
Building area: 3,527 sq. ft.
Total floor area: 4,848 sq. ft.

SATOSHI MATSUOKA + YUKI TAMURA
EBISU PROJECT

Tokyo, Japan
Design: 2017-
Construction: 2018-

Site plan S=1:2000

Birds' eye view from east

Northwest elevation

This is a project for a housing which consists of three houses and an underground parking in a dense residential area of Tokyo. The plot of the site is deep in depth but very close to adjacent buildings. Moreover, the site faces a street on the north side and there is a three-meters high retaining wall at the back of the plot. Though we cannot get much daylight, there are breezes and small alleys in its complicated neighborhood.

We designed a fish-bone-shaped plan with 3.2 meters square towers jointed at an angle of 45 degrees. To respond to each small situations of surroundings, we made triangular courtyards to have setbacks from the neighborhood, and obtained ventilations and views towards the backside. Four towers surrounded by courtyards line up one behind another from the facing street to the retaining walls, and bay windows in trapezoid plane shapes are attached to their exterior walls. Diverse bay windows function also as niches, sun rooms and part of living spaces. Each towers has four different facades with bay windows, which give people a feeling of living inside projecting space of the windows. Each houses is composed of four to six floors of towers, so that they form a continuous but diverse windowscape.

Towers consist of four or five floors and are 10 meters high. Each towers has different floor levels and ceiling heights from the towers next to it to make views from each towers varied.

The sequential views towards outside are at an angle of 45 degrees in succession just like a folding screen depicting scenery, while the interior space expands and shrinks, to emphasizes the void going through the towers. The interior scenery has longer range than the exterior views, and is unfolded along the walls. Facades repeat bay windows, and such windowscape continues to the end of the site like a townscape.

Architects: MATSUOKASATOSHITAMURAYUKI—Satoshi Matsuoka, Yuki Tamura, principals-in-charge; Kohei Fukino, project team
Consultants: TECTONICA—Yoshinori Suzuki, structural; MISAWA A.project—Sigeru Oshima, producer
Structural system: reinforced concrete
Major materials: concrete, glass, wood
Site area: 95 m²
Building area: 56 m²
Total floor area: 151 m²

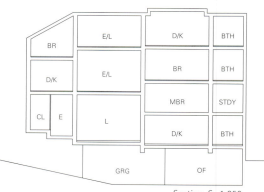

Section S=1:250

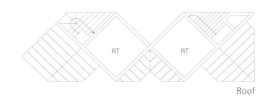
Roof

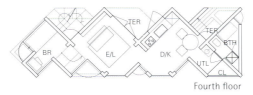
Fourth floor

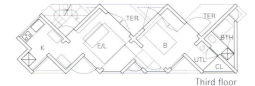
Third floor

Second floor

First floor S=1:250

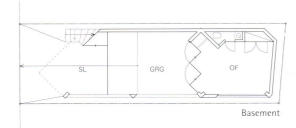
Basement

都内の建て込んだ住宅地に3戸の集合住宅と地下駐車場，小さなオフィスを計画する。敷地は奥行きが深く，隣家が境界線ぎりぎりまで迫る。北側接道の敷地の最奥には3メートルの擁壁があり，採光条件はよくないが，周囲の入り組んだ建物群の隙間には，風の通り道や小さな抜けがところどころに見られる。

計画は一辺3.2メートルの正方形のタワーを45度振ってつなげたフィッシュボーン・プラン。周辺の状況に応えるため，三角形の庭で周囲から引きをとり，採光と通風，奥行き方向へのビューを確保した。庭に囲まれたタワーが前面道路から擁壁まで4棟連なり，その周囲に台形平面のベイウィンドウが取り付く。大小のベイウィンドウはニッチやサンルーム，居室の一部をなす。タワーごとで四面異なるベイウィンドウに囲まれ，四周に張り出した出窓の中に暮らす感覚をもつ。各戸は四つから六つのタワー平面によって構成され，多様な窓辺が連続する住宅となる。

タワーの断面は，地上10メートルのなかに地下階を含めて四層と五層の2種類で構成する。フィッシュボーンの一つの正方形タワーを単位にスキップして，隣り合うタワーのレベル差と天井高の差異がフィッシュボーンの一山一山からの眺めを特別なものにする。

外への眺めは45度振られた近景が屏風絵のように断続的に連なる一方，室内どうしは広がっては萎み，複数のタワーを貫通する抜けが強調される。外の風景の射程より長い室内の風景が壁面に沿って展開される。ファサードはベイウィンドウが反復され，窓辺の点景が街並みのように敷地の奥まで連続する。

Model photos: Ayane Hirose

IRISARRI-PIÑERA
SURF AND YOGA MONITOR

Doniños, Ferrol, Galicia, Spain
Design: 2016-17
Construction: 2018-19

South view

The project parts from an idea that integrates several necessities and concepts in a sole edification.

The personal domestic program joins the desire to add spaces where the house's owner can share with other people experiences around two activities, surf and yoga, of which she is an instructor.

These spaces for temporary use are integrated in turn with an understanding of the housing program as something evolutive in time, paced to the changes in the vital needs of the owner. The organization therefore parts from a system of hierarchies and degrees of privacy and independence on demand.

Minimizing resources generates the need of utilizing a strategy of multi-use changing spaces, so that less space is built, but at the same time the level of relations between them is increased, enabling a richer world of personal relationships.

The project is located on a plot characterized by a steep slope from the road, facing south and overlooking the valley and lagoon of Doniños, coinciding in this case the most interesting views with the best sunlight and orientation. It is also noteworthy that this unevenness makes the home have a discreet and minimal presence as seen from the level of the public road, while at the same time respecting the sunlight and privacy of neighboring homes.
It is intended as a construction that integrates itself into the landscape, which only alters slightly the area, and that is why the project is based on the idea of "laying" pieces, maintaining the runoff and the nature of the place.

It is a flexible organization that allows a certain use linked to the outside of the parcel according to its uses, and thus collecting the tradition in terms of holding a strong relationship with the environment and the area. The housing is solved by understanding the program in a flexible approach that allows independence of use, transferring this strategy to the architecture in a way that the volume appears as a sum of small pieces that are added to create a subtle set of scale, thus becoming integrated into the traditional way of occupying rural territory.

Four pieces with the most fixed and private program support an open and permeable space, open to multiple uses and distributions, and which is situated in a suspended position, leaving the ground to flow freely under it. The four pieces, according to their position and the slope of the terrain, generate complementary spaces above or below the level common to them all.

The place invites to participate in nature, and the building contributes to this by generating different garden-spaces with varying degrees of privacy.

Structurally, it is expected to be solved with a light structure of minimum supports, so that the later of terrain and the runoff are altered as little as possible. A building that minimizes its ecological print, and that is posed with dry construction of maximum energetic efficiency, with a use of bioclimatic architecture in terms of a volumetric of rain architecture, and galleries facing south.

Location

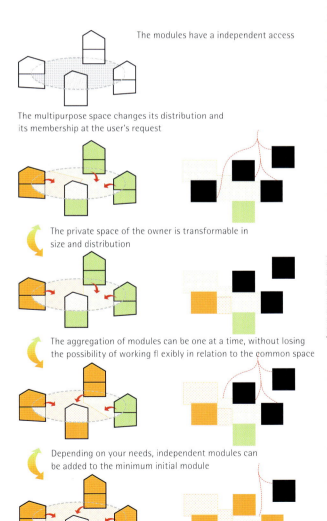
Diagram

First floor

Upper ground level

Lower ground level S=1:400

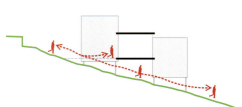

The construction tries to respect the original land and nature, supporting itself only on separate supports

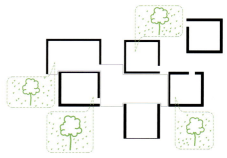

The independent modules adjust to the terrain and organize semi-private garden areas

Garden diagram

South elevation S=1:400

Section

North elevation

Architects: Irisarri-Piñera—
Guadalupe Piñera, Jesus Irisarri, principals-in-charge; Alexandre Martinez, architect; project team
Structural system: steel and wood
Major materials: steel and wood
Site area: 1,228 m²
Building area: 203 m²
Total floor area: 34,034 m²
Cost of construction: 240.000 euros

Yoga space on upper ground level

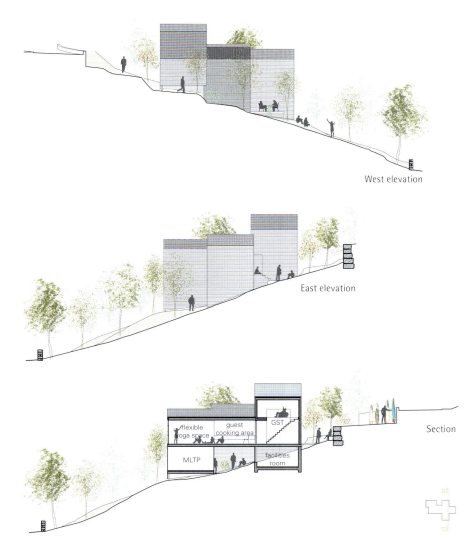

West elevation

East elevation

Section

この計画は，複数の与条件やコンセプトを単一の提案として統合させるというアイディアに端を発する。

個人住宅のプログラムに，施主が人々と2種類の体験——自身が指導者を務めるサーフィンとヨガ——を共有できる空間を加えるという希望が重ねられている。

一時的に利用されるこれらの空間は，時とともに展開し，施主の生活の変化に対応可能な居住プログラムと統合される。住宅の構成は，要求に応じたプライバシーや独立性の程度やヒエラルキーのシステムが基盤となっている。

材料を最小限に抑えると変化に富む多目的の空間という考え方を活用することが必要となり，建てられる空間は少なくなるが，空間同士の関係は深まり，いっそう豊かな人間関係の世界が築かれる。

この住宅の敷地は，道路から伸びる急傾斜の坂道が特徴となっている。ここでは，最良の日当りや方位の条件が最も興味深い眺望と一致し，南向きの敷地からはドニニョスの渓谷や潟の眺めを望むことができる。さらに土地の高低差のおかげで，住宅は近隣住居の採光やプライバシーを妨げないこと，さらに一般道から眺めると控え目でミニマルな存在として現れることも注目に値するだろう。

今回目指したのは，周囲にはわずかな変化しかもたらさない，ランドスケープと一体となるような建物で，雨水流出や土地の性質にいかなる変化も加えない，要素を「据える」というアイディアの実現を目標とした。

この住宅は，用途に応じて住宅の外部と関連のある使い方ができる，フレキシブルな構成であり，この意味において，この住宅では周囲の環境や地域と強いつながりをもつという伝統が取り戻されている。独立した使い方が可能な，柔軟なアプローチを通じてプログラムを理解し，この考えを建築へ転用すると，ヴォリュームは微妙にスケールの異なる小さな要素の集約として立ち上がり，地方の土地を占める伝統的な手法と重ねられる。

最も固定された，プライベートなプログラムを含む四つの要素が，様々な用途や配置に対応した，オープンでアクセスしやすいスペースを支えている。このスペースは地面から自由に漂うように空中に浮かんでいる。四つの要素はそれぞれの配置と土地の傾斜に応じて，共有スペースの階の上下に補足的な空間を生み出している。

自然に溶け込むよう誘いかけてくる土地に応えるように，建物にはさまざまなレベルでプライバシーが保たれた庭が複数設けられている。

構造面においては，地形や雨水流出への将来的な影響が最小限に留められるよう，最小限の支持材を用いた軽い構造を用いる。この住宅は，エネルギー効率を最大限に高めた乾式工法を採用し，雨水の活用や南向きのギャラリーを備える。環境面での影響を最小限に留めた人間と気候の関係を考慮した建物となる。

KATSUFUMI KUBOTA
K-VILLA

Nasu, Tochigi, Japan
Design: 2015-17
Construction: 2018-

Model photos: Ayane Hirose

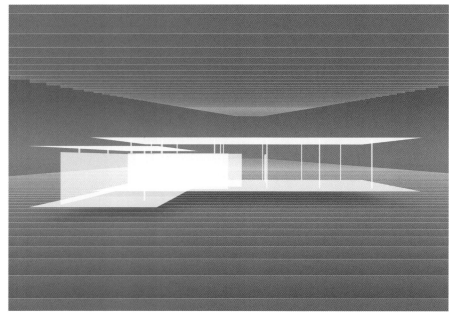

Perspective

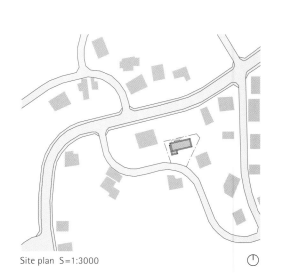

Site plan S=1:3000

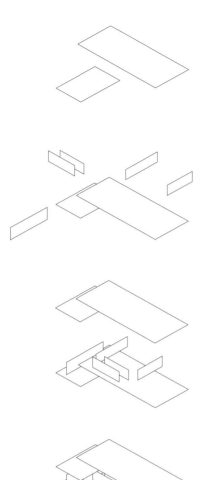

Diagram

The site is on a corner of Nasu Kogen highlands located on the northern part of Tochigi prefecture. Within these expansive highlands, rich and profound nature pulsate in the beautiful light penetrating through the forests and the refreshing breeze blowing in the air, moving from darkness to light, and stillness to motion.

The pressures of relating with others, however small and common they may be, cause our hearts to close, stagnate and obscure without our knowing. Our desires to be liberated from these pressures push us to update ourselves through superficial entertainment and joy and yet, our hearts remain clenched still, slowly eating away our energy to live. In order to reverse and break away from this flow, we must connect our hearts to an infinitely freer power, and to inspire a breath of new life. The building we create here will be planned so that it functions as a medium that induces response and fosters a relationship between both sides.

A life with nature is greatly different from merely enjoying the scenery from a large window. We explore the ways of a house that enables the residents to live each day as if they are always standing in a field, underneath the trees, whenever and wherever they may be. Every element, from the indispensable walls, floors and roof down to materials and detail, is fundamentally reevaluated and sublimated from concrete substance to abstract existence, ultimately leading to the abstraction of the house itself. In a fragile and transparent house without material qualities, the heart becomes unified with grand and boundless nature; here, an infinite and energetic life force pours in, letting one take back the desire for freedom and life. In *K-Villa*, we aimed to create such a house that revives and overflows the heart with joy.
Katsufumi Kubota

今回の敷地は，栃木県の北部に位置する那須高原の一角にある。伸びやかに広がる高原の中，林立する木立の狭間から漏れ入る光の美しさや吹き抜ける風の清々しさ，闇から光，静から動へと，豊かで深遠な〈自然〉が脈動する。

人にとって他との関わりによる重圧はもちろん，日常的な小さな関わりでさえも煩わしく，無意識の内に〈心〉は閉ざされ，淀み濁っていく。それを起因とした自由への渇望が，表層的な楽しみや歓びを追い求めアップデートを試みるが，それでもなお〈心〉は強く閉じられて，生きる力は徐々に蝕まれる。こうした流れを断ち切り反転させるには，大きく無限で自由な力と〈心〉を繋ぎ，〈心〉に新たな息吹を吹き込む事が必須だ。此処で創る〈建築〉は，両者の関わりを誘発し，反応を促す触媒として機能するように計画を進めていく。

〈自然〉と共にある生活，それは大きな窓から自然感を味わうこととは，まるで異なる。どこにいても野に居るような，何をしていても木立の下にあるような，そんな日々を営む〈建築〉の在り方を模索する。真に必要な壁と床そして屋根，さらに素材からディテールに至るまで，全ての意味を原点から見直して，具象的な物質から抽象的な存在へと昇華させ，〈建築〉の存在さえも抽象化する。物質性が失われた儚く透明な〈建築〉は，壮大で無限な〈自然〉と〈心〉を一つに融け合わせ，〈心〉に限り無い自由と躍動する生命力を注ぎ込み，生きる力と自由を取り戻す。こうして〈心〉を蘇生させ，歓びに溢れた〈建築〉を目指したのが「K-VILLA」である。

（窪田勝文）

Architects: Kubota Architect Atelier—Katsufumi Kubota, principal-in-charge; Kazuya Toizaki, Kazusa Kubota, Masayuki Kubota, project team
Consultants: Takeuchi Partners Architect Engineer's Office Co.,Ltd.—Kinji Takeuchi, structural
Structural system: reinforced concrete
Major materials: exposed concrete
Site area: 516.00 m²
Building area: 104.47 m²
Total floor area: 95.00 m²

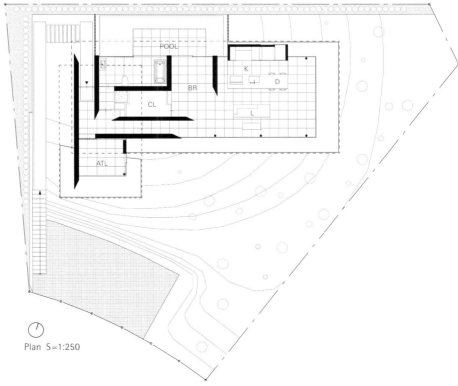

Plan S=1:250

View from east

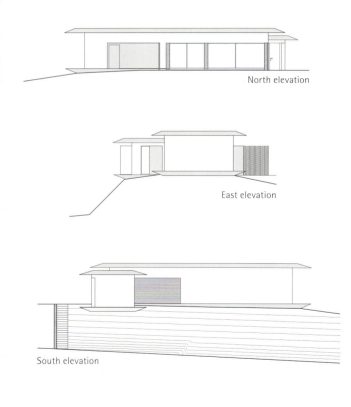

North elevation

East elevation

South elevation

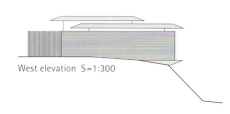
West elevation S=1:300

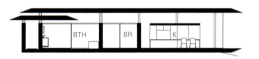

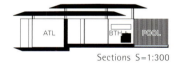
Sections S=1:300

Kitchen/dining/living room: looking east

STEVEN EHRLICH + TAKASHI YANAI
BAXTER STREET RESIDENCE

Silverlake, CA, U.S.A.
Design: 2016-17
Construction: 2018-19

View from northwest

Tucked into the hills east of Silver Lake Reservoir, the Baxter Street Residence is a reimaging of modern living. Questioning the formal confines and traditional understanding of house as structure located within context of site, we asked ourselves, "What if the house is the site?"

Designing the street-side entry gate as the front door, the pool deck as the main living area, and the gardens as the private retreat—the residence sits in conversation with mid-century modern masterpieces. These include Neutra's *VDL House* to the north, Lautner's "lost" *Jules Salkin Residence* to the east, and the *Reiner-Burchill (Silvertop) Residence* to the west; all works exploring contemporary ideas of residential dwelling.

On site, black masonry walls follow the existing topography, carving into the hillside to preserve remnants of the adjacent famed Villa Capistrano Gardens, originally designed for Julian Eltinge, America's first drag superstar.

Gently perched on these walls is a quiet modern architectural volume, opportunely angled to capture sweeping views of the reservoir.

Designed for an aesthete, with a punk and vintage edge, the residence is the creative collaboration of local artisans banded together to answer the call to capture the Silver Lake spirit.

シルバー・レイク貯水池の東側の丘に建てられた「バクスター・ストリート・レジデンス」は，現代的な暮らしの姿を再び想像し直そうというものである。形状に関する制約や，敷地のコンテクスト内に位置する構造としての住宅という従来の理解に疑問を投げかけることで，「〈住宅〉を〈敷地〉と見た場合はどうなるのか？」と自問している。

正面玄関となる道路側の入口ゲート，主要な居住エリアであるプールデッキ，プライベートな憩いの場である数カ所の庭を設計している。この住宅は現代建築のマスターピースであるミッドセンチュリー住宅との対話の中にあり，北側にはノイトラの「VDLリサーチハウス」，東側にはラトナーの"失われてしまった"「ジュールズ・サルキン・レジデンス」，そして西側に「ライナー・バークヒル（シルバートップ）レジデンス」があるが，これらの作品はすべて，住宅にまつわる現代的なアイディアを探求したものである。

敷地では，黒い石積みの壁が既存の地形に従って伸びつつ丘の中腹を切り開いている。この壁が，アメリカ初のドラッグクイーンとして知られるジュリアン・エルティンジのために当初デザインされた，敷地に隣接する有名なヴィラ・カピストラーノ庭園の面影を残す。

この壁の上には，静謐で現代建築的な姿を持つヴォリュームが貯水池を一望する眺めを取り込むのに絶妙な角度を成し，穏やかに建っている。

厳しい審美眼を持ち，パンクやヴィンテージに傾倒する住人のために設計されたこの住宅は，「シルバーレイク魂」を表現するための呼びかけに応えて団結した地元の職人による，創造的なコラボレーションである。

Vicinity map

Original Villa Capistrano Gardens with view of Silver Lake Reservoir beyond, Circa 1920

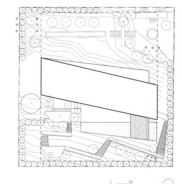

Site diagrams

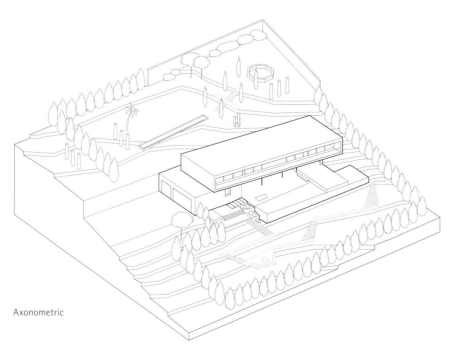

Axonometric

Architects: EHRLICH YANAI RHEE CHANEY
Architects—Takashi Yanai, design principal;
Steven Ehrlich, principal; Jeehye Kim, project architect; Jessica Moon, Melissa Cataldo, Gibran Villalobos, Erin Wong, project team
Consultants: David Lau, structural;
T Engineering, civil engineering;
Terremoto, landscape
General contractor: Dave King
Structural system: masonry, concrete, steel and wood construction
Major materials: custom back CMU block, shosugiban wood siding, custom tile
Site area: 20,000 sq. ft.
Building area: 3,500 sq. ft.
Total floor area: 6,500 sq. ft.

Living area

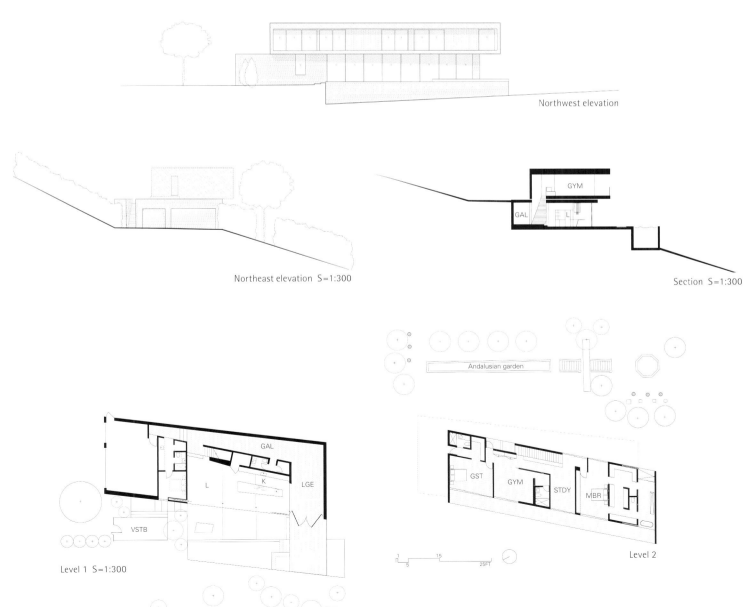

Northwest elevation

Northeast elevation S=1:300

Section S=1:300

Level 1 S=1:300

Level 2

MAKOTO TAKEI + CHIE NABESHIMA / TNA
M-PROJECT

Michigan, U.S.A.
Design: 2017-18
Construction: 2018-

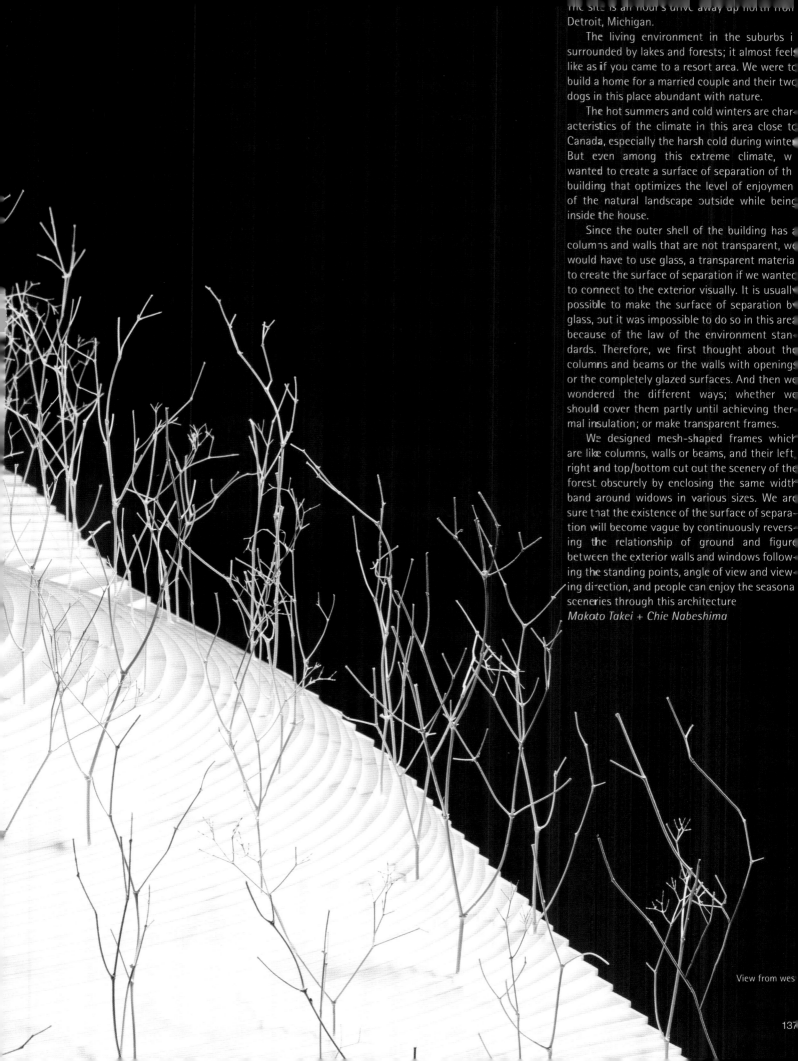

The site is an hour's drive away up north from Detroit, Michigan.

The living environment in the suburbs is surrounded by lakes and forests; it almost feels like as if you came to a resort area. We were to build a home for a married couple and their two dogs in this place abundant with nature.

The hot summers and cold winters are characteristics of the climate in this area close to Canada, especially the harsh cold during winter. But even among this extreme climate, we wanted to create a surface of separation of the building that optimizes the level of enjoyment of the natural landscape outside while being inside the house.

Since the outer shell of the building has a columns and walls that are not transparent, we would have to use glass, a transparent material to create the surface of separation if we wanted to connect to the exterior visually. It is usually possible to make the surface of separation by glass, but it was impossible to do so in this area because of the law of the environment standards. Therefore, we first thought about the columns and beams or the walls with openings or the completely glazed surfaces. And then we wondered the different ways; whether we should cover them partly until achieving thermal insulation; or make transparent frames.

We designed mesh-shaped frames which are like columns, walls or beams, and their left, right and top/bottom cut out the scenery of the forest obscurely by enclosing the same width band around widows in various sizes. We are sure that the existence of the surface of separation will become vague by continuously reversing the relationship of ground and figure between the exterior walls and windows following the standing points, angle of view and viewing direction, and people can enjoy the seasonal sceneries through this architecture
Makoto Takei + Chie Nabeshima

View from west

Section S=1:250

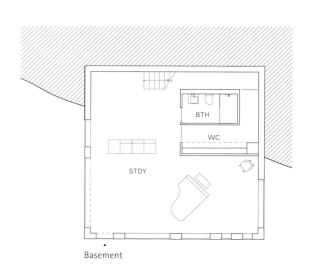
Basement

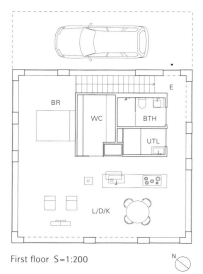
First floor S=1:200

Northwest elevation

Model photos: Ayane Hirose 　　　　　　　　　　　　　　　　Southwest elevation

敷地はミシガン州のデトロイトから車で1時間ほど北上したところにある。

郊外の住環境は湖と森に囲まれ，別荘地にでも来たかのように感じる。そういった自然豊かな場所に夫婦と犬2匹の家を建てることになった。

カナダに近いこのエリアは暑い夏と寒い冬が特徴の気候で，特に冬の寒さが厳しい。そのような過酷な気候の中でも，家の中に居ながら外部の大自然の景色を最大限ありのままに享受できるような建物の境界面を考えることにした。

建物の外殻には柱や壁がありそれは不透明であるので，もし外部と視覚的に繋がろうとすると，ガラスという透明な素材で境界面をつくることになる。ガラスだけで境界面をつくることは可能であるが，この地域は環境基準の法律上，不可能であった。そこで，外と内を隔てる境界が，建築の外壁を成立させるために必要な柱や梁，あるいはそれを覆う壁に窓を穿ったものか，あるいは外観が全てガラスで覆われていて，それを断熱性能が確保されるまで部分的に塞いでいくのか，そのどちらでもない透過性のある骨格にならないか，と考えた。

同じ幅の帯を大小様々な大きさの窓の周りに巡らせ，柱のような，壁のような，梁のような，左右，天地が曖昧な網目状のフレーミングに森の景色が切り取られることを考えた。立つ位置や見る角度や方向によって，外壁と窓の地と図の関係が反転し続けることで境界面の存在は薄れ，四季折々の自然を建築を通して楽しめるに違いない。

（武井誠＋鍋島千恵）

Architects: TNA—
Makoto Takei, Chie Nabeshima, principals-in-charge; Kei Tanaka, project team
Consultants: Jun Sato Structural Engineers, structural
Structural system: wood frame
Major materials: mortar
Site area: 2,615.3 m²
Building area: 83.06 m²
Total floor area: 168.34 m²

STUDIO TONTON
RT HOUSE

Surabaya, East Java, Indonesia
Design: 2017
Construction: 2018-19

Site plan S=1:10000

Overlooking from east

This project is situated in a dense residential area, completed with a pleasant direct view towards big lake of a golf course. The main concept of this house is to accommodate the client's interest in art pieces, therefore this house is the intermixture space between living and artworks showcase. The house was designed with strong geometry and introverted character which resulted in a more solid facade at the front to avoid excess infiltrated sunlight. On the contrary it has a big opening on the rear area to capture alluring natural view.

Rather than a collection of rooms, this house was designed as a series of boxes made out of each independent structure. The main space divided into eight structural cores; fifth of them that located at the front area were planned to become gallery and the other cores are designed to accommodate more private function of the house. The gallery space were planned to have an expansive space with various height, providing abundant room to show large scale artworks, and also enables guests to experience diverse spatial quality while exploring the volumes.

The individual boxes are connected with a transparent glass roof which transform the in between space into a unique semipublic interior space. It will enhance visual interaction among the cores and bring livelier atmosphere into the house. These semipublic spaces were accessed by stairs that designed to have multi-orientation with each other. Moreover shifted voids that created will bring vertical connection between floors and also produce immersive experience of shadow play. This entire shift of elements adds richness to the spatial mood within the house.

Materials used on this project for the external walls are made by concrete with additional local ulin wood cladding as a facade in several cores, while the internal walls are all using exposed concrete as a finishing. Warm and neutral colored materials were picked to bring abundance for the living aspects and also strengthen the artworks within the architecture.

As the respect of nature, green space were brought back to the architecture by transforming the cores as a giant planter. With thick layer of soil layer, these planters also function as storm-water basins for detention and retention to support in high density dwelling. The design was aimed to give positive impact for the neighborhood environments.

ZONING

MASSING DISTRIBUTION

ADDITIONAL GREENERIES

Diagrams STACKING + LAYERING

DAYLIGHT RESPONSE

FACADE APPLICATION

View from street on north

West elevation

North elevation

First floor

Second floor

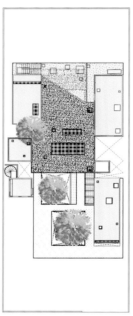
Roof

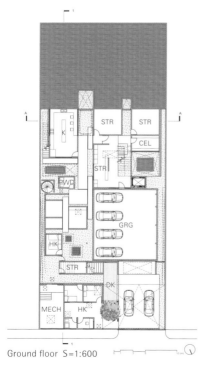
Ground floor S=1:600

Second mezzanine

Third floor

Architects: Studio TonTon—
Antony Liu, principal-in-charge;
Louis Satria Purwanto, Heddy Purnomo,
Monica Marcellina, project team
Consultants: Hadi Yahya and Associates,
structural; PT. Makesthi Enggal Engineering,
mechanical; Studio TonTon, interior design
General contractor: PT. Karya 2 Ton
Structural system: steel and concrete system
Major materials: exposed concrete, glass, Ulin wood
Site area: 1,000 m²
Building area: 600 m²
Total floor area: 1,590 m²

South elevation

East elevation

このプロジェクトは密集した住宅地に位置し、目の前にはゴルフコースの巨大な湖に向けた心地よい眺望が広がっている。クライアントの芸術作品に対する関心に応えることがこの住宅の中核となるコンセプトであったので、住宅は住むための場所と芸術作品のショーケースを掛け合わせたような空間となった。住宅は強力な幾何形態と内向的性格を持ち、正面は非常に重厚なファサードによって太陽光が過度に浸透してくることがないように計画された。その一方で住宅の背後には巨大な開口部を設け、魅惑的な自然への眺望を得ることができる。住宅は個室の集合体というよりはむしろ、各々が独立した構造を持つボックスの連続となるように計画されている。メインスペースは8個の構造体に分割された。正面に配置された5番目のボックスはギャラリーとして計画され、その他の構造体は住宅のよりプライベートな機能が収められている。ギャラリースペースはさまざまな高さからなるゆったりとした空間を持つように計画された。そのため大型の芸術作品を展示することができるように十分な余地を持ち、ゲストがヴォリュームの中を歩き回りながら様々な性格の空間を味わうことができるようになっている。

各々のボックスを透明なガラスの屋根で結ぶことにより、隙間の空間は独特のセミパブリックな内部空間へと変化する。それにより、構造体同士に視覚的な交わりが生まれ、より生きいきとした雰囲気が生み出されるようになる。これらのセミパブリックスペースは、お互いに向きが同じにならないように計画された階段からアクセスすることができる。さらにはヴォイドのずれが床同士の間に垂直のつながりをもたらし、影の戯れの中へと入り込んでゆくかのような体験を生み出してくれる。こういった要素のずれは全体として、住宅内部の空間の雰囲気に豊かさを加えてくれる。

このプロジェクトの外壁の素材にはコンクリートが使用され、部分的にはウリンと呼ばれるこの地域特有の木材でいくつかの構造体のファサードを覆い、内部の壁は全て打放しコンクリートによって仕上げられている。生活の豊かさを演出し、建築内の芸術作品の存在を強めるために、温かみのあるニュートラルな色合いの素材が選定された。

自然への敬意の表現としてコアを巨大なプランターへと変容させることにより、緑の空間を建築内部へと引き込んだ。土壌の層を厚くすることにより、これらのプランターは豪雨の際は貯水槽として機能し、住宅密集地における生活を支える役割を果たす。周辺環境に対してプラスの影響を与えることを意識して設計された。

Living/dining room on first floor

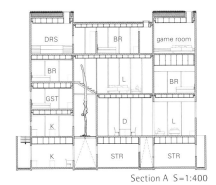
Section A　S=1:400

Section 1

143

The site opens up to the landscape of the sky that looks over the far away town of Karuizawa, the landscape of continuous mountain ranges and the rich landscape of the forest that stands on the slope within tree groves. Landscape and scenery are similar words that express what you can see with your eyes. Landscape has a strong visual implication that allows us to view as it is, and scenery has a strong spiritual implication that gives us a subject of appreciation.

In other words, the scenery can be created depending on the operation of architecture. We wanted to create a place where people can enjoy the abundant scenery by distinguishing the great landscape of Karuizawa using slabs that cut out the scenery.

The composition is simple. The upper and lower slabs cut out the landscape while creating three sceneries, and including the vertical circulations they connect as a sequence. We want to create an experience where the outside world feels like a film by framing the landscape like a photograph or a movie. We want people to feel that they are inside a film by creating distance with the long and deep slab, including the sounds of nature like the sound of rain and birds chirping.

The arrangement was determined like deciding the angle of a photograph when one observes the place on the spot, by arranging the direction of each floor at the respective place where it creates a fitting scenery. The composition that looks like bridges hanging over each other emphasize the slab, and it is intended to make a scenery that is continuous by distorting the scale of the residence combined together with the surrounding landscape.

We think that the scenery that is framed like documenting a photograph will remain in memory as a spatial experience and of nature that is continuously changing.

MAKOTO TANIJIRI + AI YOSHIDA / SUPPOSE DESIGN OFFICE
HOUSE IN KARUIZAWA

Karuizawa, Nagano, Japan
Design: 2017-18
Construction: 2018-19

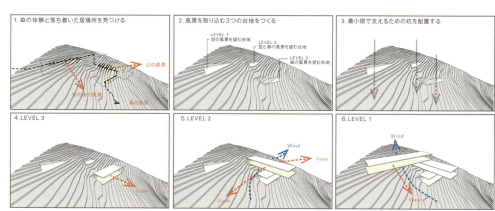

Diagram

View from south

View from east

View from southeast　　　　　　　　　　　　　　　　　　　　　　　　　　　　　　　　　　Model photo: Nohara Yamazaki

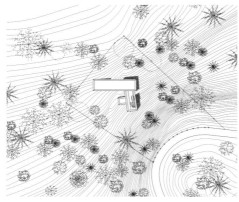

Site plan　S=1:3000

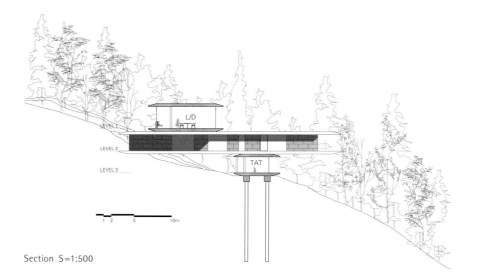

Section　S=1:500

　遠く軽井沢の街を眺める空の風景，連なる山脈の風景，木立の間の斜面に森の豊かな風景が広がる敷地である。その目に見えるものを表わす言葉として風景と景色と近しい表現がある。風景は視覚的な意味合いが強く，ありのままの眺め，景色は精神的な意味合いが強く，鑑賞としての対象となるようである。
　つまり景色は建築の操作によってつくることができる。軽井沢の雄大な風景をスラブで切り取り顕然化させることで豊かな景色を堪能できる場所を実現させた

いと考えた。
　構成はシンプルである。上下のスラブで風景を切り取りながら三つの景色をつくり縦動線を含めシークエンスとしてつないでいる。風景を写真や映画の様にフレーミングすることで外の世界がフィルムの中のように感じる不思議な体験をつくりだしたい。雨音や鳥の声など自然の音さえも，長く深いスラブで距離感をつくることでフィルムの中にあるように感じられるのではないだろうか。

　配置については現地を観察し写真のアングルを決めるようにそれぞれにあった景色をつくれる場所に各層向きを決め配置している。スラブを強調した橋を架けあうような構成は，連続性を持ち住宅のスケールを歪ませ周囲の風景と相まって景色となるよう意図している。
　写真に記録するようにフレーミングされた景色は，刻々と変わる自然の変化と空間を体験として記憶に残るのではないかと考えた。

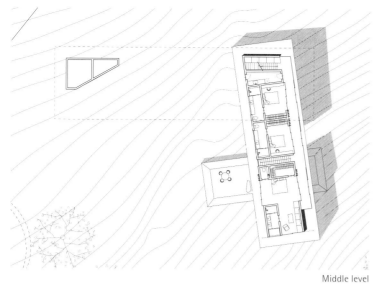

Middle level

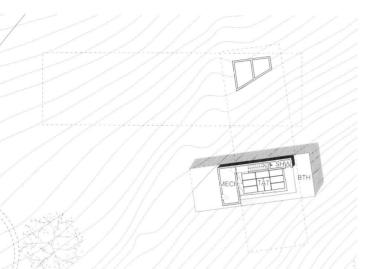

Lower level

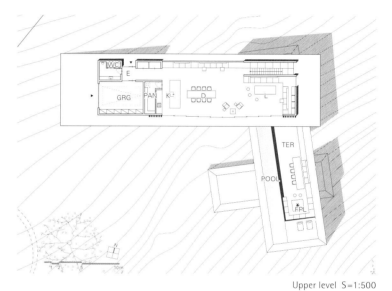

Upper level S=1:500

Architects: SUPPOSE DESIGN OFFICE—
Makoto Tanijiri, Ai Yoshida, principals-in-charge; Lorenzo Sanna, project team
Consultants: TECTONICA INC—
Yoshinori Suzuki, structural; Zo Consulting Engineers—Noriko Ito, mechanical
Structural system: reinforced concrete
Major materials: exposed concrete, stone pitching, exterior; exposed concrete with dust proof finishing, stone pitching, interior
Site area: 5,917.00 m²
Building area: 519.28 m²
Total floor area: 390.11 m²

View toward living room and terrace from dining room

BGP ARQUITECTURA
JOJUTLA HOUSE

Condesa, Mexico City, Mexico
Design: 2017
Construction: 2018-

View from street

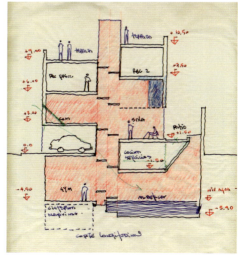

Sketch

This single family house is designed in half-level floors and a basement; in order to avoid halls and long distance circulations, a grand central staircase articulates the distribution of the rooms on all floors.

Due to the small area of the site (137 square meters) and given that walls usually take up 15% of construction area, the project's walls are made with thin sheets of marble, glass or steel; replacing regular thickness walls and allowing more efficient spaces.

The house offers a unique answer to the architectural program; clearly separating the more public areas on the ground floor from the private ones on the upper floors. The basement is flooded with a large interior pool, and gym. The ground floor has the garage and main entry; from there you can access half-floor above the living room and a library. The kitchen and dining room with a pantry are on the second level and the third, fourth levels hold two bedrooms. The master bedroom on the fifth level has connection with the roof garden.

The main facade is made of poured in-place concrete and has vertical recessed windows on the sides that generate subtle lightning to the living spaces.

To provide the house with the maximum possible natural lightning while not blocking the views and communication between the areas of the house, each step of the central staircase is made of clear transparent glass, also delimited by two large mirrors extended from the basement to the third floor, creating an infinite visual effect. The back glass facade allows natural light to the rooms, and a sloped patio at the back allows the sunlight entrance to the ground floor areas; including a horizontal dome at the edge of the pool.

View toward living room from patio

Staircase on first floor

Architects: bgp arquitectura—
Bernardo Gómez-Pimienta,
Luis Enrique Mendoza, principals-in-charge;
Regina Nájera, Alba Silva, César Gálvez,
project team
Consultants: bgp arquitectura, interior
Structural system: concrete walls and slab,
steel beams
Major materials: concrete, steel, marble, clear
glass
Site area: 137 m²
Building area: 104.70 m²
Total floor area: 133.89 m²

Pool

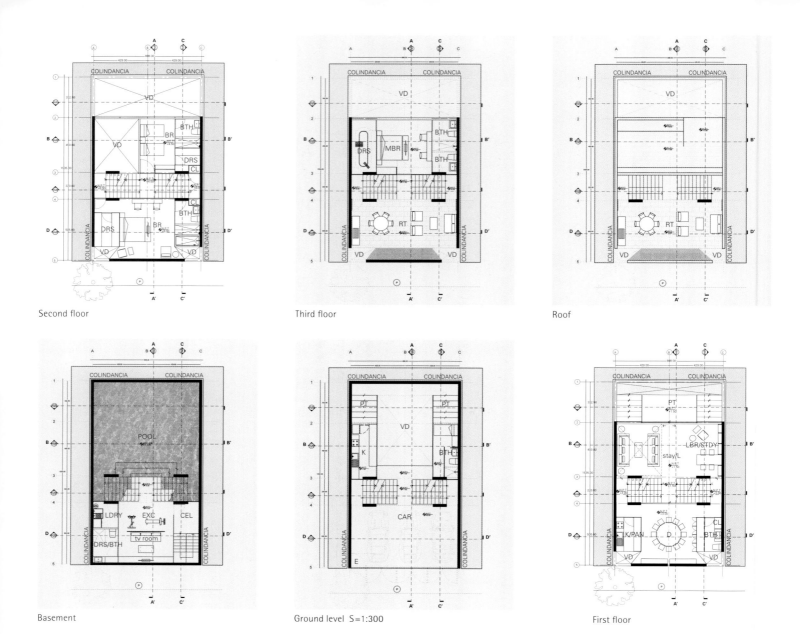

Second floor

Third floor

Roof

Basement

Ground level S=1:300

First floor

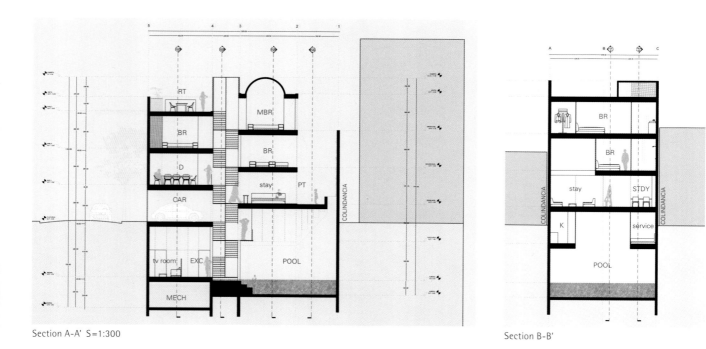

Section A-A' S=1:300

Section B-B'

Dining room

Master bedroom

この核家族用の住宅は，高さを半階分ずらしたフロアと地下室で構成されている。廊下や長い距離の動線を避けるために，中央の大階段によって全フロアの部屋の配置が定められている。

敷地面積が狭く(137平方メートル)さらに通常に壁が建築面積の15％を占めることから，より効率性の高い空間を実現させるよう普段用いられる厚さのある壁に代わるものとして，このプロジェクトでは薄い大理石板，ガラス板やスティール板が壁として用いられている。

この住宅では，1階のパブリックエリアを上階のプライベート空間と明確に切り離し，建築プログラムに対するユニークな回答を提示している。地下には大きな屋内プールとジムを設けている。1階にはガレージと正面玄関があり，ここから半階上にある居間とライブラリーへアクセスすることができる。2階は台所とパントリー付きの書屋どうとなっており，3，4階には2部屋の寝室が占めている。5階にある主寝室の奥にはルーフガーデンが続く。

正面ファサードには現場打ちコンクリートが用いられている。両端には縦長のはめ殺し窓を設け，リビング空間には，ほのかな光が届けられる。

採光を最大限確保しながら，エリア間の眺めやコミュニケーションが遮断されないよう，中央階段の踏面は透明なガラス製となっている。さらに，階段の境界は地下から3階にかけて伸びる2枚の巨大な鏡によって定められているため，無限に広がる視覚効果が生まれている。背面のガラスのファサードからは日光が室内へと射し込んでいる。傾斜した裏のパティオは，プール脇にある横長のドームを含む，1階に陽の光を取り込んでいる。

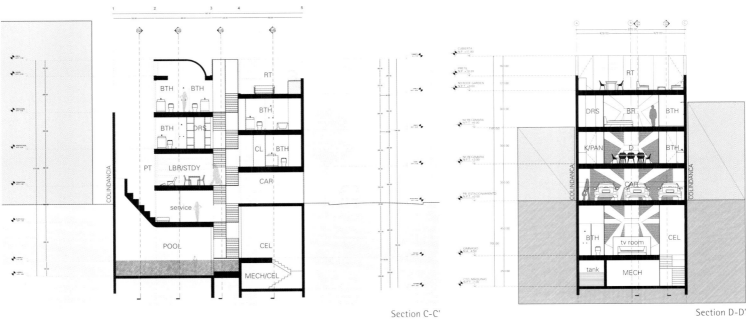

Section C-C'　　　Section D-D'

NITSCHE ARQUITETOS
ILHABELA HOUSE

Ilhabela, São Paulo, Brazil
Design: 2017-18
Construction: 2018-19

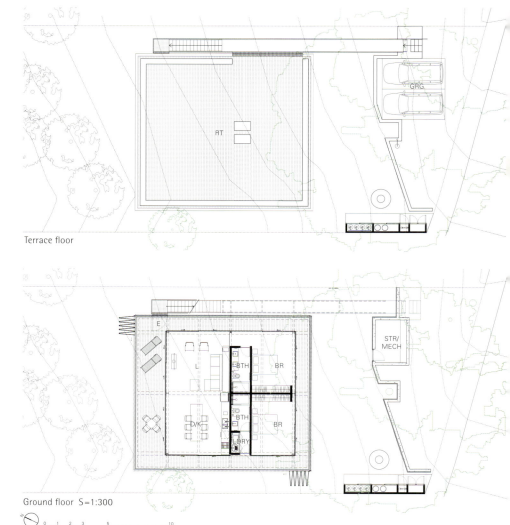

Terrace floor

Ground floor S=1:300

This small beach hideaway privileges the nature trying to interfere minimally. The precast light structure optimizes the construction in this area of difficult access. From the road you can see only the belvedere platform, which works as a roof. Underneath this, the simple program of two bedrooms, living room and kitchen reinforce the spatial amplitude. When the brises and windows are open, the house turns into a large veranda overlooking the sea.

View from east: approach leads to roof terrace and stair to main living area

小さな砂浜にある隠れ家は，自然の恩恵を享受するものであり，それに対する干渉が最小限になるように試みている。プレキャストの軽快な構造は，アクセスの難しい場所における建設を効率良くしている。道路からは，屋根として機能する見晴台のプラットフォームが唯一見えるだけである。この下部の，寝室2部屋，居室，台所というシンプルなプログラムは，空間的な広さを強調する。日除け戸と窓を開け放つと，住宅は，海を望む大きなベランダへと変化する。

View toward northwest: shade closed (above), shade opened (below)

Architects: Nitsche Arquitetos—
Lua Nitsche, Pedro Nitsche, principals-in-charge; André Scarpa,
Fernanda Veríssimo, Marcelo Anaf,
Rodrigo Tamburus, Rosário Pinho, Gil Barbieri,
project team
Consultants: Miguel Maratá, structural;
Zamaro—Marcelo Zamaro, mechanical; Nitsche

Arquitetos, interior design
Structural system: concrete and steel
Major materials: steel, glass, concrete and wood
Site area: 748 m²
Building area: 170 m²
Total floor area: 170 m²

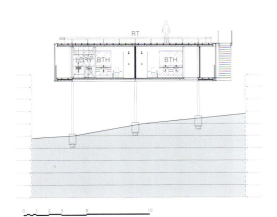

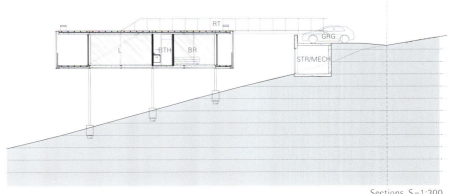

Sections S=1:300

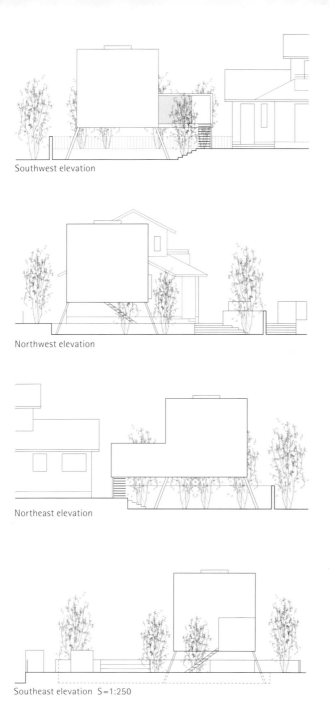

Southwest elevation

Northwest elevation

Northeast elevation

Southeast elevation S=1:250

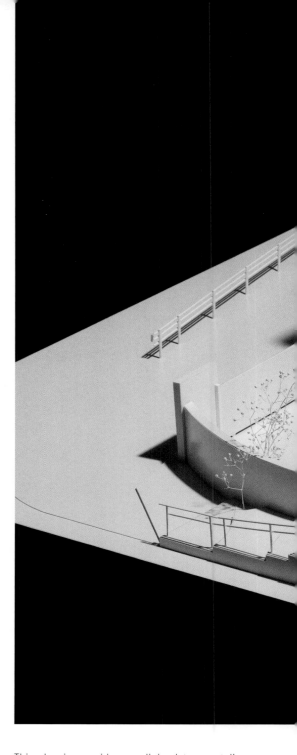

SHIGERU FUSE
HOUSE IN HITACHINAKA

Ibaraki, Japan
Design: 2017-18
Construction: 2018-

This plan is a residence adjoined to an atelier and gallery. Around the site, residences and fields scatter; with an industrial complex to the north, this is a typical suburban landscape facing a 16 meters-wide major road with heavy traffic to the north-west.

The client is a textile artist who wanted to build an atelier and gallery space on an existing parking lot because the atelier in the main house has become too small and also in order to hold exhibitions periodically. This space—in order to use it as an atelier in every day life, and as a gallery for exhibitions—is necessary to have a suitable light environment for an atelier and walls for a gallery. To achieve that, a compact volume was established as a large exhibition wall, and I proposed a cross section where only

Overlooking from south

diffused light can shine onto the wall. The 5.4 x 5.4 x 5.4 meters volume is supported with round pillars arranged at 20 degrees opening to the bottom. Pillars bearing both vertical load and sharing stress made it possible to have a sense of it floating. The volume of the loft hangs like a nest of boxes inside the cuboid that is supported by round pillars diffuses natural light from the ceiling, and it lights up the four side of walls on each side of 4.8 meters high.

This project is composed of a simple cross section with minimal elements that contains the interior space at a scale with significance. The simple exterior of the building that floats within the scale of the town will become a landmark of the suburban.

Shigeru Fuse

この計画は，住宅に併設されるアトリエ兼ギャラリーである。敷地周辺は住宅と畑が点在し，北側には工場団地，北西に幅16メートルの比較的交通量の多い幹線道路に面する典型的な郊外の風景である。

テキスタイル作家のクライアントは，母屋の工房が手狭になり，定期的な展覧会を行うため，既存の駐車場の上にアトリエ兼ギャラリーのスペースを要望された。このスペースは，日常的にはアトリエとして使用し，展覧会の会期にはギャラリーとして使用するため，アトリエの光環境とギャラリーの壁面が必要であった。そのため，コンパクトなヴォリュームにできるだけ大きな展示壁面を確保し，展示壁には拡散光だけが入る断面計画を考えた。5.4×5.4×5.4メートルの建物ヴォリュームは，20度下方が開いた丸柱を配置し，鉛直力と地震力を同時に負担することで軽やかに浮かせることを可能にした。

丸柱に支えられた立方体のボックスの中に入れ子のように吊られたロフトのヴォリュームが，トップライトから入る自然光を拡散光にし，高さ4.8メートルの4辺の壁を照射する。

この建築は，最小限の要素で構成されたシンプルな断面に，抑揚のあるスケールを内部空間に内包する。そして，街のスケールに浮いたシンプルな建物の外観は，郊外の風景のランドマークとなるだろう。

（布施茂）

Overall view from west

Site plan S=1:4000

Architects: fuse-atelier + fuse-studio (Musashino Art University)—
Shigeru Fuse, principal-in-charge (fuse-atelier/Musashino Art University);
Youhei Yamada, Kouki Ito, Hidenori Jyuna, Yamato Watanabe, Hidetaka Yonezawa, (fuse-studio), project team
Consultants: Konishi Structural Engineers + konishi-studio(Musashino Art University)—
Yasutaka Konishi, structural
Structural system: steel
Major materials: acrylic silicone coating, exterior; plaster board + AEP (wall, ceiling), concrete finishing with trowel (floor), interior
Site area: 1,148.14 m²
Building area: 35.25 m²
Total floor area: 78.49 m²

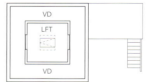

Third floor

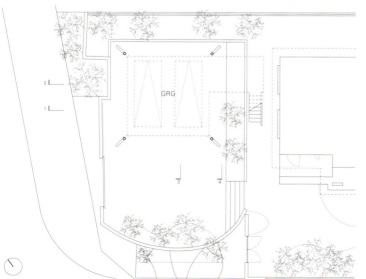

First floor S=1:250

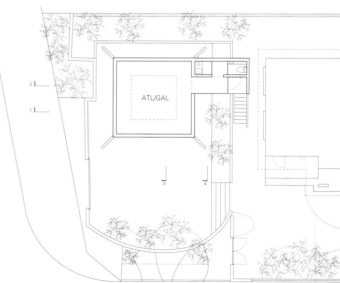

Second floor

156

Second floor: view from entrance toward atelier and gallery

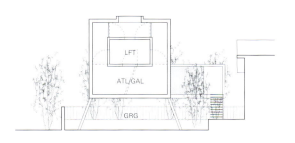

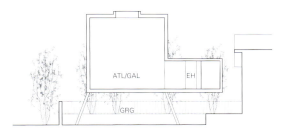

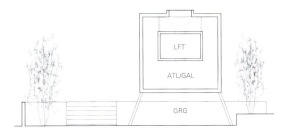

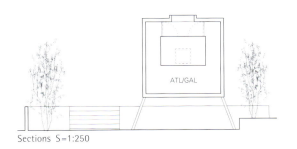
Sections S=1:250

Model photos: Ayane Hirose   Loft hanged from ceiling

Atelier and gallery/loft

HIROYUKI ARIMA
IN PARK SLOPE

Park Slope, Brooklyn, New York, NY, U.S.A.
Design: 2017-18
Construction: 2018-19

Aerial view from north

New York's Park Slope neighborhood is a quiet residential area characterized by rows brownstone buildings. It is a relaxed environment that stretches over a slightly sloping terrain that declines towards Prospect Park, a popular recreational park for the local residents. An old, two-story building stands here, housing the artworks and records of the sculptor Toshio Sasaki. This is where we are working on a combined program that integrates his artworks with other features. A gallery and memorial site will be installed on the building rooftop to exhibit the artworks. Below will be turned into an atelier, residence, hotel, and cafe. The building is narrow, with 7 meters of frontage and 40 meters depth, with an alley connecting these areas. The site was formerly a stone dealer's studio with a crane installed underneath the high ceilings. The artist made use of this machine in his vigorous creative endeavors, and the studio, even after his death, continues to serve young artists as an atelier and residence. This project will reorganize this program to reach out and be more open to the public, continuing to rewrite the history of this location as a place of creative practice. Sculptures by Toshio Sasaki were created for the purpose of "shaking up existing values to find new." Harmony that lies beyond his art is neither generic nor simple; it is simultaneously a new and delicate composition, exchange, and poetry that capture the uniqueness of each location. This is especially evident in his work "Inversion of Light" which was submitted for the World Trade Center memorial. His work was based on the concepts of "life and eternity" and "living memorial"; various social issues expand like a mandala over ground zero, using light, water, and earth elements as reactors to turn conflict into harmony and pass down memory to the new generation.

My new design will further elaborate on these ideas. I believe that we, as human beings, find, respond, change, and remember through experience.
Hiroyuki Arima

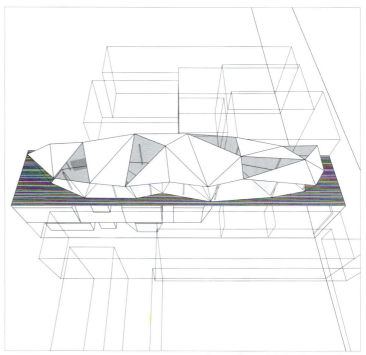

Perspective: aerial view from northwest

Northeast elevation

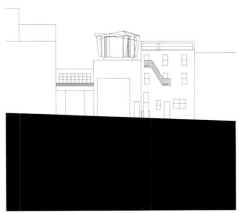

Northeast elevation S=1:600

Model photos: Ayane Hirose

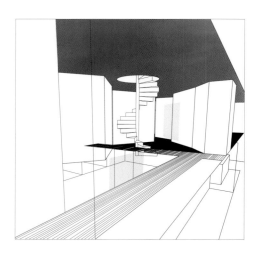
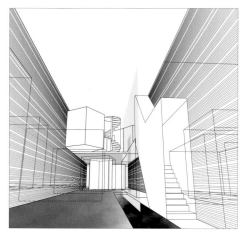
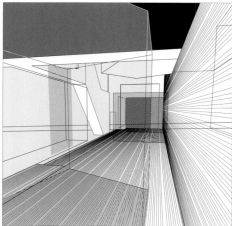
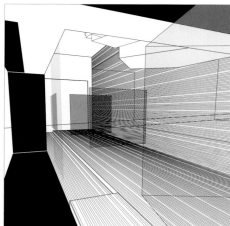

Perspectives

Architects: Hiroyuki Arima + Urban Fourth—
Hiroyuki Arima, principal-in-charge;
Hozumi Tsunekawa, project team
Structural system: RC + wooden
Major materials: glass, wooden boards
Site area: 308.4 m²
Building area: 308.4 m²
Total floor area: 637.8 m²

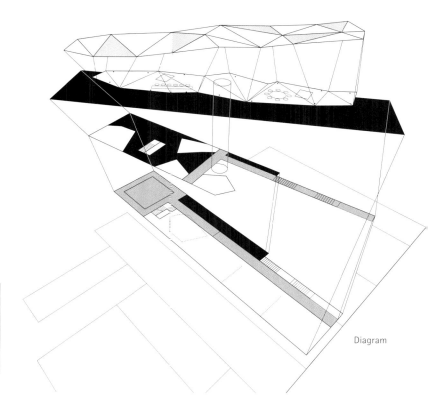

Diagram

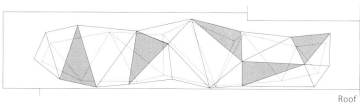

Roof

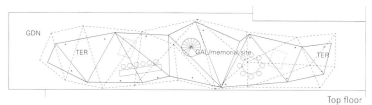

Top floor

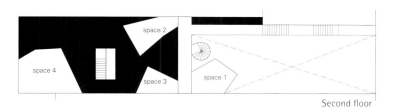

Second floor

First floor S=1:400

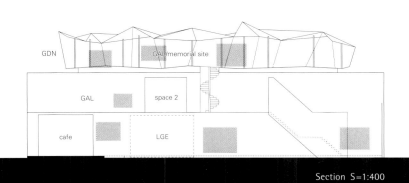

Section S=1:400

ニューヨークのパークスロープはブラウンストーンの建物が特徴の落ち着いたエリアである。市民の憩いの場であるプロスペクトパークに向かってなだらかに傾斜していて全体に優しい環境に包まれている。2階建の古い建物があって，その中に彫刻家佐々木敏雄のこれまでのアートピースや記録が保管されていて，それを中心に他要素を複合構成するプログラムを構想している。ルーフトップに作品を展示するgallery & memorial siteをセットする予定だ。下階にはアトリエ，レジデンス，ホテル，カフェが各所にある。建物は間口7メートル奥行40メートルほどの細長い形状で，alleyが各エリアをつなぐ。元々は石材業の工房であり天井が高くクレーンがセットされていた。それを使用し創作活動は精力的に進められ，彼が亡くなった後も，スタジオは若いアーティストのアトリエ+レジデンスとして今も稼働していて，このプロジェクトはそれを組み替えて街に開き延長させる。過去の実践の場であったという「記憶」が今後さらに上書きされるだろう。佐々木敏雄の彫刻は「既存価値を揺り動かし新しい価値に出会うこと」を目的に創造されている。彼の造形の先にあるのは一般的な単純な調和ではない。それぞれの場の個性を捉えた繊細で新しい「構成」であり「交換」であり「詩」である。その特徴はWTCテロの後にその悲劇を悼んで構想されたメモリアルのための作品「光の反転」に顕著だ。「生命と永遠」「生きる記念碑」という彼が示したコンセプトには，対立している様々な社会的ISSUEが「光」「水」「土」という素材をリアクターとしながら，グランドゼロの場に曼荼羅のように広がり，「対立を融和に」「記憶を新しい次元につなげる」ことを表現していた。

私の考察する新しい構成は，それをさらに発展させるものとして行われる。人々は体験を通して，見出し，反応し，あるいは変化し記憶する。

（有馬裕之）

ANDRA MATIN
PERERENAN HOUSE

Bali, Indonesia
Design: 2017-18
Construction: 2018-19

View from northeast

Terrace

Located in Pererenan, Bali, just northeast from Seminyak, The house situated on part of a contoured land with total land area of 6,000 square meters, owned by the house owner and their extended family.

Taking inspiration from "Rumah Panjang" from Borneo, the house sits on a row of thin columns and almost entirely covered in reclaimed iron woods. The master bedroom and 2 children bedrooms are placed opposite of each other, connected by a private common area. The entire house volume and upper terraces are completely covered by a wide single shield roof made from bamboo shingles, as a protection from rain and glare, while framing the surrounding views at the same time.

The public function such as house entrance, living, dining, and kitchen sits directly on the site, conforming to the existing contour, thus creating a play of height on the lower level. A library in inserted in between the upper house and the lower function as a transitional space between the public and the private.

There is a 7 meter-height difference from the main road and the lowest level of the site. The highest point of the site are functioned as parking area and entry point with an access to a small guesthouse and service area, all made from rammed earth. From the main entrance, the owner has a direct access that takes them directly to the common area on the upper level. The guest on the other hand, will be taken toward a footpath along the contoured site on the side of the house before finally arrive at the house entrance. The wide house entrance terrace provides an unobstructed view to the pool/ natural pond and the lush vegetation of the contoured land.

Master bedroom

View from south

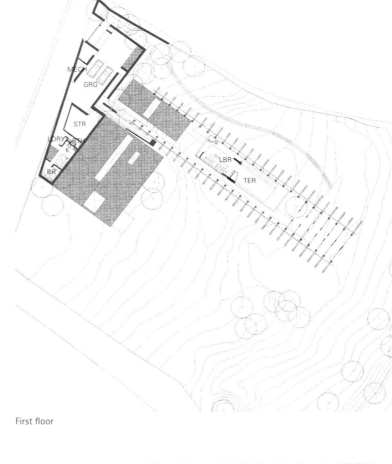

First floor

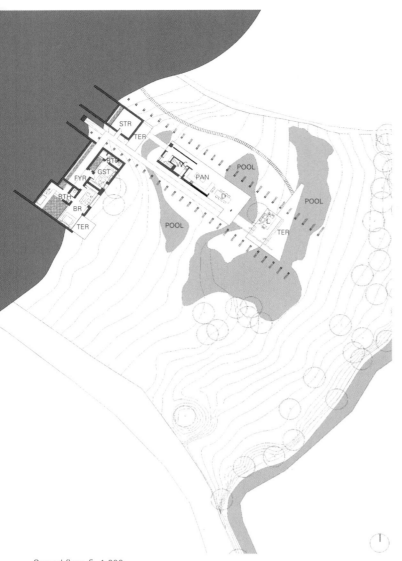

Ground floor S=1:800

Site plan S=1:5000

バリ，セミニヤクのすぐ北東にあるベレレナンに位置するこの住宅は，地域全体で6,000平米の起伏のある土地の一部に存在し，住宅のオーナーとその拡大家族によって所有されている。

ボルネオに由来する「ルマー・パンジャン」からインスピレーションを受けたこの住宅は，薄い柱の列の上に乗っており，ほぼ全体にわたって再利用された硬質木材によって覆われている。主寝室と二人の子供の寝室は，それぞれ反対側に位置し，プライベートな共有スペースによって接続されている。家全体のヴォリュームと上部テラスは，竹板からつくられた幅の広い一枚の遮蔽屋根によって完全に覆われており，雨や強い光からの防護となると同時に，周辺の眺望を切り取っている。

住宅の玄関，居間，食堂，台所といったパブリックな機能は敷地に直接配置されており，既存の起伏に適応することで低層部における高さの変化をつくり出している。ライブラリーは，パブリックとプライベート間の移行的な空間として，上層部の住宅と低層部の機能の間に挿入されている。

主要道路から敷地の最も低いレベルまでには7メートルの高さの差が存在する。敷地の最高点は，小さなゲストハウスとサービスエリアへとアクセスできる，駐車場ならびに入口として機能し，それら全ては版築によってつくられている。メインの玄関からは，オーナーが上層部にある共有エリアへとすぐに行くことのできるような，直接のアクセスが存在する。他方でゲストは，最終的に住宅の入口にたどり着く前に，住宅の脇の起伏のある土地に沿った歩道に向かって進むことになる。住宅の広い玄関テラスからは，起伏のあるその土地に存在する水たまりや自然の池，生い茂った植生へと向けた，遮る物のない眺望が得られる。

Second floor　　　　　　　　　　　　　　　　　　　　　　　　　Roof

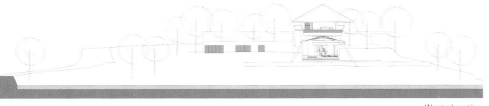

West elevation

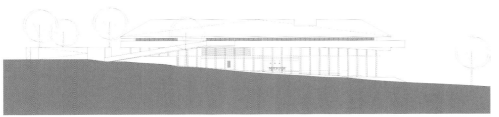

South elevation

North elevation　S=1:800

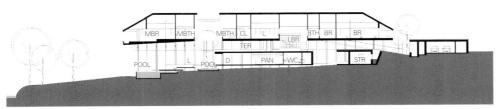

Section A-A'　S=1:800

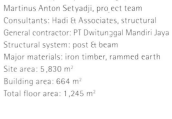

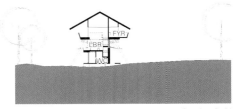

Section B-B'

Architects: andramatin—
Andra Matin, principal-in-charge;
Martinus Anton Setyadji, project team
Consultants: Hadi & Associates, structural
General contractor: PT Dwitunggal Mandiri Jaya
Structural system: post & beam
Major materials: iron timber, rammed earth
Site area: 5,830 m²
Building area: 664 m²
Total floor area: 1,245 m²

The design brief is to create a small hideaway bungalow in the middle of a 4 hectares teak plantation, located about 2,5 hours from Jakarta.

The dispersed composition of the architecture is a response to the man made grid of the teak trees, with approximately 140 meters distance from the site entrance to the front terrace. The long walks are meant as a way to experience the transition inside the forest in a slow and soothing manner.

At the center of the plantation, a small bungalow covered entirely in teak wood acts as a place to dwell or just to spend the night. The 50 meter long structure are just composed of two indoor function, one master bedroom and one living and dining area at the opposite side, both surrounded by a large terrace. All of the openings are covered in fine metal meshes to prevent insects and ensure sufficient daylight, air circulation and view.

Nearby, a slim 4 meters x 4 meters structure are built as an observation tower. The 20 meter-height will provide an unobstructed view across the teak plantation. There is a chance to catch a glimpse of the hills on the east side nearby, or the Sunda strait in distance.

View toward terrace from amphitheater

ANDRA MATIN
OMAH JATI

Anyer, Banten, West Java, Indonesia
Design: 2017-18
Construction: 2018-20

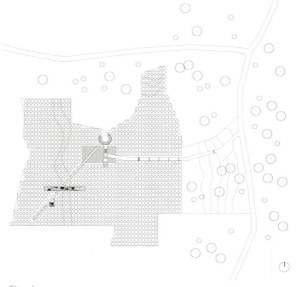

Site plan

Aerial view

View from north

設計に対する要望は，ジャカルタからおよそ2.5時間のところにある，4ヘクタールの広さのチーク・プランテーションの真ん中に，人目につかない小さなバンガローをつくることである。

この建築の分散した構成は，チークの木々からなる人工のグリッドに対する応答であり，敷地の入口から正面テラスまではおよそ140メートルの距離がある。長い歩行距離は，ゆっくりと落ち着いたやり方で森の中を移動する経験を得るための方法として意図されている。

プランテーションの中心では，チークの木のなかに完全に覆われた小さなバンガローが，住むため，あるいはただ夜を過ごすための場所としての役割を果たしている。50メートルの長さの構造物が，内部の二つの機能を正確に構成している。すなわち，一つの主寝室と，反対側にある一つの居間／食堂エリアであり，双方とも大きなテラスによって囲まれている。すべての開口部が質の良い金網で覆われており，虫を防ぐとともに，十分な昼光，空気循環，眺望を確保している。

その近くには，4メートル四方のスリムな構造物が，展望台として建てられている。その20メートルの高さによって，チークのプランテーションを見わたす，遮るもののない眺望が得られるだろう。ここでは東側付近にある丘や，遠くにあるスンダ海峡を一目見る機会も存在する。

Living room

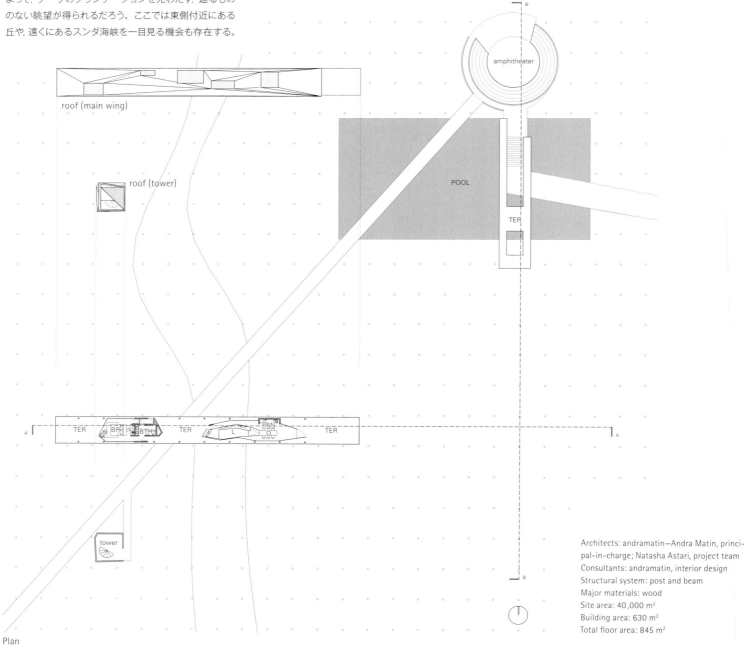

Plan

Architects: andramatin—Andra Matin, principal-in-charge; Natasha Astari, project team
Consultants: andramatin, interior design
Structural system: post and beam
Major materials: wood
Site area: 40,000 m²
Building area: 630 m²
Total floor area: 845 m²

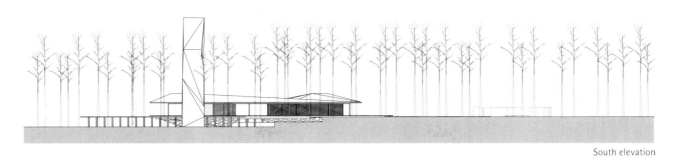
South elevation

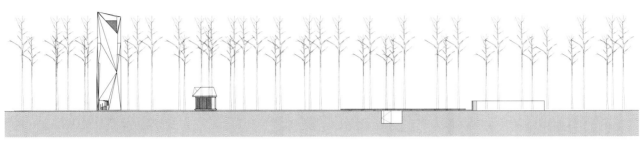
East elevation

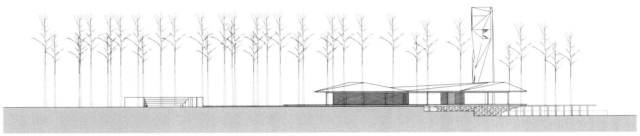
North elevation

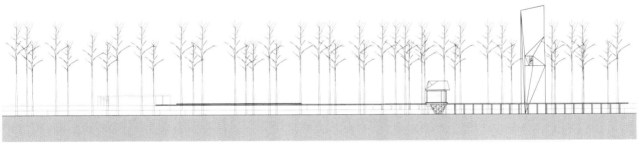
West elevation

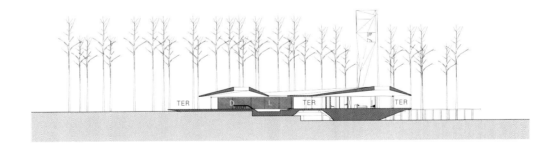
Section A-A'

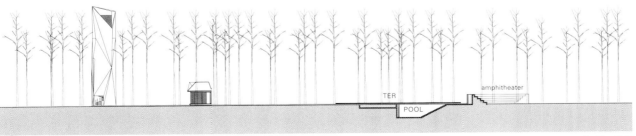
Section B-B'

FRAN SILVESTRE
ZARID HOUSE

Tarifa, Spain
Design: 2016-17
Construction: 2018-19

Located on the beach of Cabo de Plata, known as the Beach of the Germans on the Andalusian coast of Tarifa, there is an uneven place with a horizontal view over the Atlantic Ocean.

To optimize the vision of the landscape, a series of slender spaces are intertwined as they adapt to the descending topography. Each of these pieces is deposited half a floor below the previous one. This way, its alternating arrangement allows all the spaces to have a direct view over the beach.

This form of aggregation minimizes its pres-

ence in the landscape, and adapts to the slope as a sort of ladder. A system of terraces that produces continuous interiors. To the southwest we find the views over the landscape, to the northeast there are enclosed courtyards and gardens that thanks to the natural ventilation mitigate the hot days and give shelter from the winds that characterize Tarifa.

The program is organized in half-levels, each piece corresponds to a different use. The main bedroom is located at the top. Half floor below the day zone is arranged at an intermedi-

ate level, while the rest of the bedrooms are placed at the bottom.

In the intersection between the pieces is located the communications core, with smooth ladders, almost ramps. This central space proposes a route through different spaces with a great spatial heterogeneity, a walk that allows us to continue through the roof generating the fiction of a loop, a walk that we could imagine as limitless.

Evening view from southwest

Sketch

Architects: Fran Silvestre Arquitectos—
Fran Silvestre, principal-in-charge;
Fran Ayala, Alvaro Olivares, Eduardo Sancho,
María Masià, Pablo Camarasa, Sandra Insa,
Santiago Dueña, Ricardo Candela,
David Sastre, Estefanía Soriano,
Sevak Asatrián, Esther Sanchís, Vicente Picó,
Rubén March, José Manuel Arnao,
Rosa Juanes, Sergio Llobregat, Juan Martínez,
Paz Garcia, project team
Consultants: Estructuras Singulares UPV,
structural; Alfaro Hofmann, interior design
General contractor: Nuam
Structural system: concrete wall system, EIFS
Site area: 2,753.78 m^2
Building area: 434.18 m^2
Total floor area: 654.81 m^2

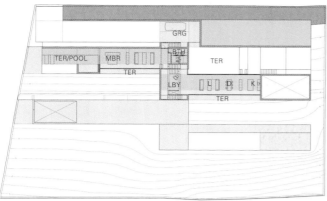
Level 0/+1 S=1:800

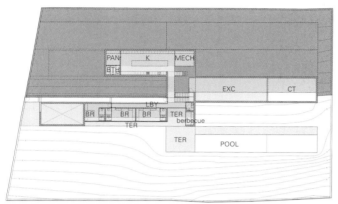
Level -2/-1

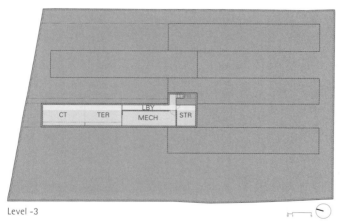
Level -3

Terrace along living room

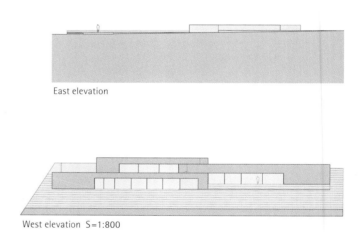
East elevation

West elevation S=1:800

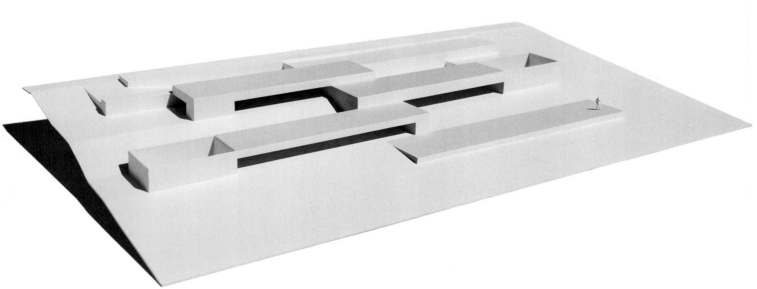

アンダルシア州の海岸都市であるタリファに位置し、「ザ・ビーチ・オブ・ジャーマンズ」として知られるカボ・デ・プラタ海岸に、大西洋へと水平な視界が広がる起伏の多い場所がある。

この地形の視界を最適化する目的で、傾斜した地形に対応する一連の細長い空間を地形に織り込むように配置している。これらの空間は、それぞれ前の空間より半階分ずつ沈み込むように配置されている。こうすることによって、互い違いに配置された全ての空間から海岸への視界が遮る物なく確保される。

集合体により形成されるこの形状は、景観の中でその存在を最小化し、一種の梯子の形として傾斜地に適応している。連続する内部空間を生み出すテラス方式。南西方向にかけては景観への眺めが広がり、北東方向には自然換気によって暑い日の空気を和らげ、タリファの特徴である強い風から保護するために取り囲まれた中庭と庭園がある。

プログラムは半層ごとに構成され、それぞれの空間が異なる使用方法に対応している。主寝室は最上部に位置している。半階層分下にある日中を過ごす場所は中間階層として設けられ、その他の寝室が最下層に配置されている。

各空間の交差部分にはコミュニケーションのためのコアとなる空間が設けられ、まるで傾斜路のようにスムーズな梯子を備えている。この中央空間は、著しく異種混交的な性格を持つ別空間へと通じる遊歩道となるよう意図している。そしてまた、ループとしての機能を生み出す屋根を通して、歩き続けられる道を、無限に感じられる道を提案する。

Ocean view from terrrace

View toward kitchen/dining room from terrace

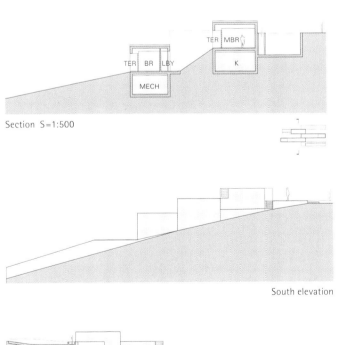

Section S=1:500

South elevation

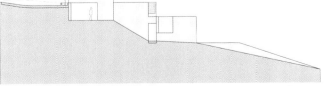

North elevation S=1:500

Lobby

Photo: Nohara Yamazaki

VO TRONG NGHIA
THANG HOUSE

Danang city, Vietnam
Design: 2014-15
Construction: 2017-18

Section perspective

174

Inspired by his childhood imagination of a country house full of rich tropical greenery, grasslands and fresh air, the owner always had a desire to own a similar house which is located right in the heart of Danang City, Vietnam.

The design team had to propose a solution in limited area of land (250 sqm). The strategy was to create a green lung for the house to breathe by dividing the land into two parallel parts: one for the garden with a huge green wall alongside; other for the living space which has majority of its windows & doors facing towards the green lung with the purpose of bringing natural light, fresh air and the aroma of grass and flowers to every single corner of the house.

The green area lost due to construction work was compensated by a fruit garden on roof top that gets sunlight and shelters the building. The roof garden included 9 tree boxes interspersed with gaps provide more greenery view under natural day & night light. This has not only contributed to the greening of the city but also creates space for urban agriculture to serve daily fresh vegetable and fruit for family. The perfect combination of farming with a panorama view of an emerging coastal city would surely relieve a person from the burden of a hectic city life.

To help the house operate more sustainably and economically, an automatic watering system recycles and circulates water from fish pond to the roof garden and vice versa, solar water heating and solar panel system installed on top produce energy for a family sized home. The design aims to make the building self-sufficient in green food production and to minimize energy consumption.

The house comprises of four main boxes— one big volume under the roof and three smaller inside the big one. These are extended and hanged over the garden to make space for bedrooms and living room. While the big box is covered by grey stone for a deep and charming feeling of the common space, the small ones are covered by white brick for an enlightening and warm feeling of living space. People can travel through different spatial in-house atmosphere. The narrow roof gaps allow the entry of natural light subtly and sufficiently for interior space. It creates an effect playing with light through the void between three levels.

This house is mainly made of local building materials which are available from nearby sources, such as the gray stone from Hoa Son rockery mine and brick from Quang Nam Province. In addition, the exposed concrete is an efficient material for low-tech construction in Vietnam and is durable under harsh local climate.

Under rapid urbanization, the lack of greenery in Vietnam cities generates various urban problems: increasing air pollution without purification, the city's inability to retain rainwater, insufficient amount of space to cool the street, and people become inactive over time. *Thang House* is one of the buildings under the "House For Trees" series and it pledges to contribute in greening of the urban landscape and improving the habitat by providing sustainable and environmentally friendly architecture. *Thang House* is yearly covered by tropical fruit trees which creates a tranquil, peaceful space for every family member and simultaneously preserves a green corner in the middle of this rapidly developing city.

Parallel garden

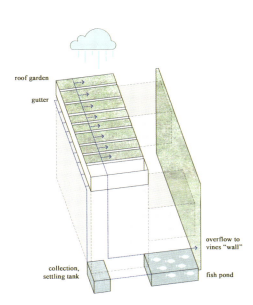

Water recycle diagram

Sectional model

First floor　S=1:300

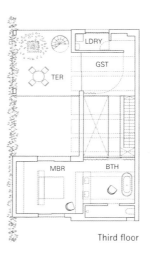

Second floor

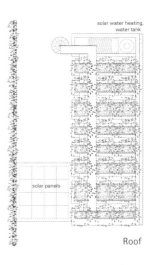

Third floor

Roof

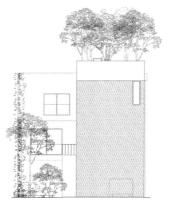

West elevation　S=1:300

East elevation

Section 1

子供の頃に想像していたような，豊かな熱帯の緑，草原，新鮮な空気に満ち溢れたカントリーハウスにインスピレーションを受けたオーナーは，これに似た住宅をベトナムのダナン市の中心部に建てる願望を常に持っていた。

設計チームは，限られた敷地（250平方メートル）のための解法を提案しなければならなかった。その設計の要は，敷地を平行な二つの部分に分割し，この住宅が呼吸するための緑の広場をつくり出すというものである。一つは巨大な緑の壁が寄り添う庭として，もう一つは自然光や新鮮な空気，芝生や花々の香りを住宅の隅々にまで取り込むために大多数の窓とドアをこの緑の広場に面して配置した，居住空間のためのものである。

建設作業により失われた緑地は，太陽光を受け，建物を保護する屋根上の果樹庭園を提供することによって補填されている。この屋上庭園には，間を空けて点在させた九つのツリーボックスが組み込まれ，自然光や夜間照明の下でより深い緑の景観を提供している。これにより，街の緑化に貢献するだけでなく，都市部において農業空間をつくり出し，家族のために新鮮な野菜や果物を日常的に提供する。注目されつつあるこの海岸都市のパノラマ風景と農業の完璧な組み合わせは，多忙を極める都市生活の負担から間違いなく人を解放することだろう。

この住宅がより持続可能に，また経済的に機能できるようにするため，自動灌漑システムによって魚用の池の水を再利用して屋上庭園へ，またその逆の方向に循環させ，その上に設置された太陽熱水器とソーラーパネルシステムによって単一家族住宅向けにエネルギーを生み出している。こうした設計により野菜などの食料を生産し，エネルギー消費を最小化することで，建物が自給自足することを目指している。

この住宅は，大きく分けて四つの箱で構成されている。一つの大きなヴォリュームの箱が屋根の下に収まり，また三つのより小さな箱がこの大きな箱の内部に収められている。これらが延長されて庭の上に張り出し，一連の寝室と居間のための空間をつくり出している。大きな箱は，公共空間として魅力的で深みのある雰囲気を醸し出すよう灰色の石で覆われ，小さな箱は，明解でありながら温かな雰囲気を持つ生活空間のために白

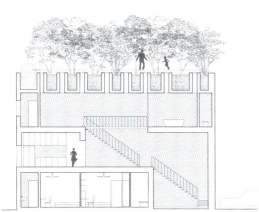

Section 2

いレンガで覆われている。人々は様々な雰囲気の空間を横断できるようになっている。屋根にある細長い隙間は，十分な量の自然光を繊細に内部空間へと届けている。これは三層を貫くヴォイドを通じて，光と戯れるような効果を生み出している。

この住宅は，主に地元の建材によって建てられている。これらはホアソンの鉱山から産出される灰色の石材やクアンナム省で生産されるレンガなど，近くの供給源から入手可能なものである。さらに，ベトナムにおいて打放しコンクリートはローテク建設のために効率的な素材であり，地元の厳しい気候の下でも耐久性がある。

急速な都市化の中で，ベトナムの都市部では緑地が欠乏し，空気が浄化されることなく汚染が進んだり，雨水を保持する能力がなかったり，道路を冷やすのに必要な空間が欠けているために人々が次第に活力を失っているなど，様々な都市問題が発生している。タン・ハウスは"樹木のための住宅"シリーズの下で進められた建物の一つで，都市景観の緑化や，住空間の向上によって持続可能で環境に優しい建築を提供し，貢献することを約束している。タン・ハウスは年間を通じて枯れることのない熱帯の果樹で覆われているため，家族の各メンバーのために穏やかで心休まる空間をつくり出すと同時に，この急速に発展する都市のただ中に緑の一画を確保している。

Architects: Vo Trong Nghia Architects—
Vo Trong Nghia, principal-in-charge;
Kosuke Nishijima, Le Phuong Uyen, project team
Consultants: Vo Trong Nghia Architects, structural/MEP/interior design/landscape;
General contractor: Mr.Thang
Structural system: composite steel and concrete
Major materials: Natural stone, concrete and brick
Site area: 250 m²
Building area: 140 m²
Total floor area: 250 m²

KEISUKE MAEDA
HOUSE IN ONNASON

Okinawa, Japan
Design: 2015-18

Model photos: Ayane Hirose

"Te-ge" (relaxed) spirit of warm tropical weather

Although Okinawa enjoys the blessings of a rich natural environment, it also endures typhoons of unimaginable brutality. Such survival has become an intimate part of everyday life, bringing about some uniquely Okinawan architecture inspired by its natural surroundings. Since the era of the Ryukyu Kingdom, this has been continually passed down, changing its form through generations. The loggia spaces underneath the eaves called *amahaji* which lessen the damages from wind, rain and sunlight; adaptation to heat environment through traditional *nuchijya* wooden construction; post-war measures to fight against the weather using reinforced concrete; and the unique inter-personal relationships inspired by distinct local climate called the *Okinawan time*—we sought to come up with a new form of architecture by contemplating how to stand by, as well as face, the people and nature of this place.

The site is in Onna, which is located in the center of the main land of Okinawa. Although sunset over the East China Sea can be seen past National road 58 on the front, the site is also approximately 2 meters lower than street level, requiring a three-level structure to secure the view. The building is made of three layers of reinforced concrete, and is uniformly 10 meters in height, width, and depth. The roof is a wooden framework that houses a large, expansive space, which can also adapt to the heat environment. In order to protect privacy and block street noise from the National road, the second floor is closed from the outside, allowing ventilation through decorative concrete blocks. For the first and third floors, *amehaji* spaces are created using the characteristically Okinawan three-centered arch motif with openings on the four outer layers, giving rise to a new sense of continuity between the indoors and outdoors.
Keisuke Maeda

Site plan S=1:10000

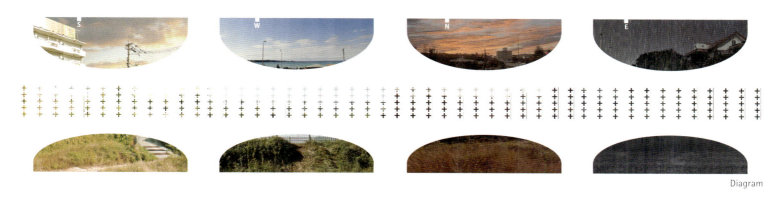

Diagram

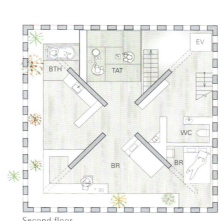

First floor S=1:200

Second floor

Third floor

南国の気候が生み出すテーゲーな空気感

沖縄という地域は豊かな自然環境の恩恵を享受する一方，台風時には想像を絶する猛威にさらされる。それは日常の生活と密接な関係を生み，沖縄特有の自然環境から導かれた建築が，琉球王国の時代より変遷しながらも現代まで脈々と受け継がれている。風雨や直射光を軽減する雨端(アマハジ)空間，伝統的な貫木屋(ヌチジャー)の木造による熱環境への順応や，戦後普及したRC造による気象への対抗。また沖縄時間(ウチナータイム)と言われる風土が生み出す人と人との関わりなど。この地における人と自然に対してどのように寄り添い，どのように対峙しなければならないのかを思考しながら新たな姿形を目指した。

敷地は沖縄本島の中央部に位置する恩納村。前面の国道58号線越しに東シナ海の夕日が望める立地である一方，道路面から2メートルほど窪んだところに敷地レベルが位置し，眺望の確保には3層構成にする必要があった。建築全体は幅・奥行・高さ方向を約10×10×10メートルの3層RC造とし，屋根部に関しては木質架構によっておおらかな大空間をつくりながら熱環境にも順応できる形式としている。2層部分は国道からの車の騒音やプライバシーの関係から，外部に対して閉じつつも通風を花ブロックによって取り入れた。1層及び3層に関しては沖縄特有の三心円弧をモチーフに外皮4面の開口がつくる雨端空間によって内外の新たな連続性を生み出している。

（前田圭介）

Architects: UID—Keisuke Maeda, principal-in-charge; Hiroyuki Ueda, Shohei Yaura, project team
Consultants: Konishi Structural Engineers—Yasutaka Konishi, Takuya Asamitsu, Junpei Sato, structural
General contractor: Taiko Kensetsu Co.,Ltd. Tatsuhide Miyazato, Masatomo Higa, Yoshitaka Higa
Structural system: RC
Major materials: structural plywood formwork concrete, decorative concrete block, exterior; PVC flooring (floor), structural plywood formwork concrete (wall, ceiling), interior
Building of Scale: Three story house
Site area: 596.71 m²
Building area: 101.002 m²
Total floor area: 239.8 m²

Sectional perspective S=1:120

Living room on third floor

This plot is located in an older residential area near to Morcote, it has a panoramic view of Lake Lugano and mountains towards the west.

Different sized and differently proportioned closed natural stone cubes generate interspaces, which are covered by a large floating cube. This space is only separated from the outer space only by a fine glass membrane. The closed cubes themselves contain smaller secondary rooms, such as library, bathroom or storage rooms, which, depending on the function, receive larger or smaller courtyards for their illumination.

The composition of these volumes creates the atmosphere of a Mediterranean village.

With the outbuilding, including guest apartment and double garage, the entrance situation for the entire property is created.

A spacious forecourt behind the house is created by the volumes of the guest house and main house, where you can either enter to the guest house, outdoor pergola or to the main house, it's the main meeting point for all.

The interior of the main house is optimized by several roof lights, which not only generate a warm lighting mood together with the wooden ceiling beams, but also the atmosphere of an external space, inside and outside merge into each other, forming a coherent spatial continuum.

WESPI DE MEURON ROMEO ARCHITECTS
PROJECT NEW HOUSE IN MORCOTE

Morcote, Ticino, Switzerland
Design: 2015-16

View from north

Roof

Ground floor S=1:500

Basement

Living/dining room/kitchen

Bathroom. View toward pool

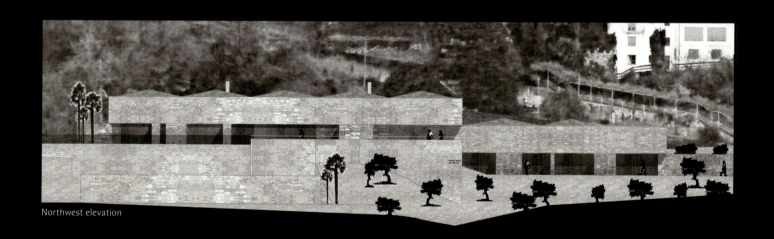
Northwest elevation

Southeast elevation   S=1:400

Lounge and loggia

この土地はモルコテ近郊の古い住宅地区に位置しており，西に向かってルガーノ湖と山々のパノラミックな眺望が広がっている。

異なるサイズとプロポーションを持った，閉じた自然石の直方体が隙間の空間をつくり出し，それらは大きな浮遊する直方体によって覆われている。この空間を外部空間から隔てるのは，純度の高いガラスの皮膜だけである。閉じた直方体自体にも，より小さい副次的な部屋が含まれており，読書室，浴室，倉庫といったそれらの部屋には，機能に応じて採光のための大小の中庭が与えられている。

それらのヴォリュームによってつくり出された構成は，地中海の村のような雰囲気を醸し出している。

ゲスト用のアパートメントと車2台分の車庫が入った離れがあることで，敷地全体の入口となる状況がつくり出されている。

住宅に面した広々とした前庭は，ゲストハウスと母屋のヴォリュームによってつくり出され，そこからゲストハウス，屋外のパーゴラ，母屋のいずれにも入ることができるような，みんなのための主要な待合いの場となっている。

母屋の内部空間はいくつかの天窓によって最大限の効果を与えられている。それらは木材でできた屋根の梁と一体となって暖かな灯りのムードをもたらすだけでなく，外部空間の雰囲気をもつくり出し，内部と外部が相互に溶け合い，ひとつながりの空間連続体を形成している。

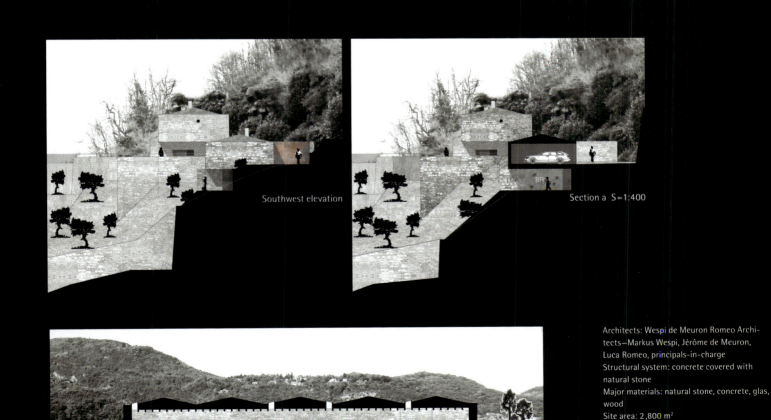

Southwest elevation

Section a S=1:400

Section b

Architects: Wespi de Meuron Romeo Architects—Markus Wespi, Jérôme de Meuron, Luca Romeo, principals-in-charge
Structural system: concrete covered with natural stone
Major materials: natural stone, concrete, glas, wood
Site area: 2,800 m²
Building area: 750 m²
Total floor area: 500 m²

PROFILE

AIRES MATEUS

Manuel Aires Mateus
1: 1963, Lisbon, Portugal
2: graduate from Faculdade de Arquitectura / U.T.L in 1986
3: collaborated with Arch. Gonçalo Byrne since 1983
4: started developing own projects as authors with Francisco Aires Mateus since 1988

Francisco Aires Mateus
1: 1964, Lisbon, Portugal
2: graduate from Faculdade de Arquitectura / U.T.L in 1987
3: Arch. Gonçalo Byrne since 1983
4: started developing own projects as authors with Manuel Aires Mateus since 1988

A: Aires Mateus e Associados
B: Rua Silva Carvalho 193, 1250-250 Lisboa, Portugal
C: www.airesmateus.com
D: m@airesmateus.com

© AMA

ALPHAVILLE

Kentaro Takeguchi
竹口健太郎
1: 1971, Kyoto
2: studied in Architectural Association School of Architecture under FOA, U.K., 1996; graduated from master course, School of Architecture, Kyoto University, 1998
4: 1998, Kyoto

Asako Yamamoto
山本麻子
1: 1971, Shiga
2: studied in l' Ecole d' Architecture de Paris, La Villette, France, 1996; graduated from master course, School of Architecture, Kyoto University, 1997
3: worked at Riken Yamamoto & Fieldshop
4: 1998, Kyoto

A: ALPHAVILLE architects Co., Ltd. / アルファヴィル
B: Kyoto, Japan / 〒615-0007 京都府京都市右京区西院上花田町32
C: a-ville.net   D: 001@a-ville.net; 002@a-ville.net

Hiroyuki Arima
有馬裕之
1: 1956, Kagoshima, Japan
2: graduated from Kyoto Institute of Technology
4: 1990

A: Hiroyuki Arima+Urban Fourth Co.,Ltd. / 有馬裕之＋Urban Fourth
B: Fukuoka, Japan / 〒815-0083 福岡県福岡市南区高宮4-14-6
C: www.urbanfourth.jp
D: info@urbanfourth.jp

BERCY CHEN

Thomas Bercy
1: Belgium
2: studied four years in fine arts and two years in architecture at Beaux-Arts School in Brussels; received Bachelor of Architecture and Civil Engeneering at University of Texas in Austin; studied Urbanism at La Pontificia Universidad Catolica de Chile in Santiago
3: Samyn and Partners, MJ Neal Architects
4: 2001, Austin, Texas

Calvin Chen
1: 1974, Taipei, Taiwan
2: graduated from University of Texas at Austin in 1998 with professional degree in Architecture; studied at St. Peter's Lutheran College in Brisbane, Australia
3: Max Levy Architect, Susman Tisdale Gayle, MJ Neal Architects
4: 2001, Austin, Texas

A: Bercy Chen Studio LP
B: 1111 E, 11th Street Suite 200, Austin Texas 78702, USA
C: bcarc.com
D: info@bcarc.com

bgp arquitectura

Bernardo Gómez-Pimienta
1: 1961, Brussels, Belgium 2: graduated from Anahuac University, Mexico (Bachelor of Architecture) in 1986 and Columbia University (Master of Architecture) in 1987 3: TEN Arquitectos co-director, 1987-2003 4: 2003, Mexico City

A: bgp arquitectura B: 23 Ave Maria Street, Santa Catarina Neighborhood, Coyoacan, 04010, Mexico City, Mexico
C: www.bgp.com.mx D: ivanreytarara@gmail.com

© Guillermo Kahlo

Tatiana Bilbao

1: 1972, Mexico City, Mexico
2: graduated from Architecture and Urbanism at Universidad Iberoamericana in 1996 3: Advisor for Urban Projects at Urban Housing and Development Department of Mexico City in 1998-99
4: 2004

A: Tatiana Bilbao Estudio B: Paseo de la Reforma 382-4, Colonia Juárez, Delegación Cuauhtémoc, CP 06600 México, CDMX, México
C: www.tatianabilbao.com D: press@tatianabilbao.com

© Roberto Sánchez

Will Bruder

1: 1946, Milwaukee, Wisconsin USA 2: received Bachelor of Fine Arts–Sculpture, University of Wisconsin-Milwaukee in 1969
3: apprenticeship with Paolo Soleri Cosanti foundation, and Gunnar Birkerts Associates Architects 4: 1974

A: Will Bruder Architects
B: 4200 North Central Av., Phoenix, Arizona 85012, USA
C: www.willbruderarchitects.com
D: studio@willbruderarchitects.com

CHENCHOW LITTLE

Tony Chenchow
1: 1967, Sydney, Australia
2: awarded degree in Architecture, University of New South Wales in 1993
4: founded Chenchow Little with Stephanie Little in 2004

Stephanie Little
1: 1970, Griffith, Australia
2: awarded degree in Architecture, University of New South Wales in 1994
4: founded Chenchow Little with Tony Chenchow in 2004

A: Chenchow Little Pty. Ltd.
B: Studio 3, 151 Foveaux Street, Surry Hills NSW 2010, Australia
C: www.chenchowlittle.com
D: mail@chenchowlittle.com

STEVEN EHRLICH + TAKASHI YANAI

Steven Ehrlich (right)
1: 1946, New York, New York, USA
2: graduated from Rensselaer Polytechnic Institute (Bachelor of Architecture, Bachelor of Science)
4: 1975, Los Angeles

Takashi Yanai (left)
1: 1968, Tokyo, Japan
2: graduated from Harvard GSD (Master of Architecture)
3: worked at an architectural publisher in Tokyo for four years; joined Ehrlich Architects since 2002

A: Ehrlich Yanai Rhee Chaney Architects
B: 10865 Washington Blvd. Culver City, California 90232, USA
C: eyrc.com
D: info@eyrc.com

BIOGRAPHY
1. birth year and place
2. educational background
3. work experience before starting own practice
4. when and where starting own practice

OFFICE INFORMATION
A. office name
B. address (main office)
C. website
D. e-mail address

ENSAMBLE STUDIO

Antón García-Abril (left)
1: 1969, Madrid, Spain
2: 1995, Master's Degree in Architecture by School of Architecture of Polytechnic University of Madrid; 2007, European PhD in Architecture; research scientist of POPlab at Massachusetts Institute of Technology (MIT) since 2012 4: 2000, founder and principal of Ensamble Studio; 2012, founder and director of POPlab at Massachusetts Institute of Technology (MIT)

Débora Mesa (right)
1: 1981, Madrid, Spain
2: 2006, Master's Degree in Architecture by School of Architecture of Polytechnic University of Madrid; International PhD Candidate and research scientist of POPlab at Massachusetts Institute of Technology (MIT) since 2012 4: 2003, Architect in Ensamble Studio; 2010, Principal of Ensamble Studio; 2012, Founder and Research Director of POPlab at Massachusetts Institute of Technology (MIT)

A: Ensamble Studio
B: Calle Cabo Candelaria 9 B, 28290, Las Rozas, Madrid, Spain
C: www.ensamble.info D: ensamble@ensamble-studio.com

GRUPO SP

Alvaro Puntoni
1: 1965, São Paulo, SP, Brazil
2: received Bachelor of Architecture (1987), Master degree (1999) and Ph.D. (2005) from FAUUSP/Faculty of Architecture and Urbanism of the University of São Paulo
3: worked with Angelo Bucci, 1987-96 and 2002-04, when they founded SPBR architects
4: founded Grupo SP in 2004

João Sodré
1: 1978, São Paulo, SP, Brazil
2: received Bachelor of Architecture (2005) and Master degree (2010) from FAUUSP/Faculty of Architecture and Urbanism of the University of São Paulo
4: partner of Grupo SP since 2004

A: Grupo SP Arquitetos
B: Rua General Jardin 645 cj. 52 01223 011 São Paulo, SP, Brazil
C: www.gruposp.arq.br
D: contato@gruposp.arq.br

Sou Fujimoto
藤本壮介

1: 1971, Hokkaido, Japan
2: graduated from University of Tokyo, Faculty of Engineering, Department of Architecture (Bachelor of Architecture) in 1994
4: 2000

A: Sou Fujimoto Architects / 藤本壮介建築設計事務所 B: Tokyo, Japan / 〒162-0807 東京都新宿区東榎町10-3 市川製本ビル6F
C: www.sou-fujimoto.net D: project@sou-fujimoto.net

Tomohiro Hata
畑友洋

1: 1978, Hyogo, Japan
2: graduated from Department of Architecture, Kyoto University in 2001; received Master of Architecture, Kyoto University in 2003
3: worked at Shin Takamatsu and Associates 4: 2006

A: Tomohiro Hata Architect and Associates / 畑友洋建築設計事務所
B: Kobe, Japan / 〒651-0082 神戸市中央区小野浜1-4デザイン・クリエイティブセンター神戸 #201 C: www.hata-archi.com D: office@hata-archi.com

---

Takashi Fujino
藤野高志

1: 1975, Gunma, Japan
2: received Master degree from Department of Architecture, Tohoku University 3: worked at Shimizu Corporation and Haryu Wood Studio
4: 2006

A: Ikimono Architects / 生物建築舎 B: Gunma, Japan / 〒370-0042 群馬県高崎市貝沢町323-1 C: sites.google.com/site/ikimonokenchiku
D: ikimonokenchiku@gmail.com

IRISARRI+PIÑERA

Jesús Irisarri Castro (left)
1: 1958, Vigo, Spain
2: graduated from Escuela Técnica Superior de Arquitectura de Coruña
4: 1989, Vigo with Guadalupe P. Manso

Guadalupe Piñera Manso (right)
1: 1960, Madrid, Spain
2: graduated from Escuela Técnica Superior de Arquitectura de Coruña
4: 1989, Vigo with Jesús I. Castro

A: Irisarri-Piñera SLNEP
B: Plaza de Portugal 2-9B, Vigo-Spain
D: irisarripinera@coag.es

Shigeru Fuse
布施茂

1: 1960, Chiba, Japan
2: graduated from Department of Architecture, Musashino Art University in 1984
3: worked at Daiichi-Kobo Associates 4: 2003

A: fuse-atelier
B: Chiba, Japan/ 〒261-0026 千葉県千葉市美浜区幕張西6-19-6
C: www.fuse-a.com D: fuse@fuse-a.com

Sean Godsell

1: 1960, Melbourne, Australia
2: received Bachelor of Architecture (Hons) from Melbourne University; received Master of Architecture from RMIT University
3: worked at Sir Denys Lasdun 4: 1994, Melbourne, Australia

A: Sean Godsell Architects
B: Level 2/49 Exhibition street, Melbourne, Victoria, Australia
C: www.seangodsell.com D: info@seangodsell.com

© Earl Carter

Albert Kalach

1: 1960, Mexico City, México
2: graduated from Universidad Iberoamericana, 1981 and Cornell University 1984
4: 1984, Mexico City

A: Taller de Arquitectura 'X'
B: 41 Av Constituyentes Hidalgo CDMX, 11850, México
C: www.kalach.com

GRUPO ARANEA

Francisco Leiva Ivorra

1: 1972, Alicante, Spain
2: graduated from Universidad Politécnica de Valencia
4: 1998

A: Grupo Aranea
B: Avenida General Marvá, n°7, 1°B, cp/ 03005, Alicante, Spain
C: www.grupoaranea.net D: info@grupoaranea.net

Hirotaka Kidosaki
城戸崎博孝

1: 1942, Tokyo, Japan
2: graduated from Nihon University in 1966; Master course of University of Sheffield in 1977 3: worked at Kenzo Tange Associates, 1979-93; Architect 5 Partnership, 1993-2005 4: 2000

A: Kidosaki Architects Studio / 城戸崎建築研究室
B: Tokyo, Japan / 〒104-0061 東京都中央区銀座1-5-12
C: www.kidosaki.com D: info@kidosaki.com

187

Mathias Klotz
1: 1965, Viña del Mar, Chile
2: received architecture degree from Pontificia Universidad Católica de Chile in 1991
4: started own studio in 1991

A: Mathias Klotz arquitectos
B: Alonso de Monroy 2869 of 401, Vitacura, Santiago de Chile
C: www.mathiasklotz.com D: estudio@mathiasklotz.com

Katsufumi Kubota
窪田勝文
1: 1957, Yamaguchi, Japan
2: graduated from Nihon University, Faculty of Engineering, Department of Architecture (Bachelor) in 1981
3: K Construction Research 4: 1988

A: Kubota Architect Atelier / 窪田建築アトリエ
B: Yamaguchi, Japan / 〒740-0017 山口県岩国市今津町1-8-24
C: www.katsufumikubota.jp D: info@katsufumikubota.jp

Kengo Kuma
隈研吾
1: 1954, Kanagawa, Japan
2: graduated from University of Tokyo (Bachelor) and received Master of Architecture in 1979 4: established Spatial Design Studio, Tokyo in 1987; established private practice in Tokyo in 1990

A: Kengo Kuma & Associates / 隈研吾建築都市設計事務所
B: Tokyo, Japan / 〒107-0062 東京都港区南青山2-24-8
C: www.kkaa.co.jp D: kuma@ba2.so-net.ne.jp

Keisuke Maeda
前田圭介
1: 1974, Hiroshima, Japan
2: graduated from Kokushikan University, Faculty of Engineering, Department of Architecture (Bachelor) in 1998 3: 2003

A: UID
B: Hiroshima, Japan / 〒720-0082 広島県福山市木之庄町3-10-20 森×hako 2F
C: www.maeda-inc.jp/uid D: uid@maeda-inc.jp

© UID

SHINGO MASUDA + KATSUHISA OTSUBO

Shingo Masuda
増田信吾
1: 1982, Tokyo, Japan
2: graduated from Department of Architecture, Musashino Art University in 2007
4: 2007

Katsuhisa Otsubo
大坪克亘
1: 1983, Saitama, Japan
2: graduated from Department of Architecture, Tokyo University of the Arts in 2007
4: 2007

A: Shingo Masuda + Katsuhisa Otsubo Architects
B: Tokyo, Japan / 〒112-0012 東京都文京区大塚4-10-9 津久井ビル1/F
C: salad-net.jp
D: contact@salad-net.jp

Gurjit Singh Matharoo
1: 1966, Ajmer, India
2: received Bachelor of Architecture from School of Architecture CEPT in Ahmedabad, India
4: 1991

A: Matharoo Associates
B: 16, Laxmi Nivas Society, Near Jalaram Mandir, Paldi, Ahmedabad - 380007, India
C: www.matharooassociates.com D: studio@matharooassociates.com

Andra Matin
1: 1962, Bandung, Indonesia
2: graduated from Parahyangan Catholic University, Bandung, 1981
3: worked at Graha Cipta Hadiprana
4: 1998, Jakarta

A: andramatin
B: Jl. Manyar III Blok 03 no. 4-6 Bintaro Jaya, Jakarta 12330, Indonesia
C: www.andramatin.com D: admin@andramatin.com

MATSUOKASATOSHITAMURAYUKI

Satoshi Matsuoka
松岡聡
1: 1973, Aichi, Japan
2: graduated from Department of Architecture, Kyoto University in 1977; received Master of Engineering in Architecture, University of Tokyo in 2000 and Master of Science in Advanced Architectural Design from Columbia University in 2001
3: worked at UNStudio, MVRDV, and SANAA, 2002-05 4: established MATSUOKASATOSHITAMURAYUKI with Yuki Tamura, 2005

Yuki Tamura
田村裕希
1: 1977, Tokyo Japan
2: graduated from Nihon University in 2000; received Master of Architecture, Tokyo University of the Arts in 2004
3: worked at SANAA, 2004-05 4: established MATSUOKASATOSHITAMURAYUKI with Satoshi Matsuoka, 2005

A: MATSUOKASATOSHITAMURAYUKI / 松岡聡田村裕希
B: Tokyo, Japan / 〒103-0024 東京都中央区日本橋小舟町8-7 東京糖商ビル3F C: www.matsuokasatoshitamurayuki.com
D: office@matsuokasatoshitamurayuki.com

Erika Nakagawa
中川エリカ
1: 1983, Tokyo, Japan 2: graduated from Yokohama National University in 2005; graduate school of Tokyo University of Arts in 2007
3: worked for ON design 4: 2014

A: erika nakagawa office / 中川エリカ建築設計事務所
B: Tokyo, Japan / 〒154-0005 東京都世田谷区三宿2-27-8 #303
C: erikanakagawa.com
D: erikanakagawa.office@gmail.com

Ryue Nishizawa
西沢立衛
1: 1966, Tokyo, Japan 2: graduated from Yokohama National University
3: joined Kazuyo Sejima & Associates in 1990 4: established SANAA with Kazuyo Sejima in 1995; established own office in 1997

A: Office of Ryue Nishizawa / 西沢立衛建築設計事務所
B: Tokyo, Japan / 〒135-0053 東京都江東区辰巳1-5-27
C: www.ryuenishizawa.com
D: office@ryuenishizawa.com

ONISHIMAKI+HYAKUDAYUKI / O+H

Maki Onishi
大西麻貴
1: 1983, Aichi, Japan
2: graduated from Department of Architecture, Kyoto University in 2006; received Master of Architecture, University of Tokyo in 2008
4: established onishimaki+hyakudayuki / o+h with Yuki Hyakuda in 2008

Yuki Hyakuda
百田有希
1: 1982, Hyogo, Japan
2: graduated from Department of Architecture, Kyoto University in 2006; received Master of Architecture, Kyoto University in 2008
3: worked at Toyo Ito & Associates, Architects, 2009-14
4: established onishimaki+hyakudayuki / o+h with Maki Onishi in 2008

A: onishimaki+hyakudayuki / o+h
B: Tokyo, Japan/ 〒103-0007 東京都中央区日本橋浜町3-10-1山岸ビル1階
C: www.onishihyakuda.jp D: info@onishihyakuda.jp

BIOGRAPHY
1. birth year and place
2. educational background
3. work experience before starting own practice
4. when and where starting own practice

OFFICE INFORMATION
A. office name
B. address (main office)
C. website
D. e-mail address

NITSCHE ARQUITETOS

Lua Nitsche (center right)
1: 1972, São Paulo, Brazil
2: graduated from Faculty of Architecture and Urbanism of University of São Paulo/FAUUSP in 1996
3: worked at Felipe Crescenti; André Vainer & Guilherme Paoliello; Isay Weinfeld 4: 2001, São Paulo

Pedro Nitsche (center left)
1: 1975, São Paulo, Brazil
2: graduated from Faculty of Architecture and Urbanism of University of São Paulo/FAUUSP in 2000
3: worked at Ruy Ohtake; Construtora Fazer; Edson Elito; Piratininga; Andrade Morettin 4: 2001, São Paulo

João Nitsche (right)
1: 1979, São Paulo, Brazil
2: graduated from Faculty of Fine Arts of Armando Alvares Penteado Foundation/FAAP in 2004
4: 2009, São Paulo

André Scarpa (left)
1: 1983, São Paulo, Brazil
2: graduated from the Faculty of Architecture of University of Porto/FAUP in 2009
3: worked at António Madureira; Álvaro Siza
4: joined Nitsche Arquitetos in 2012

A: Nitsche Arquitetos
B: Rua General Jardim 645 cj. 12 São Paulo, SP, 01223-011, Brazil C: www.nitsche.com.br
D: nitsche@nitsche.com.br

Smiljan Radic

1: 1965, Santiago, Chile
2: graduated from Pontificia Universidad Católica de Chile in 1989; studied at Istitutto Universitario di Architettura di Venezia in Italy
4: 1995, Chile

A: Smiljan Radic Clarke
B: Los Conquistadores 1700 p.20 A, Providencia, Santiago, Chile
D: smiljanradic@gmail.com

RICA STUDIO*

Iñaqui Carnicero (left)
1: 1973, Madrid, Spain
2: awarded architect and international Phd from Polytechnic University of Madrid
4: 2000

Lorena del Río (right)
1: 1981, Madrid, Spain
2: received Bachelor's and Master's degrees in Architecture from Polytechnic University of Madrid in 2008; Ph.D. Candidate
4: 2008

A: RICA Studio*
B: Avenida del Rodeo 47, Torreldores 28250 Madrid, Spain; 1105 Taughannock Blvd 14850 Ithaca, NY, USA
C: www.ricastudio.com
D: info@ricastudio.com

Hiroshi Sambuichi
三分一博志

1: 1968
2: graduated from Architecture and Building Engineering, Faculty of Science and Technology, Tokyo University of Science
3: worked at Shinichi Ogawa & Associates

A: Sambuichi Architects / 三分一博志建築設計事務所
B: Hiroshima, Japan / 広島県広島市中区中島町8-3-302
D: samb@d2.dion.ne.jp

selgascano

José Selgas
1: 1965, Madrid, Spain
2: graduated from Superior Technical School of Architecture of Madrid (ETSAM) in 1992
3: worked with Francesco Venecia on Naples, 1994-95
4: 1996

Lucía Cano
1: 1965, Madrid, Spain
2: graduated from Superior Technical School of Architecture of Madrid (ETSAM) in 1992
3: work with Julio Cano Lasso until 1996 and member of Cano Lasso Studio, 1997-2003
4: 1996

A: selgascano
B: Avenue Casa Quemada 1, Madrid 28023, Spain
C: www.selgascano.com D: info@selgascano.com

Yo Shimada
島田陽

1: 1972, Hyogo, Japan
2: graduated from Kyoto City University of Art in 1995; graduated from post graduate course in 1997
4: 1997

A: TATO ARCHITECTS / タトアーキテクツ/島田陽建築設計事務所
B: Hyogo, Japan / 〒650-0002 兵庫県神戸市中央区北野町2-13-23
C: www.tat-o.com D: info@tat-o.com

Fran Silvestre

1: 1976, Valencia, Spain 2: graduated as Architect (building specialty) from ETSAV/Escuela Técnica Superior de Arquitectura, Valencia in 2001; graduated as Architect (urban planning specialty) from TU/e (Technische Universiteit Eindhoven, The Netherlands) in 2002 4: 2007

A: Fran Silvestre Arquitectos B: San Vicente Martir, 160 1, 46007, Valencia, Spain C: www.fransilvestrearquitectos.com
D: media@fransilvestrearqutiectos.com

SPBR ARQUITETOS

Angelo Bucci
1: 1963, Orlândia, São Paulo, Brazil
2: received Master degree in 1998 and Ph.D. in 2005 from FAUUSP/Faculty of Architecture and Urbanism of the University of São Paulo
4: 2003, São Paulo, Brazil

A: spbr arquitetos
B: Av. Faria Lima, 1234, cj. 121 01451-001, São Paulo, SP, Brazil
C: www.spbr.arq.br D: spbr@spbr.arq.br

© Ana Ottoni

STUDIO TONTON

Antony Liu
1: 1967, Jakarta, Indonesia
2: received Bachelor of Architecture from Tarumanagara University
3: partner architect at PT. Pakar Cipta Graha in Jakarta
4: 1999, Gading Serpong, Tangerang, Indonesia

A: Antony Liu + Architects / Studio TonTon B: Paramount Hill Golf – GGB No. 35, Gading Serpong, Tangerang 15332 - Indonesia
C: www.studiotonton.com D: studiotonton@gmail.com

Peter Stutchbury

1: 1954, Sydney, Australia
2: Graduated from University of Newcastle in 1978
3: Nielsen Warren Architects, 1982 and Quay partnership, 1979-80
4: established own practice in 1981

A: Peter Stutchbury Architecture
B: 5/364 Barrenjoey Road, Newport, NSW, 2106, Australia
C: www.peterstutchbury.com.au
D: admin@peterstutchbury.com.au

189

SUPPOSE DESIGN OFFICE

Makoto Tanijiri
谷尻誠
1: 1974, Hiroshima, Japan
2: graduated from Anabuki Design College
3: worked at Motokane Architect Office, 1994-99; worked at HAL Architects, 1999-2000
4: established Suppose design office, 2000; SUPPOSE DESIGN OFFICE Co.,Ltd. with Ai Yoshida, 2014

Ai Yoshida
吉田愛
1: 1974, Hiroshima, Japan
2: graduated from Anabuki Design College
3: worked at Izutsu Co., Ltd., 1994; worked at KIKUCHIDESIGN, 1996-98; worked at Suppose design office since 2001
4: established SUPPOSE DESIGN OFFICE Co.,Ltd. with Makoto Tanijiri, 2014

A: SUPPOSE DESIGN OFFICE / サポーズデザインオフィス
B: Hiroshima, Japan / 〒730-0843 広島市中区舟入本町15-1
C: www.suppose.jp D: info@suppose.jp

TNA

© 堀田貞雄

Makoto Takei (left)
武井 誠
1: 1974, Tokyo, Japan
2: graduated from Department of Architecture, Tokai University in 1997 3: Tsukamoto Laboratory, Graduate School of Science and Engineering, Tokyo Institute of Technology + Atelier Bow-Wow, 1997-99; worked at Tezuka Architects, 1999-2004
4: 2004

Chie Nabeshima (right)
鍋島千恵
1: 1975, Kanagawa, Japan
2: graduated from Department of Architecture, Nihon University in 1998
3: worked at Tezuka Architects, 1998-2004
4: 2004

A: TNA / TNA一級建築士事務所
B: Tokyo, Japan / 〒162-0065 東京都新宿区住吉町9-7-3F
C: www.tna-arch.com D: mail@tna-arch.com

Vo Trong Nghia

1: 1976, Quang Binh Province, Vietnam
2: studied architecture at University of Tokyo before returning to Vietnam to establish own practice
4: 2006, Vietnam

A: Vo Trong Nghia Architects
B: 8 Floor, 70 Pham Ngoc Thach Street, Ward 6, District 3, Ho Chi Minh City, Vietnam C: votrongnghia.com D: hcmc@vtnaa.com

WESPI DE MEURON ROMEO

Markus Wespi
1: 1957, St. Gallen, Switzerland
2: autoeducated
3: worked at André M. Studer, 1975-82; Ernst E. Anderegg, 1983; Fred Cramer, 1983; Franco S. Ponti
4: started own practice since 1984; worked with Jérôme de Meuron since 1998; office Wespi de Meuron Romeo Architects since 2012

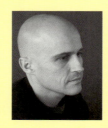

Jérôme de Meuron
1: 1971, Münsingen, Switzerland
2: studies at Technical School in Burgdorf 1993-96; architectural practical stay in Ghana (Africa) 1996-97
4: work with Markus Wespi since 1998; Office Wespi de Meuron Romeo Architects since 2012

Luca Romeo
1: 1984, Locarno, Switzerland
2: studies at Technical School in Lugano-Trevano 2003-06
3: worked at Sergio Cattaneo, 2000-03 and 2006-11
4: work with Markus Wespi and Jérôme de Meuron since 2011; Office Wespi de Meuron Romeo Architects since 2012

A: Wespi de Meuron Romeo Architects
B: Via G. Branca Masa 9 6578 Caviano Switzerland
C: www.wdmra.ch
D: info@wdmra.ch

Akira Yoneda

米田 明

1: 1959, Hyogo, Japan
2: received Bachelor degree in 1982, Master degree in 1984 from University of Tokyo; Master of Architecture in 1991 from Harvard University 3: worked at Takenaka Corporation, 1984-89 4: 1991

A: architecton / 建築設計事務所 アーキテクトン
B: Tokyo, Japan / 〒151-0071 東京都渋谷区本町1-7-16-612
D: a-tecton@pj8.so-net.ne.jp

*: photos by GA photographers

EXHIBITION
GA HOUSES PROJECT 2018
Saturday, 24 March—Sunday, 3 June

開館時間：12:00－6:30 pm　会期中無休
入場料：600円（前売券・団体10名以上：500円）

〒151-0051 東京都渋谷区千駄ヶ谷3-12-14 | tel: (03)3403-1581 | www.ga-ada.co.jp

Exhibition "GA HOUSES Project 2017" © GA photgraphers

GA HOUSES SPECIAL
MASTERPIECES
1945-1970 & 1971-2000 & 2001-2015

Today we are proud to present the third installment of the MASTERPIECES series, following up the previous two volumes showcasing the cream of Post-war residential projects realized around the globe.
Volume One covers the years from 1945 to 1970. A selection of more than 50 houses of late Modernism, from the rehabilitation period just after the WWII up to the times of Cultural Revolution. Works by the modern masters of Europe and America attaining maturity and those of their followers full of bloom depict a generation shift from old to new.
Volume Two covers the years from 1971 to 2000. A selection of more than 50 houses from a time of major transition headed for the new possibilities of 21st century, starting from the rise of Post-Modernism and ending with the chaotic fin de siecle.
Volume Three covers the years from 2001 to 2015. Enter the 21st century, with the Internet reaching the masses, the world is seeing a diversification of 'residential values.' While Japan, South America, Australia and Asia are stepping up their presence, we keep a close watch as to where the residential architecture is headed.
The three-volume series is a comprehensive collection of 'best architectures' of the Postwar 70 years from around the world.

戦後，世界中で実現された住宅作品から，選りすぐりの名作を紹介した2巻に続く，第3巻を上梓いたしました。
第1巻は，1945年から70年。第2次世界大戦終結直後の復興期から文化革命前後まで，モダニズム後期の住宅50余軒を紹介します。ヨーロッパやアメリカの近代の巨匠達の円熟期の作品と，そのフォロワー達の若々しい住宅，新旧の世代交代の時代の住宅建築と言えます。
第2巻は，1971年から2000年。ポストモダンの隆盛から混沌とした世紀末までの50余軒。建築界が大きくシフトしていき，21世紀の可能性に繋がっていく時代の住宅建築が収録されています。
第3巻は，2001年から2015年。21世紀を迎え，インターネットが浸透し〈住宅の価値〉が多様化した現代。日本，南米，オーストラリア，アジアの存在感が増すなか，住宅建築はどこに向かうのか。
3巻合わせて，戦後70年間の世界の〈ベスト建築〉を総覧するシリーズです。

English and Japanese texts, Size: 300×228mm
¥3,800

01 1945-1970

Alvar Aalto; Francisco Artigas; Atelier 5; Luis Barragán; Sergio Bernardes; Antonio Bonet; José Antonio Coderch; Charles & Ray Eames; Craig Ellwood; Ralph Erskine; Albert Frey; Bruce Goff; Michael Graves; Herbert Greene; Joaquim Guedes; Arata Isozaki; Gwathmey Henderson Siegel; Philip Johnson; Louis I. Kahn; Raymond Kappe; Kiyonori Kikutake; Edward A. Killingsworth; Pierre Koenig; John Lautner; Le Corbusier; Richard Meier; Paulo A. Mendes da Rocha; Mies van der Rohe; MLTW; Luigi Moretti; Richard Neutra; Oscar Niemeyer; Juan O'Gorman; Jean Prouvé; Paul Rudolph & Ralph S. Twitchell; Richard & Su Rogers; Eero Saarinen; & Alexander Girard; Carlo Scarpa; Tobia Scarpa; Robert Venturi & John Rauch; Vittoriano Viganò; Frank Lloyd Wright

284 total pages, 76 in colors **43 architects, 51 works**

02 1971-2000

Tadao Ando; Arquitectonica; Mario Botta; Marcel Breuer; William P. Bruder; Frank O. Gehry; Michael Graves; Gwathmey Siegel; Hiroshi Hara; Steven Holl; Kei'ichi Irie; Osamu Ishiyama; Franklin D. Israel; Toyo Ito; Hugh Newell Jacobsen; John M. Johansen; Alberto Kalach; Rem Koolhaas; Kruek & Olsen; John Lautner; Ricardo Legorreta; Mark Mack; Mecanoo; Richard Meier; Enric Miralles; Morphosis; José Oubrerie; Eric Owen Moss; Toru Murakami; Barton Myers; Edward R. Niles; Charlotte Perriand; Antoine Predock; Bart Prince; Foto Architects; Paul Rudolph; Carlo Scarpa; Scogin Elam and Bray; Kazuyo Sejima; Kazuo Shinohara; Álvaro Siza; Robert Stern; Tod Williams Billie Tsien; Riken Yamamoto; Carlos Zapata

296 total pages, 120 in colors **45 architects, 53 works**

03 2001-2015

Aires Mateus; Tadao Ando; Jun Aoki; Hiroyuki Arima; Atelier Bow-wow; Bercy Chen; Blank Studio; Randy Brown; Will Bruder; doubleNegatives Architecture; Georg Driendl; Steven Ehrlich; EMBT; Masaki Endoh; Terunobu Fujimori; Sou Fujimoto; Antón García-Abril; Sean Godsell; Steven Holl; Kei'ichi Irie; Osamu Ishiyama; Alberto Kalach; Katsufumi Kubota; Kengo Kuma; Keisuke Maeda; Gurjit Singh Matharoo; Andra Matin; Glenn Murcutt; Ryue Nishizawa; Smiljan Radic; Hiroshi Sambuichi; selgascano; Kazuyo Sejima; Álvaro Siza; Ettore Sottsass; SPBR Arquitetos; Studio Mumbai; Peter Stutchbury; Ryoji Suzuki; Makoto Takei + Chie Nabeshima/TNA; Wespi de Meuron Romeo Architects; Akira Yoneda;

296 total pages, 156 in colors **42 architects, 55 works**

GA DOCUMENT
Global Architecture

GA DOCUMENT presents the finest in international design, focusing on architectures that expresses our times and striving to record the history of contemporary architecture. International scholars and critics provide insightful texts to further inform the reader of the most up-to-date ideas and events in the profession.

多様に広がり，変化を見せる世界の現代建築の動向をデザインの問題を中心に取り上げ，現代建築の完全な記録をめざしつつ，時代の流れに柔軟に対応した独自の視点から作品をセレクションし，新鮮な情報を世界に向けて発信する唯一のグローバルな建築専門誌。

English and Japanese texts, Size: 300×257mm ¥3,200+tax

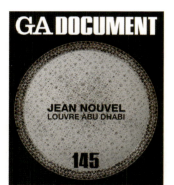

Special Issue:
Jean Nouvel Louvre Abu Dhabi
Interview:
Hala Warde Story of Louvre Abu Dhabi
—
特集：
ジャン・ヌヴェル ルーヴル・アブダビ
インタヴュー：
ハラ・ワルデ ストーリー・オブ・ルーヴル・アブダビ

112 total pages, 88 in colors

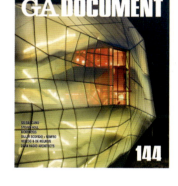

Works:
selgascano Plasencia Congress Center;
Steven Holl Lewis Arts Complex, Princeton University; **Morphosis** Emma and Georgina Bloomberg Center; **Diller Scofidio + Renfro** Roy and Diana Vagelos Education Center; **Herzog & de Meuron** 56 Leonard Street; **Zaha Hadid Architects** 520 West 28th; Mathematics: the Winton Gallery Science Museum

作品：
セルガスカーノ：スティーヴン・ホール：
モーフォシス：ディラー／スコフィディオ+レンフロ：
ヘルツォーク&ド・ムーロン：ザハ・ハディド・アーキテクツ

132 total pages, 96 in colors

Works:
Renzo Piano Building Workshop & Luis Vidal + Architects Centro Botín; **Eric Owen Moss** Vespertine; **Patkau Architects** Audain Art Museum; **Dorell Ghotmeh Tane** Estonian National Museum / Memory Field; **Snøhetta** Lascaux IV: International Centre for Cave Art ; **David Chipperfield** Inagawa Cemetery Chapel and Visitor Centre; and other

作品：
レンゾ・ピアノ&ルイス・ヴィダル+アーキテクツ：
エリック・オーウェン・モス：パトカウ・アーキテクツ：
田根剛+リナ・ゴットメ+ダン・ドレル：スノヘッタ：
ディヴィッド・チッパーフィールド，他

132 total pages, 90 in colors

Special Issue
INTERNATIONAL 2017
Projects: Aires Mateus / Tadao Ando / BIG
Shigeru Ban / Tatiana Bilbao / Coop Himmelblau
Atelier Deshaus / Elemental + Ecól architetti
Ensamble Studio / Sou Fujimoto / Frank O. Gehry
Norman Foster + Rubio Arquitectura / Zaha Hadid
Heatherwick Studio / Steven Holl / Toyo Ito
Junya Ishigami / JKMM Achitects / Kengo Kuma
Christian Kerez / Li Xiaodong / Daniel Libeskind
MAD Architects / Morphosis / O'Donnell + Tuomey
MVRDV / Jean Nouvel / selgascano / Snøhetta
Renzo Piano Building Workshop / spbr arquitetos
UNStudio / Riken Yamamoto

196 total pages, 158 in colors

Works:
Herzog & de Meuron Elbphilharmonie Hamburg;
Frank O. Gehry Pierre Boulez Saal; **Aires Mateus** Architecture Faculty in Tournai; Meeting Centre in Grândola; **OMA** Alexis de Tocqueville Library;
Álvaro Siza Nadir Afonso Foundation; **Álvaro Slza & Eduardo Souto de Moura** International Museum of Contemporary Sculpture & Abade Pedrosa Municipal Museum; **selgascano** Second Home Lisbon

作品：
ヘルツォーク&ド・ムーロン：フランク・O・ゲーリー：
アイレス・マテウス：OMA：アルヴァロ・シザ：エドゥアルド・
ソウト・デ・モウラ：セルガスカーノ

136 total pages, 94 in colors

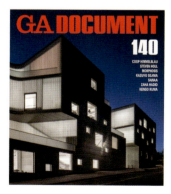

Works:
Coop Himmelblau Museum of Contemporary Art & Planning Exhibition (MOCAPE);
Steven Holl University of Iowa, Visual Arts Building;
Morphosis Taubman Complex, Lawrence Technological University; **Kazuyo Sejima** Sumida Hokusai Museum; **SANAA** Maru; **Zaha Hadid** Port House, Heydar Aliyev Center; **Kengo Kuma** Under One Roof Project for EPFL ArtLab Building

作品：
コープ・ヒンメルブラウ：スティーヴン・ホール：
モーフォシス：妹島和世：SANAA：ザハ・ハディド：隈研吾

144 total pages, 90 in colors

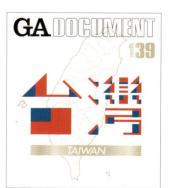

Special Issue: TAIWAN
Essay: Soutetsu Sha
Works: Toyo Ito; Norihiko Dan;
Terunobu Fujimori; Riken Yamamoto
Projects: SANAA; Mecanoo; Kengo Kuma; Akihisa Hirata; Steven Holl; OMA;
Norman Foster; Sou Fujimoto and others

特集：台湾
エッセイ：謝宗哲
作品：伊東豊雄：團紀彦：藤森照信：山本理顕
プロジェクト：SANAA：メカノー：隈研吾：平田晃久：
スティーヴン・ホール：OMA：ノーマン・フォスター：
藤本壮介，他

156 total pages, 96 in colors

Works:
Zaha Hadid Salerno Maritime Terminal;
BIG/Bjarke Ingels Group Serpentine Gallery Pavilion 2016; **Herzog & de Meuron** The New Tate Modern; **OMA** Pierre Lassonde Pavilion;
Snøhetta San Francisco Museum of Modern Art Expansion; Ryerson University Student Learning Centre;
Fernando Menis CKK Jordanki;
UNStudio Arnhem Central Transfer Terminal

作品：
ザハ・ハディド：BIG／ビャルケ・インゲルス・グループ：ヘルツォーク&ド・ムーロン：OMA：
スノヘッタ：フェルナンド・メニス：UNスタジオ

144 total pages, 90 in color